Conor B P9-CDJ-626

GUARDIANS OF
THE
PEACE

PRENDEVILLE PUBLISHING LIMITED

Prendeville Publishing Limited, an English company, whose
registered office is at 17 Brudenell Road, London SW17 8DB,
England.

First Published in 1974 by Gill and Macmillan Ltd Dublin and in
London through association with the Macmillan Publishers
Group and printed by Bristol Typesetting Co. Ltd, Bristol,
England. This edition is published by Prendeville Publishing Ltd,
London. It is a facsimile of the 1974 edition with some
modifications to the original text. Additional typesetting for this
edition: *The Point*, London, Photo reprographics: *Kingswood Steele Ltd*,
London. 'Frame grabbing' from *British Movietone News'* newsreel:
Printout Video Publishing, London.

British Library Cataloguing in Publication Data.
A Catalogue record of this book is available from the British
Library

ISBN 0 9535697 1 3
Printed by ColourBooks Ltd, Dublin.

For my wife, Ann

Contents

List of Illustrations

Introduction

One of the most instructive tests of a democracy is the way its police services operate. In their relationship with the community, in their accountability, in their operations and in their overall patterns of behaviour, the police are almost invariably a mirror-image of the broad values of the society they serve. In few countries is this as true as in the Republic of Ireland.

At the opening of the 21st Century, Ireland's national police force, the Garda Siochana, may appear little different from a myriad of other services provided by the State. It discharges its functions with efficiency, in much the same fashion as any other civil police organisation in Western Europe. This is as it should be. The best policing is surely that which is discharged unobtrusively and which the community takes for granted. But there was a time when the establishment of a native police force, routinely unarmed, presented a daunting challenge to the vision and the stability of the young State. It was, moreover, to test the discipline, the endurance and sometimes the courage of the several thousands of young men who had the task of making it a reality on the ground.

This book was written at a time when some of the political figures who were involved in the foundation of the force were still living, as were quite a few of its founding members. Its purpose was to record their account of one of the most enduring enterprises of independent Ireland and to place it in a political, historical and social context. In the quarter century since the publication of *Guardians of the Peace* all of the founding members of the Garda Siochana who assisted me in my undertaking have passed on. When I began my research in the early 1970s, I realised it was important to get their accounts at first hand before the march of time would make it impossible. Few archival sources were open to me and in the main I relied for documentary support on a small store of private papers and official documents - Routine Orders, for example, or published material such as the Garda Review; the Garda Pensioners' magazine, An Siothadoir or the Garda Siochana Code. The Mulcahy papers in the archives of University College

Dublin and some papers provided by the late Mr Ernest Blythe gave me an insight into government thinking. Some former members of the force allowed me access to personal diaries or written accounts of particular events.

In the intervening period, a great array of sources has opened up. State papers have been made available with the passage of time and many valuable documents have been turned over to the Garda Museum, which did not exist 26 years ago. Moreover, there has been extensive and valuable scholarship into the history of Irish policing. In short, a great deal more is now known about the establishment and development of Ireland's national police force than when I finished my work in 1973.

The option has therefore existed of revising *Guardians of the Peace* in the light of all that has been learned since and to amend or alter the undoubted misinterpretations and omissions which were embodied in my narrative. After consultation with Bill Dee, at whose initiative this re-publication is taking place, I decided not to do so but to allow the original version, with its imperfections and its incomplete perspective, to stand virtually as it was written. There is one signal exception. It concerns the narrative in Chapter 10 of the supposed preparations by General Eoin O'Duffy to stage a *coup d'etat* against the incoming Fianna Fail government. Relying wholly as it did, on the information of one witness, this account should have been qualified when first published. The matter is addressed in this edition, I believe, with the balance and the qualifications which it lacked when first written.

The book was scarcely published when the power-sharing administration in Northern Ireland, set up under the Sunningdale Agreement, collapsed. Northern Ireland faced into more than twenty years of violence and the course of events for the whole island was changed. Policing, North and South, was to undergo extraordinary change as well. The Garda Siochana did not face unrestrained paramilitary violence as did the Royal Ulster Constabulary. Nonetheless, gardai were obliged to engage with the rise of politically-inspired violence. Some died while many others were wounded. The development of the force was shaped in considerable measure by the security requirements which flowed from the Northern Ireland crisis.

The crisis of the North forced change upon the Garda Siochana. But this was not the only influence for change which was brought to bear upon it. A conjunction of factors emerged in the 1970s which, in some ways, altered the Garda Siochana almost beyond recognition from the slow-moving, reactive organisation which I described when this book was first published. And yet, in other very fundamental ways, the Garda Siochana of the 21st Century must be remarkable for the extent to which it has not changed at all since its foundation. Indeed, one might go further and observe that in certain aspects it has not changed since the era of its predecessor force, the Royal Irish Constabulary.

Contemporaneously with the crisis of the North, the pace of social and economic change quickened within the Republic of Ireland. Rising living standards and a relaxation of social mores were accompanied by a rising crime rate. Armed crime overflowed from the North. Ordinary criminals quickly saw that guns could yield profitable results and the armed criminal became a reality in the cities and towns. As Ireland became more urbanised, international linkages increased. Organised crime grew and developed in the urban areas. The drugs trade, in particular, came to dominate whole areas of Dublin and other cities. The Garda Siochana was facing into a period in which crime would become highly profitable, ruthlessly violent where necessary and organised, in some instances, at business-school levels of efficiency.

Somewhat more recently, evidence began to emerge, confirming what many had long suspected; that Irish society harboured many dark secrets, injustices and inequalities under its patina of religious devotionalism and social conformity. It became clear that crime grew, in considerable measure, from conditions of social deprivation, especially in the larger cities and towns. Extensive problems of sexual abuse of vulnerable children, sometimes at the hands of those into whose care they had been entrusted, came to light. More slowly, but no less surely, it began to become clear that white-collar crime and corruption were widespread within supposedly respectable strata of Irish society and that they reached into the heart of the administrative and political establishments.

The Garda Siochana of the 1970s, 1980s and 1990s found itself obliged to adapt to this increasingly complex society in which traditional assumptions about right and wrong were often inverted. The simplicities and certainties of earlier times were no more. Most of the authority institutions in Ireland found themselves facing challenges to their credibility and confidence - the political establishment, the churches, big business, the banks, the professions, even the courts. The Garda Siochana was only one of many institutions obliged to face up to new realities, new demands and new challenges.

The story of the modern Garda Siochana responding to change is almost a perfect metaphor of modern Ireland facing the same challenge. Todays' Garda Siochana is more highly trained and educated, better equipped than when this book was written. It is backed with a range of specialised services which were unimaginable a quarter of a century ago. Its members are better paid and provided for. And while its ranks are still predominantly male, the numbers of female members have steadily increased. It has at times leaped forward to embrace change, as with the establishment of the fine Training College at Templemore. At other times it has had to be dragged kicking towards reform. Today, it is undoubtedly more honest about its own shortcomings. As with many other organisations, it has abandoned or broken out of time-honoured conventions. Gardai have engaged in what is effectively strike action, to the dismay of many of those who would still wish the force to discharge a vocational or exemplar role in Irish society. Yet, when opinion is polled, its standing is still high among the population. Even in a society with a skills shortage and in which young people can pick and choose between attractive careers, entry to the Garda Siochana is highly prized. It is remarkable that Ireland pays its police officers better than its teachers, its nurses and the bulk of its civil servants.

It is not the function of this introduction to seek to evaluate how well or otherwise the Garda Siochana has responded to these changes in the society it serves. That would require another book which, no doubt, will be written one day if it is not already in preparation by some commentator or analyst. But it is important to understand that whatever has been the story of the Garda since 1974 it has been built upon the foundations described in this book. The modern Garda Siochana draws on the strengths and, equally, labours under the disabilities which derive from its historical inheritance.

At this writing, the future of policing in Northern Ireland, now at peace for the first time in more than 30 years, is under review. The report of the Commission under the chairmanship of Mr Chris Patten has recommended the disbandment in all but name of the Royal Ulster Constabulary and the setting up of a powerful new police authority comprising representatives drawn from all the main political parties. Patten proposes the establishment of new linkages at local level between the police and the community and a simplification of the command structure within a newly-named Northern Ireland Police Service. If these changes are put in place, the result will be a significant divergence between the constitutional bases of Ireland's two police forces. Northern Ireland's police will be statutorily linked to the community and set apart from the authority of central government. The Garda Siochana will continue to operate as an arm of government, a centrally-controlled service of the State, directed by a commissioner and senior officers who are appointed directly by central government. How long that disharmony can endure must be a fascinating question.

In addressing this and other questions on Irish policing, past and present, it is now possible to refer the reader to a much more comprehensive bibliography than in 1974. The incomplete picture painted in these pages is greatly amplified by a number of works which have been published in recent years and which must be especially recommended. Primary among these are Gregory Allen's *The Garda Siochana;* Liam McNiffe's *A History of The Garda Siochana;* Eunan O'Halpin's *Defending the State;* and Dermot P J Walsh's *The*

Irish Police. A number of personal accounts of life in the Garda Siochana have been published, including Tim Doyle's *Peaks and Valleys* and Tim Leahy's *Memoirs of a Garda Superintendent.* John D Brewer has produced a remarkable oral history of the RIC while Stephen Ball has edited *A Policeman's Ireland* - the Recollections of Samuel Waters RIC as part of the Cork University Press's splendid series Irish Narratives. Jim Herlihy has produced valuable work on the RIC, including a complete copy of the RIC list. Donal O'Sullivan, a former Chief Superintendent of the Garda Siochana, has produced a fine overview of policing in Ireland between 1822 and 1922 - *The Irish Constabulary.* There has been extensive work on the history and contemporary conditions of the Royal Ulster Constabulary. Chris Ryder's *The RUC, a Force Under Fire* is essential reading. So too is Sir John Hermon's *Holding the Line.* Completeness requires a reading also of John Stalker's account of his time in Northern Ireland, entitled simply *Stalker.* Excellent insights into the Dublin crime underworld have been provided by Paul Williams in *The General* and *Gangland* and by Paul Reynolds's *King Scum.*

The story told in *Guardians of the Peace* is part of a longer and wider narrative. But it is a story which still has relevance as Ireland moves, hopefully, to a new era of peace and stability. It is above all a chronicle of the idealism and the imperfections of ordinary men presented by history with the discharging of a rather extraordinary task.

I would like to thank the Managing Director of Prendeville Publishing, Mr Bill Dee, whose imaginative approach and enthusiasm has made possible this re-publication of *Guardians of the Peace.* My thanks also to Inspector John Duffy and his staff at the Garda Museum, Dublin Castle, whose kindness and co-operation is highly-valued. I would also like to acknowledge the contribution of many former and serving members of the Garda Siochana, and their families, who have added to the store of knowledge of Irish policing history over the years.

Conor Brady
Dublin, May 2000

1 The Irish Garrison 1812-1913

In a period of just under seven months—from February to August 1922—the 10,000 men of the Royal Irish Constabulary, the organisation which had formed the backbone of British administration in rural Ireland for over a hundred years, disappeared from the towns and villages where they and their predecessors had enforced the writ of the Crown on four generations of their fellow Irishmen. They made their way in small detachments of ten or twelve, usually under the grudging protection of an Irish Republican Army escort party, to the nearest military camp or railway station thence to depart to England or America or the police forces of the colonies or in some cases to Belfast, where the government of Northern Ireland was recruiting a new police force. By the autumn of 1922 the once familiar bottle-green uniform of the 'Peelers' had vanished for ever from the countryside of twenty-six Irish counties.

In the momentous events of those troubled months the passing of the R I C was scarcely noticed, and not at all regretted, by the people among whom they had lived and worked.

Their inglorious end was understandable, for the force had all but ceased to function in a police role for over two years. Its ranks had been depleted by resignations, its morale had been broken by the success of the Sinn Féin boycott and the I R A guerilla campaign. Above all, its acceptability among the people had been irrevocably lost through the excesses of the Black and Tans and Auxiliaries. And yet nothing symbolised more clearly the changes which were taking place in Ireland than the disbandment of the R I C. It was the end of the force which had embodied the strength of the alien power; the R I C had not only symbolised, but made meaningful with their very presence, the control which Britain had exercised over Ireland and the Irish people. The constabulary had represented the Dublin Castle administration in a host of matters, mainly quite unconnected with police work. They looked after the school attendance regulations, the Weights and Measures Acts, and agricultural statistics; they had a hand in the regulation of virtually every aspect of life in rural Ireland. No farmer, shopkeeper or tradesman could hide anything from the Peelers for it was their duty to know everything about everyone. They were the eyes and ears of the Castle, and where necessary they were its strong right hand. They were, in short, the single, strong and utterly reliable service which had enabled Britain to hold Ireland in a condition of relative tranquillity in the previous hundred years.

The R I C had been a unique institution. It combined the functions of a rural gendarmerie, a civil police and—outside of the larger towns—a rudimentary civil service. Nurtured on classical colonial lines, it had served as a model for policing the other troublesome subject races of the Empire who could not be left to look after themselves and who could not be left under the permanent care of the army. The basic concept was that of a native force, raised from the sturdier elements of the peasantry and rigorously drilled, trained and officered by Englishmen. Well armed and equipped, they were spread throughout the country in compact small detachments within easy reach of one another in event of serious disturbance. In slightly varying forms this model was used for the policing of India, Canada and Africa with considerable success. In Ireland too it was highly effective and proved its worth in suppressing the Fenian risings of 1848 and 1867, while in the earlier decades of the century it had been the Tory government's sole effective weapon in dealing with the combined evils of agrarian outrage and sectarian strife.

The Royal Irish Constabulary owed its origins to Robert Peel, more celebrated in police history as the founder of the London Metropolitan Police—the legendary Bobbies. The two systems, of necessity, were worlds apart, for Londoners would not have policemen patrolling their streets with carbines slung across their backs and bayonets and revolvers in their belts. But it throws an interesting sidelight on the nature of British administration in Ireland in the years immediately after the Union that two entirely different police systems should be developed for a supposedly 'united' kingdom. Britain got an unarmed policeman, answerable not to central government but to a watch committee and depending in the last analysis on the moral support of the community to enable him to enforce the law. Ireland, by contrast, got an armed garrison, rigidly disciplined and directly controlled by Dublin Castle, operating with the backing of the Martini-Carbine, the bayonet and the sword rather than the support of the community.

In September 1812 Peel arrived in Ireland as Chief Secretary to find the country in the preliminary stages of total chaos. There was a mounting toll of violence and destruction all over the country which neither the civil nor military authorities appeared capable of controlling. The militia's manpower had been drained off in order to cope with the continental wars and the medieval policing system had been entirely overrun by the scale of violence and outrage. Probably most serious of all, the local magistracy system was riddled with abuse and corruption and in the few districts where sufficient organised strength was available to put down crime there was not the inclination among the supposed leaders of society.

Ireland was beset by a major threat to public order in the form of secret societies, which had become a dominant feature in the pattern of Irish rural life since the 1760s. These illegal, oath-bound combinations of men were motivated primarily by agrarian grievances, though in the North the basic issues were confused by sectarian differences, frequently fostered by a reactionary ruling class. The political ideologies of French and American republicanism also had a small, but by no means insignificant, influence among urban intellectuals (many of them Ulster Presbyterians) and were largely responsible for the formation of the United Irishmen and the abortive rebellions of 1798 and 1803.

The principal secret societies—the Whiteboys, Rightboys and Ribbonmen—had a membership of several thousand among the lowest stratum of society—the landless labourers and cottiers. The main waves of their activity occurred in periods of greatest economic distress, when high rents, tithes and dues coincided with low wages and potato shortage to cause considerable hardship. In such periods agrarian outrages were common and vast areas of the country, particularly the South and South-west, were plunged into disorder. It was frequently necessary to call in special army detachments or *ad hoc* bodies of militia to control the eruption of violence, and although they were generally successful in armed confrontations or punitive expeditions, they were of little use in a purely preventive capacity.

The outbreak of the Napoleonic War and the subsequent withdrawal of much of the garrison for service in Europe gave an additional sense of urgency to the government's approach to the problem of secret societies. Although the vast majority of the peasants who participated in rural agitation had little interest in the political ideas of Bonapartism, the timid and isolated Protestant Ascendancy now saw them as a grave menace both to the security of the state and to their own safety. The authorities, whether influenced by these exaggerated fears or by more sinister motives, kept alive the illusion of a nationwide conspiracy to bring about a French invasion in which the Grand Army would be joined by the insurgent hordes of Catholic Irish, all intent on a final massacre of their hated masters. But even if the secret societies were misrepresented, their activities continued to have a severely disruptive effect throughout the country.

To cope with this dangerous situation on behalf of the Crown, Peel found at his disposal an antiquated police system which had carried over without improvement since the Middle Ages, a magistracy which was almost totally corrupt and inactive and a military garrison which had been reduced to a fraction of its original strength and effectiveness.

The basis of policing in rural Ireland up to this time had been a combined use of the military and the rather generously entitled 'Baronial Police'. The 'Barnies' as they were more commonly known, were, in the main, deserving pensioners who were appointed by the local magistrates through the County Grand Juries. Pay was very poor and there was no training or proper organisation for the force. The uses to which it could be put were of necessity therefore very limited. They served writs, guarded courthouses during sittings and occasionally accompanied bailiffs' parties on seizures or evictions where no trouble was anticipated. Where anything more strenuous or dangerous was involved the military would be called in and the Barnies sent home. The system worked quite well on the whole as long as the military were available to back up the Baronial Police where necessary. In the years preceding the Act of Union the peasantry had very limited access to firearms or other weapons of war and major disturbances were rare. The peasants only became a police problem wherever large-scale evictions took place, and then they tended to stay around their native districts, sleeping in ditches and living off whatever they could beg or steal. At that stage they became a nuisance and had to be moved on. And if the Barnies were not up to the task, a detachment of Hussars could be readily made available.

But when Robert Peel arrived to take office at Dublin Castle in the autumn of 1812, that simple but adequate system had broken down. From all over the country magistrates reported grave disorders. Much of that disorder, Peel was ultimately to conclude, was their own fault, but for the present all he could have seen from the urgent notifications of the magistracy was that crime and outrage were on the increase and that the military, whom the magistrates had traditionally called upon to restore order were simply not there any more. Huge areas of the South, South-west and Midlands were under the control of outlaw gangs who would descend at night to murder and maim their opponents, burn their homes and drive off their livestock. Moreover, the secret societies had extended their ramifications everywhere, even into the remaining military detachments in the countryside, paralysing the system of informers which in the past had served as an early-warning system to the landlords and the magistrates.

But, as Peel was swiftly to realise, the problem was not simply one of a dwindling military garrison and a rise in the crime rate. The Irish magistracy itself was a corrupt institution, operating on an elaborate system of patronage and with little enthusiasm among the magistrates themselves for the preservation of the king's peace. Reports on the magistracy showed many of its number to be deceitful, violent and seditious and it was not uncommon for magistrates themselves to be convicted for customs and excise offences. In fairness, their inactivity may not have been due entirely to incompetence and indifference. In a community where secret societies, oath-bound bands and violent outrage were increasing daily, the magistrate who would dare to move against lawbreakers would have to be very sure of his own safety and there was not much to be hoped for in the way of protection from either the Barnies or the few remaining military detachments.

Since there was little prospect of bringing the military back to normal strength in the foreseeable future, Peel drew up his own plan for a police force specifically designed to meet the unique requirements of the Irish situation. The new police were to be known as the Peace Preservation Force and they were to be recruited from the ranks of the militia or disbanded regular soldiers. They were to be heavily armed, trained and under the direction of a chief officer who would also exercise some of the powers of a stipendiary magistrate. But the force was not to be allocated throughout the countryside on a permanent or general basis and thus, for the time being at any rate, one of the most distinctive characteristics of the Irish constabulary system—its placing of the police among the people on a local level—was put aside. Full control of the police was thus taken out of the hands of the magistrates, with the result that many of them adopted an uncooperative attitude towards the operations of the new force.

Furthermore, the Lord Lieutenant, Whitworth had turned down an original proposal by Peel that the new police should be recruited from the 'small farmer' class and this was to put severe limitations on the usefulness of the force as an intelligence agency since the ex-soldiers and militia men were outsiders, unknown and unaccepted in the rural communities. The Peace Preservation Force was to operate as a flexible and mobile instrument which would be drafted into troubled areas once they were proclaimed under the terms of a new and stringent Peace Preservation Act. While operating in such districts they would be directed by their chief officer who would work in co-operation with the local magistrates and the proclaimed area would bear the expense of the force itself.

In September 1814 the Barony of Middlethird in Tipperary received the first detachment of the Peace Preservation Force. The initial results were encouraging. From a condition of utter lawlessness the barony was swiftly brought to a state in which crime and outrage were for some time completely eliminated.

Applications for the use of the 'Peelers' (as the new force became known) poured into the Castle and over the next two years virtually the entire country was introduced to the force with varying degrees of success. It was particulary effective in Cork, Tipperary and Limerick, where its arrival was shortly followed by a marked decrease in crime and outrage. But it had very definite limitations due to its composition and the fact that it was not locally based. As a 'flying squad' it was highly successful, but as a police force proper, capable of anticipating and preventing crime, it had only sporadic success.

The creation of a permanent police establishment throughout the country did not come until 1822 when, in spite of the bitter opposition of the Irish members, Westminster passed an Irish Constables Act which provided for a force to be known as the County Constabulary which, though uniform in its nature throughout the whole country, was, for practical purposes, administered at county level by the magistrates and chief constables. The government had not intended to leave the force under local control but the principle of a permanent and general police system had evoked such a storm of protest in parliament that the concession had to be made. The magistrates retained the power of appointment of constables and sub-constables and this left the way open for the continuance of patronage in the force. Nevertheless, the creation of the County Constabulary firmly established the concept of a regular and general police force as a permanent feature of the Irish countryside, and because the day-to-day running of the force was under the control of the local magistrates there was little if any of the former influential opposition which had hampered the activities of the Peace Preservation Force. With the blessings of the Ascendancy class the County Constabulary dealt firmly if selectively with the law and order problems of rural Ireland for fifteen years.

In 1835 the Irish police system was reshaped into the form in which it was to endure until the end of the British rule. The reform was enacted by the Whig government and was placed specifically under the direction of the new Under-Secretary, Thomas Drummond. Drummond, who had caused outrage and anger among the Irish landowning classes by his declaration that 'property has it duties as well as its rights' had a deep understanding of Irish problems and a genuine sympathy with the lot of the Irish peasant. He immediately saw that the County Constabulary, in spite of its undoubted efficiency, was regarded by the Catholic peasantry as a partisan force—and not perhaps without good reason. The officers were exclusively Protestant and the ranks contained a disproportionately large number of Protestants as well. There were many Orange lodges in the force, often flourishing with the connivance of the magistrates; and the growth of the campaign for Catholic Emancipation in the 1820s was accompanied in many parts of the country by an undercurrent of agrarian tension. In 1826 the campaign reached a peak of excitement and turbulence when the 'forty-shilling freeholders' defied tradition and their landlords and voted for pro-Emancipation candidates. Intimidation and counter-intimidation were wide-spread, Catholic groups were organising massive protest demonstrations and marching openly, and by 1828 the government realised that it had to cope with an alarming situation of potential revolution. The police played an indistinct role throughout this difficult period, but too often their anti-Catholic sympathies became clear. The attainment of a substantial measure of Catholic Emancipation in 1829 eased political tensions but did not diminish the level of violence in rural Ireland, nor did it serve to improve relationships between the peasantry and the police. The Emancipation controversy had scarcely begun to abate when a campaign began to abolish the payment of tithes to the Established Church.

So bitter did the 'tithe war' become that it was necessary in the period 1830–32 to reintroduce the Peace Preservation Force to augment the County Constabulary in a number of areas. Yet clashes became more frequent and more serious. In December 1831 a mob of several thousand peasants attacked a detachment of police who had come to enforce the collection of tithes at Carrickshock in Co Kilkenny. Seventeen policemen, including the Chief Constable of the county, were killed and dozens more injured.

Drummond soon realised that the basic fault in the constabulary system was the degree of control which the local magistracy still maintained over it in accordance with the act of 1822. Accordingly, during the parliamentary sessions of 1835–36 he pushed a second Constabulary Bill through parliament, vesting control of a unified Irish police force for the area outside of Dublin in an Inspector-General who would be directly responsible to the Lord Lieutenant and the Chief Secretary. The power of appointment of constables and sub-constables was taken away from local magistrates, and inspectors were appointed to direct the force at county and district level. Finally, the four provincial police depots of Ballinrobe, Armagh, Ballincollig and Philipstown, which had served the needs of the County Constabulary were closed down and replaced in 1839 by a central depot at the Phoenix Park, outside Dublin. A depot reserve of about four hundred men was created to augment the normal complement wherever serious disturbances took place. The legislation providing for the continuing existence of the Peace Preservation Force was repealed and the force passed out of existence.

While the police system of rural Ireland underwent this gradual, if stormy evolution, the City of Dublin had developed its own police force in quite a different idiom, identical almost to that of London and the bigger English cities. Prior to 1842 the responsibility for maintaining the king's peace in the city and its adjoining townships had rested with the Dublin Watch or 'Tholsel Guard' as it was colloquially known. The Watch comprised a couple of dozen elderly men who patrolled the streets at night as best they could in pretentious uniforms of blue and gold. Each constable, while tottering on his rounds, was obliged to carry a lamp and a poleaxe which, together with the heavy greatcoats supplied at the expense of the city, ensured that he was sufficiently hampered not to be able to intervene in any disturbance of which he did not have very adequate advance warning. A popular verse which Trinity College undergraduates were in the habit of reciting in the city's alehouses gives some idea of the opinion which the citizenry held of these worthies :

> Through Skinners Row the toast must Go,
> And our Cheers reach Christ Church Yard,
> Till its vaults profound send back the sound,
> To Wake the Tholsel Guard.

The Tholsel Guard was phased out during the years 1808–42 by a rather haphazard series of statutes which brought into being an unarmed civil force, very similar to the London one, called the Dublin Metropolitan Police. By the end of the nineteenth century the D M P had reached a strength of 1,200 men and had earned for itself a reputation as one of the best police forces in Britain or Ireland, excelling in some respects even the celebrated London Metropolitan Police.

Until 1913, when they became the most bitter enemies of the Dublin working class through the violence of the general strike, the D M P were a force which was remarkably well adjusted to the needs and problems of the urban population among whom they lived. Their task was in every respect akin to that envisaged by Peel for the London police: 'the preservation of life and property, the prevention and detection of crime and the prevention of nuisance and abuse in public places'. Quite different was the role of Drummond's new constabulary who operated in a society where virtually all serious crime was politically inspired, where their primary purpose among the people was espionage and where the people themselves had, at best, mixed views of the police.

But the Irish Constabulary, as the new unified police was called, occupied over the next three generations, a role in the life of rural Ireland which was considerably more significant than that of the D M P in Dublin. With the gradual restoration of a measure of order into the day-to-day life of the countryside in the latter decades of the nineteenth century, the Irish Constabulary and the people coexisted with less violence, and an element of mutual respect and friendship grew up in the relationship. But in consequence the police became the object of more virulent criticism and hatred whenever that delicate equilibrium broke down. The friendliest Peeler was found to be an untrustworthy confidant or neighbour when something went wrong.

In 1848 and again in 1867 they functioned efficiently and loyally against the Fenian risings—earning on the one hand from Queen Victoria the right to be known as the Royal Irish Constabulary, and on the other an undying hatred and rancour among the rural population.

Yet it would be wrong to describe the relationship which pertained in these years between the Royal Irish Constabulary and the Irish people as one of constant enmity and mutual antagonism. The relationship functioned on two levels. Individual policemen in the community were usually respected and even popular. They were the pick of the countryside's youth, athletic, intelligent and—relative to their neighbours—well educated. They were good customers in small village stores, they could help out with official forms and documents which meant nothing to people who could neither read nor write and they made reliable and desirable sons-in-law. But on the other, more basic, level, they knew and the people knew that when a crisis would come the Peelers' first loyalty would be to the Crown. They were acceptable when things ran smoothly in the district, but when there was a whiff of dissaffection in the air they were the Castle's men and that basic factor underlay their affability.

Inevitably there was enmity and antagonism but as time went on its appearance became less and less frequent. The Peelers, on a day-to-day level, were welcome at weddings, parties or dances. If a Peeler were a good fiddler or dancer he was doubly welcome, and while his mingling too freely with the local population might prejudice his chances of future promotion, that was usually decided anyway by his religion and origins and did not therefore affect his everyday life.

There were a number of good reasons for the growing acceptance of the R I C among the people from about 1880 onwards. The fearful poverty of the Famine era became a thing of the past and the Irish peasantry had begun to savour their first experience of a little security with a modicum of comfort. The sectarian bitterness of the earlier decades of the century had largely disappeared and certainly no longer manifested itself in large-scale violence. Some progress had been made towards achieving tenant ownership of the land and there was to be a continuous advancement in this direction. In short, there had been improvements, however slight, in the lot of the Irish peasant and the main causes of outrage and violence had been somewhat alleviated.

Contemporary accounts confirm the improvement in relations at this time and the police themselves tended to attribute the phenomenon to the growing desirability and acceptability of the police as a career for young men of modest origins and some education. Up to the disbandment of the R I C in 1922 some 30,000 Irishmen had made a career out of the police and some had attained promotion to very senior ranks although these were almost exclusively the preserve of Protestant members. From 1895 onwards about half the commissioned ranks in the force were filled by men who had risen from the ranks, but the R I C cadet scheme, whereby suitable young men—usually the landless or less fortunate sons of the gentry—were given commissions at the rank of District Inspector, persisted to the end. By contrast with the D M P and British police forces, the R I C observed a rigid distinction between officers and men and the police cadet school in the Phoenix Park depot was regarded as a very suitable finishing school for the less promising sons of Eton or Harrow who did not make it to Sandhurst and who were therefore destined for a career in the constabulary. The cadet school itself was conducted much in the tradition of a lesser public school with constant wagers, dares and practical jokes passing between young cadets and officers. It was traditional that a new arrival would be persuaded, bullied and if necessary beaten into buying supplies of wine for his fellows in the mess and a favourite form of entertainment among the would-be guardians of the law was engaging two mess waiters to put on a human cockfight, battling one another with their feet while their hands would be firmly trussed behind their backs.

For the most part, the officers who left the Phoenix Park depot to take up their appointments in country districts had only a rudimentary training in professional police work. The emphasis during training was on the necessity and means of maintaining discipline among their men and the handling of disaffection and violence among the people. District Inspector George Garrow Green, who left behind a highly illuminating account of life in the R I C described his state of preparedness on leaving the Park for Listowel, Co Kerry, in terms which would hardly have elicited the approval of his comrades but which paint a fairly typical picture if one is to judge by contemporary evidence: 'I could draw a map of Chinese Tartary but had a profound contempt for Taylor on Evidence, I could form a hollow square but of the necessary steps to be taken in a murder case my head was about equally empty. With these advantages I started to assume command of a lawless station in the wilds of Kerry and to instruct the fifty peelers therein in all that pertained to crime and outrage.'

Inspector Garrow Green was not long in discovering, however, that officers of the R I C had to learn their duties very quickly. The complexities of maintaining order in large, widely scattered rural communities had to be mastered swiftly if an officer was to have the full loyalty of his men. The R I C system depended on the imposition of a rigid organisation and discipline from above, and where any link in the chain of command was broken there was always a danger that the rank-and-file constabulary might move even slightly towards a closer identification with the people.

When the underlying tension between police and people came to the surface, however, it did so with an astonishing severity and viciousness as, for instance, in July 1900 when a dispute developed in the Kilkenny-Waterford district over the employment of police pensioners on local authority work. The argument went on for months until finally the *Waterford Star*, voicing the opinion of probably a substantial body of the people, came out strongly against the idea of jobs for police pensioners and issued the declaration: 'The policeman who has done his share of the noble work of spying, evicting and batoning in Ireland should be made to seek other fields when he retires.' And yet this was in an area which had enjoyed relatively cordial relations between police and population and at a time when there was greater peace in Ireland than at any time in the preceding hundred years. Inspector Garrow Green too was under no illusions and knew that behind the good humour and the harmless roguery the ordinary people ' still looked forward to the near future and when they would have a police force of their own making'. The people, he recorded, had little of the 'old respect for the green cloth of the Irish garrison'.

Ironically, it was the unarmed and, in the main, non-political Dublin Metropolitan Police which was first to fall under the wrath of the people in the troubled years leading towards the signing of the Anglo-Irish treaty of 1921 and the setting up of the Irish Free State. The *Report of the Committee of Inquiry (Royal Irish Constabulary and Dublin Metropolitan Police)* of 1914 recorded that the R I C were, on the whole, well integrated among the people in so far as could be expected; it observed that 'the military character of the Force is passing away' and that 'the men do not, as a rule, carry arms, except for drill and for ceremonial occasions.' By that time the R I C's unarmed metropolitan sister-force had been reviled and cast aside by the working-class population of Dublin as a result of their brutality in breaking the general strike of 1913.

In 1913 the D M P was just under 1,200 strong and was still regarded as a model urban police force in international police circles. Relations between police and all classes of society were good and the police bands and mounted sections were in great demand for public functions, processions and celebrations. A celebrated tradition of physical fitness had been built up in the force and its tug-of-war team had several times carried off British and European trophies. In 1844, when the force was just over 1,000 strong, 942 members were recorded as being 5ft. 9in. or over, 153 were 6ft. 0in. or over and 36 were 6ft. 2in. or over. By tradition the tallest men policed the B District, which comprised stations at College Street, Lad Lane and Clarendon Street and which covered the south side of the city centre between the Liffey and Grand Canal Street and was bounded on the west by South Great George's Street, Aungier Street and Camden Street. In 1876 the average weight of members of the force was 12 stone 11lb and one celebrated Constable Woulfe was recorded at 20 stone with a height of 6ft. 6½in.

The D M P was part of Dublin's very life, an instituition in the capital, as much an integral part of the city as Guinness's Brewery or Nelson's Pillar.

All that changed in August 1913. Dublin was paralysed by a general lock-out as Jim Larkin, the trade union leader, organised the workers to stand up against the employers and profiteers who kept them and their families in what had become notorious as the worst slums in Europe. For reasons which have never been fully explained the police charged a huge crowd which Larkin was addressing. In the charge and in subsequent skirmishes through the centre of Dublin which lasted for several days, at least three people, including a young woman, died. The D M P were immediately identified by the Dublin working class as the agents of the employers and a rift developed which has yet to be completely rebridged.

It is difficult to pinpoint exactly the reasons for the ferocity of the Dublin police force's attacks on the strikers of 1913— the people who had adored and cheered them in the past. But it cannot have been unconnected with a growing mood of resentment and viciousness within the force at inadequate pay and worsening conditions of service.

Between 1903 and 1913 there had been a marked fall-off in the desirability of the police forces as fields of employment. Pay had not been increased to match the cost of living and the police had lost considerable ground compared with other urban occupational groups.

Resignations from both the D M P and the R I C were increasing. In 1903 there were 85 resignations from the R I C; in 1911 there were 163, and in 1913, 299. In 1901, while pay in the better British police forces varied between £1 9s. 9d. a week and £1 13s. od., the pay of the D M P constable was £1 10s. od. R I C constables received only £1 7s. od. In 1914, when British police rates jumped to £1 18s. od., for example, in the case of the Sheffield police, the D M P man was still receiving only £1 10s. od., while the R I C man had gained a shilling increase, giving him £1 8s. od. a week. By contrast, Dublin bricklayers in 1914 earned an average wage of £1 19s. 7d. a week, stonecutters earned £1 15s. 5d. a week, and plumbers earned £2 1s. 7½d. Labourers' earnings varied between £1 0s. 10d. and £1 1s. 10½d. a week.

Thus the police were in many instances earning less than the men whom they were facing on the picket lines and in the streets. Repeated appeals by the police representative bodies to improve their situation had been ignored by the authorities and one of the results was that the resentment of the Dublin police was taken out on the heads of the Dublin workers in the general strike. It was not the first or last time that Irish workers were to find themselves the first victims of discontent among their police forces.

The D M P were to remain in a condition of virtual impotence throughout the years of the struggle between the forces of Dáil Éireann and the Crown, and their rehabilitation was not even begun until 1925, when they were amalgamated with the Gárda Síochána, the Irish Free State force which was set up to replace the R I C.

The D M P had to be periodically withdrawn from the streets of the capital during the period 1919–21 and attempts which were made to arm the force were frustrated largely by the opposition of the police themselves. It was perhaps this conscious policy of opting out of the trouble that enabled the force to emerge from the period at least structurally intact. But the Royal Irish Constabulary did not have the luxury of such a choice. They were obliged to face the inevitable reckoning which their role as the Crown's first line of defence was to bring. From January 1919 onwards they began to pay the price of that role.

B

2 The Chaos of Transition 1913-22

THE year 1913 marked the beginning of the end of the tranquillity which Ireland had enjoyed almost without interruption since the last of the Fenian risings in 1867. From 1913 onwards the police were variously occupied with strikes, the revival of the Irish Republican Brotherhood and the gathering crisis of Home Rule. In 1913 Sir Edward Carson organised the Ulster Volunteers in opposition to the Home Rule Bill and later in the same year, largely as a counter to the existence of the Unionist force, the Irish Volunteers were organised under the leadership of Eóin MacNéill. In April 1916 Dublin burst into a brief but bloody rebellion which left 500 dead and 2,500 wounded on the streets of the capital. Almost from that point, as it must have appeared to Dublin Castle, a mood of bitterness and disaffection spread throughout the country.

But while Ireland had been disturbed in the years leading up to 1916, the troubles had been largely confined to Dublin and Ulster. True, there was a growth in unrest in some parts of the provinces such as Kerry, but the population on the whole was peaceable. The police were at full strength and fully alert, well aware of the dangers of German infiltration, and their intelligence reports were superbly accurate. They reported some unrest but nothing more serious from most areas. It was to take a series of those unfortunate acts of maladministration which seemed to characterise British rule in Ireland to bring the country from a condition of relative stability in the spring of 1916 to one of widespread agitation and disorder by the spring of 1919.

The first and most serious error had been made by General Sir John Maxwell, Commander-in-Chief of the British forces in Ireland and director of the troops which put down the

Easter Rising of April 1916. As soon as resistance had been crushed Maxwell had set about teaching the rebels a lesson. Fifteen of the leaders were shot over a period of weeks and in the immediate aftermath of the rebellion over 3,000 people were arrested. Of these almost 2,000 were transported to England where they were interned for periods ranging from eight to fifteen months. The severity of Maxwell's punishment and in particular the execution of the leaders was to have the ironic effect of reviving Sinn Féin's fortunes just as the organisation seemed to be on the way to obliteration in public rage and outcry against the Rising. Sinn Féin, of course, had not been responsible for the Rising but they reaped the political benefits of its blood sacrifice. When the last group of prisoners was released in 1917, they returned to heroes' welcomes amongst a people who had begun to rally around the Sinn Féin platform and who had begun to turn against the Castle administration in all its aspects with unprecedented unanimity.

The other major cause of Irish disaffection was a blunder of almost equally staggering proportions. In 1918 the British government threatened to introduce conscription into Ireland and the tumultuous reaction reinforced the gathering strength of Sinn Féin. In the event, the war was over before the issue could be decided but the eight months of controversy had brought tens of thousands of recruits into Sinn Féin and the Irish Volunteers, which were now being organised by an earnest and enthusiastic young Corkman, Michael Collins, recently freed from internment in Britain. Even the Royal Irish Constabulary and Dublin Metropolitan Police protested against the proposal but Lloyd George insisted that the Irish Conscription Bill should go on the statute book.

Thus by November 1918 Ireland was in a state of seething unrest and resentment accentuated by the first pangs of economic recession as the war drew to a close. Massive unemployment and low wages both in Dublin and the provinces heightened the tension. The men of 1916 were heroes, the bad intent of the British government had been clearly seen in the Conscription Bill, and times were hard in the country.

Ordinary people who hardly understood the relationship between Ireland and Britain suddenly found themselves estranged from the administration which directed their lives. Encouraged by Sinn Féin, they found that they could hate England and its agents with a great hatred.

Sinn Féin, which had grown but slowly since its foundation in 1905 by Arthur Griffith, a Dublin journalist, had now spread its influence into every town and village outside the north-eastern counties. In July 1917 Eamon de Valera had won a by-election victory in Clare on a Sinn Féin ticket which propounded a policy of abstentionism from Westminster and envisaged the setting up of an alternative assembly and administration for the Irish people. Shortly afterwards de Valera was elected President of both Sinn Féin and the Irish Volunteers. Immediately after the war ended the party contested the general election and captured seventy-three seats, virtually obliterating the old Irish Parliamentary Party.

On 21 January 1919 about two hundred people filed into the Dublin Mansion House to witness the elected Sinn Féin members who could be mustered declare themselves the Assembly of Ireland—Dáil Éireann. Most of the elected members were on the run or in prison. A useful 'German plot' of the previous summer had enabled the Castle to sweep up large numbers of Sinn Féin organisers for prison or internment —among them Arthur Griffith and Eamon de Valera. In the event only twenty-five members were present at the first meeting. The chair was taken by a forty-four-year-old director of a firm of ecclesiastical candlemakers, Cathal Brugha, best known to the police for his threat to shoot the cabinet ministers responsible if conscription were introduced to Ireland during the war. In its first session the Dáil issued a declaration of independence, sent messages of goodwill to other nations, issued its democratic programme and announced its intention of setting up its own machinery of state. It was a unique form of challenge to the imperial power of Great Britain and a dignified, if pretentious, opening to the campaign which was to undermine the institutions of the Castle government.

The selection of the R I C as the first target for elimination in that campaign was inevitable. In 1919 the force was almost 10,000 strong, spread through 1,200 heavily fortified barracks, well armed and superbly disciplined. In the thinly scattered and still relatively poor communities of the Irish countryside the police were often the only tangible form of authority which the people knew. They extended their influence in virtually every aspect of rural life. If they could be neutralised, the whole machinery of British government outside of Dublin would have to come to a halt.

On the principle that the first step required to topple the existing structure was to remove the supports on which it rested, the Dáil in February 1919 called for a boycott of the R I C. It was taken up with great vigour by the 1,500 Sinn Féin clubs all over Ireland and within weeks the force had been placed on the defensive and largely isolated from the community.

It was of little account that most of the men in the R I C in 1919 saw nothing reprehensible in their calling, having joined in a period of calm and reasonably good relations between the force and the people. Ireland was in a vicious and particularly ugly mood in the spring of 1919. All community life was denied the police, merchants refused to supply local barracks with goods and any who did ran the risk of retribution by Sinn Féin and the Volunteers. Policemen's families underwent intimidation in many places and in a number of instances girls who fraternised with the police were publicly humiliated and punished. Most of the R I C rank and file were Catholics but more often than not they now found themselves worshipping alone in church while the remainder of the community waited to attend whatever Mass the police did not.

It is tempting but unhelpful to speculate on whether the R I C could have withstood the pressure of a social boycott on its own. They had never been intimidated in the past by mere unpopularity and, in spite of the increase in the rate of resignations and the discontent over pay, morale was still high.

It was perhaps fortunate for the Sinn Fein party programme that on 21 January, the day the First Dáil met in Dublin, a party of Tipperary Volunteers decided to accelerate the demise of the Royal Irish Constabulary in their own way.

That afternoon a party of eight men under Dan Breen and Seán Tracy ambushed an explosives convoy which was under escort by armed RIC constables near Soloheadbeg in Tipperary. Two constables were shot dead. The ambushers took their Lee-Enfield rifles before departing with their load of gelignite.

The Soloheadbeg ambush was not the first clash between the police and the Volunteers-there had been several shooting incidents in Kerry in which the Volunteers had come of second best-but it was the first successful engagement which the forces of the Republic had fought since 1916. It set the pattern for a campaign of attacks against the police which spread all over the country in a matter of weeks. Many local Volunteer commanders were obliged to combine the attacks with arms-gathering operations and there was a high casualty rate among the attacking parties. Nevertheless, between June and December 1919 the RIC were beaten back from large areas of the countryside, barracks were burned, lines of communication were severed and eighteen constables were killed and over seventy wounded.

The withdrawal of the RIC from the countryside had several important implications for Sinn Fein and the Irish Republican Army, as the Volunteers were now known. Firstly, the way was now open for the recruitment, training and organisation of volunteers on a nation-wide basis, a task which had been impossible while the police operated in every town and village. Secondly, the Castle was now obliged to fall back on the raw force of military strength to hold the country, and the regular army garrison was unable to adapt to full police functions. Thirdly, the Castle's overall intelligence system had been neutralised and, finally, the ancillary agencies of the Crown, now without the protection of the police, were rendered ineffective. In 1918 the R I C had 1,129 stations throughout the thirty-two counties, but by early 1920 that figure had been reduced almost by half. As the police withdrew, other elements of the Castle bureaucracy ceased to function as well. Local authorities made declarations of support for Dáil Éireann, health and welfare boards reported to the Dáil's departments of state, and in county after county the Crown courts effectually ceased to operate.

The withdrawal of the R I C left a massive administrative vacuum in the community. Rates and taxes could not be gathered, court orders could not be enforced and legal debts could not be collected. In a community where deprivation and real hardship were still common, the growth of disorder was widespread and swift. As the area under R I C control diminished, the Dáil realised that to be consistent with its own claims of jurisdiction it would have to create alternative police and courts and thus in June 1919 the hitherto largely imaginary machinery of the Dáil government was extended to include a system of courts and police.

Co. Clare was the first to adopt these new institutions and by the autumn of 1919 the county had a flourishing network of both parish and district courts. A police section was drawn from the I R A which, it was hoped, would enforce the orders of the Sinn Féin courts as well as performing regular police duties. By early 1920 these courts were functioning in twenty-eight of the thirty-two counties. They were highly successful, operating—with the occasional local variation—on a code drawn up by a number of contemporary legal authorities. Barristers and solicitors pleaded before these courts, whose efficient and impartial operation became a major element in Sinn Féin propaganda to the international press.

The Republican Police were, unfortunately, less successful. On a purely practical basis, policing in a war-time situation where the enemy would not distinguish between Republican Police and army—if indeed that distinction ever existed—was largely impossible. Moreover, many battalion commanders reasoned that if a good man with a gun was available for active service, he could be put to more productive work than chasing petty criminals and moonshiners.

The wave of crime and lawlessness which followed the withdrawal of the R I C was a manifestation of long-pent-up resentment and distress among the communities of rural Ireland. Unemployment, low wages and the endemic squabbling over land had all engendered tensions and hostilities which the firm hand of the R I C had long held under control. But by the end of 1919 the smouldering bitterness and hostility had overflowed into a wave of landgrabbing, anarchy and sheer criminal lawlessness. In the South and along the western seaboard, the traditional homes of the poteen industry, there was a massive increase in illicit distillation with all its attendant evils of violence, extortion and drunkenness. Later during 1920 the poteen trade was to expand beyond its traditional geographical confines and covered almost the whole country—even Dublin City.

Real hardship too was in many instances aggravated by the disturbances. Because it was physically impossible to collect debts or enforce court orders over large areas, merchants and shopkeepers began to restrict credit and many families living on the cycle of the farming year, whereby they paid their bills at harvest or market time, found themselves in real difficulty. The inevitable consequence was a sharp increase in ordinary crime, often accompanied by violence or intimidation and often under the guise of military action on behalf of the Republic. Small communities which had never known criminal violence beyond the occasional public-house brawl now found themselves in the situation where necessity, opportunity and simple criminality all combined under the gun in an attack on the peace of the community. The breakdown of order was, furthermore, frequently taken as an opportunity for settling old scores and feuds, many of them originating from the land distribution acts of previous years.

Finally, there was simple destructiveness, usually manifesting itself in indiscriminate arson and violence. Empty R I C barracks and government buildings were a legitimate target in the context of the struggle, but too often the campaign of arson was extended to include unco-operative and unpopular merchants and businessmen, isolated farmhouses and out-houses, especially those owned by Protestants or other sup-posed supporters of Britain, as well as lifeguard and coast-guard stations.

The level of crime in the community increased steeply during the latter half of 1920. The R I C and D M P did not, of course, draw any distinction in their records between political and non-political crime, so comparisons based on their reports are of no help in estimating the crime increase—as distinct from the level of war activities—at the time. As far as the Castle statistics were concerned, the shopkeeper who was killed for the contents of his till was in the same category as the Black and Tan who died in an I R A ambush. During the month of September 1920 the newspapers recorded no fewer than twelve killings which, as far as one can judge from contemporary evidence, had no direct political connotations. Bank robberies became an everyday occurrence, many banks being robbed repeatedly with almost predictable regularity. Apart from a brief six-week period after the truce when the level of crime was to drop very noticeably, disorder and violence continued on a massive scale right up to the beginning of the Civil War when the remaining elements of order and restraint were finally swept aside.

When the truce became effective on 21 July 1921 the whole underground administration of the Irish Republic sur-faced with a newly acquired legitimacy. For a brief period of weeks nobody worried over-much where the jurisdiction of the Crown forces would end and that of Dáil Éireann and its forces begin. But in the euphoric atmosphere of new-found peace it was assumed that most things would look after them-selves and that the maintenance of order would follow auto-matically.

De Valera issued an appeal to the people to observe the truce, warning each 'individual soldier and citizen' that he had to 'regard himself as the custodian of the nation's honour'. On

27 July the Dáil's Minister for Home Affairs, Eamon Duggan, told a press conference with apparent unconcern that no arrangements had yet been made for the distribution of responsibility for law and order in rural areas. The terms of the truce were vague on the matter beyond a stipulation that the policing of Dublin would remain the duty of the D M P. The British apparently took it that the R I C and Crown courts would continue to function, while the Dáil government, for its part, had no intention whatever of suppressing the Republican police or courts. In October the Republican courts began to function openly in Dublin and a number of other centres. In Dublin they undertook prosecutions at the request of the City Corporation. Most of the prosecutions were for breaches of the Weights and Measures Acts and fines were imposed on dairymen and publicans for selling substandard produce. Within a month the Republican courts were functioning openly all over the country, hearing cases and passing judgements, often while nearby Crown courts stood empty and unattended.

The Chief Secretary, Sir Hamar Greenwood, was horrified. He begged Collins and de Valera at least to operate their courts discreetly, as he was sure to be attacked at Westminster over this flouting of the imperial power. The Dáil government was not to be moved, however, and, predictably, on 20 October 1921 Greenwood had to admit to outraged members at Westminster that the Sinn Féin courts were indeed operating in breach of the truce—'but', he pleaded, 'the government must be allowed some discretion in these matters'.

That was not the last of Greenwood's problems at Westminster arising out of the maintenance of order during the truce period. Late in July a liaison system had been organised by Austin Stack and Michael Collins to ensure adequate communication between Republican and Crown forces in every district. Again on 20 October Greenwood was asked at Westminster whether British officers were now under instructions to treat with 'murderers, robbers, and arsonists'. Much to the dismay and anger of the house, he was obliged to admit that this was indeed the case. However, in an effort to maintain the king's writ, he assured the members, Sinn Féin courts in Westmeath had been successfully suppressed.

The liaison system had, on the whole, worked quite well in maintaining the truce. Michael Staines, who had headed the Republican Police, was sent as liaison officer to Galway where a particularly sensitive and dangerous situation had arisen. Eóin O'Duffy, who was the energetic and capable O/C of Northern Command, was sent to Belfast, where the eve of the truce was marked by an Orange attack on Catholic ghettoes which left fifteen dead and a hundred wounded. O'Duffy appears to have made genuine efforts at first to co-operate with the R I C and the British Army in Belfast, but on finding that the co-operation was not reciprocated, on the night of 1 September he called out I R A snipers to defend the Catholic districts. His reported order of those days, 'Give them the lead', which confirmed his reputation as a man of firm action, was to lend an ironic touch to his subsequent appointment as Commissioner of an unarmed Irish police force.

But the liaison system could do no more than prevent major outbreaks of hostilities between the two sides. At the local level all was in chaos. In most areas there was only a token force of R I C or Republican Police and in some districts of the West and Midlands there was neither. Wherever the two existed side by side there was constant friction, often marked by violence. The R I C were still performing some basic police duties in a few areas, mainly in the counties of the Pale— Dublin, Wicklow, Kildare, Louth and Meath. In September R I C men in Drogheda evicted a group of striking workers from a foundry which they had occupied, and in some areas of Wicklow and Dublin a few regular R I C patrols begun to operate again. However, as soon as the truce was seen to be effective, the Republican Police in most districts began to insist on an authority which they had largely eschewed in the previous two years and clashes between the two police agencies became common. In October I R A volunteers had to inter-vene in Carrickmacross, Co. Monaghan, when R I C and

Republican Police tried to arrest each other in an altercation which began when members of both forces were called to deal with a man who was drunk and disorderly. In Drogheda in October a macabre game of hide and seek was played out between the two police forces for possession of a body which had been taken from the River Boyne. It was finally agreed to hold two inquests on the dead man, one for the R I C and one for the Republican Police. The jury (which was the same for both inquests) returned a verdict of death by misadventure and added a rider criticising the R I C for locking the body in a shed and going away with the key.

There were occasional instances of R I C men handing over prisoners to Sinn Féin courts and of Republican Police handing over prisoners to the R I C. On a few occasions the two forces worked together to track down armed criminals. When Mr Max Green was shot dead in St Stephen's Green in Dublin on 3 March, while trying to stop an armed robber, Metropolitan Police and Republican Police joined forces to arrest the culprits. Assistant Commissioner Barrett of the D M P writing his report of the case to the Chief Secretary remarked: 'The greatest co-operation between D M P, I R P (Irish Republican Police) and civilians was noticeable. The Assistant Commissioner got every assistance and statements from I R P officers who are prepared to give any evidence they can at the trial.'

But the manner and form of relations between the two police forces was mainly dictated by the allegiance of the local authority of the area. Where the local health boards, coroners and like officials recognised Dáil Éireann, the R I C had no choice but to recognise the *de facto* authority of the Dáil if they were to function at all. Conversely, where the authority of the Castle was still good, the Republican Police usually found themselves obliged to work in collusion with the R I C. But these orderly arrangements were rare. In most places neither agency worked with any noticeable effectiveness and any competent criminal had hardly to take their existence into account at all.

The position of the R I C had become quite invidious after the truce. Under the Government of Ireland Act of 1920 the R I C and D M P were to pass from imperial control in any event after three years. Generous retirement terms were offered to members who did not wish to serve in either force under a Belfast or Dublin government. The members of both forces were now unsure whether this would be prejudiced by the new settlement which was shaping up between the Dáil and the London government and demoralisation set in rapidly and severely. In desperation, the Representative Bodies of both forces petitioned Westminster, the govenment, and finally the king, for a speedy disbandment on the terms set out in the 1920 act.

Whatever the future held for the D M P, it was clear that the R I C would never again be able to function as a police force in rural Ireland. Even ordinary civil duties could not be performed without the risk of death or serious injury to members of the force. In March 1922 County Inspector Carroll wrote from Cork to the Inspector-General that his men were no longer prepared to carry out the innocuous task of enumerating emigrants at Cobh. It took four or five men to escort the enumerator to the quay, he said, and the lives of the enumerator and the escort constables were in constant danger: 'The R I C are risking their lives in doing work which could be done by civilians without any danger,' he added.

Furthermore, the R I C had been depleted by almost 2,000 resignations between the end of 1919 and the truce. In some instances whole barracks had resigned *en masse*. At Listowel in Kerry in June 1920 the men forced District Commissioner Ferguson Smyth to leave the barracks in rage and indignation when he had exhorted them to shoot Sinn Féiners on sight. The entire barrack party then resigned. There were similar incidents at Killarney and Tralee barracks.

The leader of the Listowel revolt, Constable Jeremiah Mee, subsequently took charge almost single-handed of the Sinn Féin campaign to bring down the police system. In October 1920 he had been authorised by the Dáil to travel throughout the country on behalf of the Department of Labour to find jobs for men who had resigned from the R I C. Earlier he had written to the Department: 'I suggest that if the Irish people are really serious about breaking up the present police force in Ireland, the first step is to safeguard the interests of those who have already come out and are now willing to assist us in our fight against oppression . . . If this were to be done all over Ireland, in my humble opinion police would resign by the hundred, the Volunteer ranks would be greatly strengthened with good fighting material and English rule in Ireland, if not completely broken, would at least be seriously shaken.'

But Constable Mee also drew attention to the growing effectiveness of the Black and Tans and, with a shrewd policeman's instinct, pointed out: 'Unless the Irish police are taken out at once, it will be useless bringing them out later as the Black and Tans will have a thorough knowledge of the country and will be able to do police work without the assistance of the Irish police.'

Collaboration with the Black and Tans was probably the final nail in the coffin of the R I C as far as the Irish people were concerned. Any man who did not come out of the force once the methods of the Tans became known had finally elected to stand for the Crown against the Irish people—or such at any rate was the general feeling when the scores came to be settled late in 1921.

Sinn Féin had done what it could to make the lot of resigned R I C men an easier one. They had appealed to the Irish Transport and General Workers Union to assist in the re-employment of policemen who had left their livelihood to support the Republic, and Sinn Féin clubs throughout the country had been asked to make special efforts to welcome back local men who had left the police. A circular of July 1920 had told the clubs:

Every man of Irish birth should get a chance of becoming a loyal citizen of the Irish Republic and of earning an honest living in

Ireland. This is true even of those Irishmen who are so unfortunate at present to be engaged in doing the work of the enemy
in Ireland as members of the R I C. Many of these men joined
without any clear understanding of what they were doing. They
were young, they had no knowledge of Irish history, the national
tradition may have been weak in their own family or in their
native place.

It should now be made clear that those who resign will not be
regarded as enemies of Ireland but will be granted every opportunity to make up for the past. Men who resign should get
credit for an honest intention. They should be welcomed back to
their native place. The local Sinn Féin club should try to help
them in the same way it helps another person in need of
employment. In case nothing can be done locally a communication should be sent to headquarters. A fund is being provided
to assist in cases of special hardship.

But by July 1921 there was little sympathy left between
the Irish people and the Royal Irish Constabulary, and shortly
after the truce Collins and Greenwood agreed in London that
the force would have to be disbanded. The D M P would be
kept on under whatever government would be created by the
settlement. The D M P had not earned anything like the
odium of the R I C, if one excepted the notorious G Division,
the 'political' wing which operated from the Castle.

Collins was also aware that the new state would need a core
of professionally trained police to form the backbone of whatever new force would be set up to replace the R I C. The first
steps to create that replacement force were not to be taken
until February of the following year but immediately the truce
was signed, Collins set about organising the nucleus of a
detective force over which he would have direct control. This
force would serve a number of purposes. He needed a body of
men which he could use to apply pressure in sensitive areas
without involving the army and thus prejudicing the truce. He
needed a protective corps for himself and the other members
of the Dáil government and for his double agents in the
British services in Dublin, who were now in constant danger

of reprisals from the British secret service. In particular, Collins was worried about the safety of his former double agents in the G Division and the secret service, Broy, Neligan and MacNamara. Finally, there was an urgent need to provide an agency which would cut down the worst excesses of criminal violence—by the gun if necessary. The new force was about a hundred strong, heavily armed and principally drawn from the intelligence units of the I R A brigades throughout the country. They were known initially as the Protective Corps and subsequently named, somewhat face-tiously, the C I D. They operated in plain clothes from their headquarters at Oriel House in Westland Row and were in a short time to become known as the 'Oriel House men'.

From August 1921 until November 1923 when they were disbanded Oriel House and its detectives became a feared institution, not only in Dublin but throughout the country. They were headed by Pat Moynihan, one of Collins's most trusted agents, who had played a vital role in his intelligence network while employed in the investigation branch of the Post Office. Moynihan had three lieutenants, Joe Kinsella, a 1916 veteran who had acted as arms and explosives distribution organiser during the war from his office at the Inchicore Rail Yard, Finion O'Driscoll, a tough intelligence officer from Cork, and Peter Ennis, who was subsequently to become head of the Gárda Síochána's Special Branch. Moynihan was conferred with the title of Director, Ennis with that of Superintendent, and O'Driscoll, Kinsella and several others with the title of Inspector. The men's pay ranged from £6 to £3 a week with keep in Oriel House.

With ruthless and often brutal efficiency Oriel House began to put down crime not only in Dublin but anywhere within striking distance of a fast car. Their brief was an open one and they co-operated variously with the R I C, the Republican Police, the British Army, the D M P and, on at least one occasion, with the Black and Tans. Their statutory basis was doubtful and it was unclear for a time to which government department they were responsible—Defence or Home Affairs.

For the most part they simply reported to Collins. Their standing orders fell somewhat short of a blanket 'Shoot first and then ask questions' but members frequently considered it necessary to equip themselves with Lewis guns and Mills bombs before setting out to make arrests or sometimes merely to conduct interrogations.

Oriel House swiftly assumed a reputation for effective, if unorthodox methods for the suppression of crime. In late 1922 and early 1923 evidence came to light of the maltreatment of prisoners and Republican supporters were to allege that a number of murders and assassinations had been committed or instigated by Oriel House men. The building itself became a focal point for nightly attacks both by Anti-Treatyites and loyalist elements and the Lewis gunners on the roof of Oriel House were engaged in more or less constant sniping with the Officer Training Corps of Trinity College and with Anti-Treaty I R A men on the roofs of buildings in nearby Brunswick Street. In October 1921 four landmines were placed at the rear of the building which, had they gone off, would certainly have buried alive approximately seventy prisoners and staff inside at the time. In the event only one of the mines exploded, plunging the building into darkness, bringing down ceilings, floors and even internal walls. Joe Kinsella, flung from his desk on the first floor, emptied his revolver into a ledger which came flying up the stairs with the force of the blast, thinking it was the first of an attacking party coming through the door. In the basement, detectives who had been guarding a number of prisoners were rescued by their charges who had literally been blown out of their cells. In the event the only casualties were three of the attacking party who were captured at Westland Row station and executed by firing squad.

The first serious breaches of the truce began to occur in September as the nature of the London negotiations became clear and the first rumours of a split within Sinn Féin began to leak out. As violence began to increase again, the efforts of the few active R I C men and Republican Police were completely overwhelmed. Unrestrained now by any bonds of honour and fanned by bitter disillusionment and hatred, the violence which had been barely controlled, finally spilled over into anarchy and open war.

Late in August 1921 a series of violent armed raids took place throughout small towns in the South. On 4 September a twenty-three-year-old retarded youth, Edward O'Connor, a discharged Dublin Fusilier, was taken from his home near Mount Street in Dublin by a group of six armed men and shot dead. On 9 September two R I C constables were kidnapped and disappeared near Bandon, Co. Cork. These were the first killings in what was to be a two-year period of bloodshed, unredeemed by few, if any, acts of valour or personal sacrifice. Robbery, intimidation, arson and kidnapping swiftly followed on a scale unprecedented even in the violence of the previous three years. By October attacks on police barracks had resumed on a large scale in contravention of the truce.

The Treaty, signed on 6 December confirmed the Collins-Greenwood agreement for the disbandment of the R I C, but it marked the complete abandonment of hope for a peaceful settlement of the differences within the Dáil.

During the next two months the wretched remnants of the R I C became the focal point for the attacks of all violent extremists; 425 of its members had been killed and 725 wounded during the period from January 1919 to July 1921 but the casualties of December 1921 to February 1922 were the most bitter of their losses. On 13 December Sergeant Maher was shot dead while walking unarmed across the village green at Ballybunion, Co. Kerry. On 14 December Sergeant Enright was killed and Constable Timoney seriously wounded while they attended a race-meeting, unarmed and in civilian clothes, at Kilmallock, Co. Limerick.

On 15 December Constable Mooney was shot while waiting at Carlow railway station, and in Lisdoonvarna, Co. Clare, on 3 February two off-duty constables were shot dead while leaving a public house. Between December and February 82 attacks were recorded on the police resulting in 12 deaths and

27 seriously wounded. In February and March 1922 the killings continued, often as demobilising constables evacuated their barracks or visited families and friends before departing. On 17 March armed men entered the wards of Galway hospital and shot dead two policemen and a civilian lying helpless in their beds. By the beginning of February the few remaining R I C garrisons throughout the country were in a state of terror and living virtually under siege. They eagerly received the I R A parties which took possession of the barracks in accordance with the terms of the Treaty.

On 10 February Lieutenant Wogan Brown was shot dead in broad daylight by armed men as he walked down the main street of Kildare, having just handed over £800 pay for his men at the Artillery Barracks. The assailants were locally known. In anger and indignation the *Irish Times* of the following day asked the Provisional Government of the emerging Irish Free State what plans it had for creating a police force. In the same issue the newspaper's Donegal correspondent reported that the county had deteriorated into a condition 'of complete brigandage'. The Cork correspondent reported that a 'great terror' hung over the city as chaos and violence rose 'unchecked by any'.

The *Irish Times* leader of the day warned the government that its prime duty would be to put down lawlessness and pointed out : 'The Provisional Government has many urgent duties but its first and most urgent duty is the restoration of and maintenance of public order. . . Crimes of violence and robbery have become alarmingly frequent in Dublin and the provinces. . . The immediate problem of finances will be vastly simplified if the Provisional Government can offer as its pledge a peaceful and crimeless Ireland.'

Three days after the murder of Lieutenant Wogan Brown, Churchill announced the suspension of troop withdrawals from Ireland because of the growing disorder. It was probably no more than a tactical move to bring further pressure to bear on the Provisional Government to take a harder line with the Anti-Treaty group, but Collins immediately cabled to say that three men had been arrested for the murder and they would, if convicted, face the supreme penalty. It was significant that, while the text of his telegram to Churchill was made public, Collins gave no indication, such as might have been expected in the circumstances, that plans were already well under way for the creation of a new police force—the Civic Guard. He had his good reasons for not doing that because the seemingly straightforward task of creating a new police had become an issue of great contention within the Provisional Government and within the leadership of Sinn Féin.

3 Steps towards Order 1922

THE Dáil government was aware from a very early stage
of the huge problems which it would encounter in endeavour-
ing to restore the rule of law once the struggle with the British
was over : this was clear from the fact that as early as August
1921, within three weeks of the truce coming into effect,
Collins and Sir Hamar Greenwood were discussing the future
of the Irish police forces. It was at this meeting that the decision in principle was taken to disband the R I C and to
keep on the D M P, although the details of this agreement
were not to be worked out until the following January. In
addition, Collins had begun to seek the advice of his contacts
in the R I C and D M P as early as September 1921. Most
of his agents in the Castle security forces had surfaced by this
time and two in particular had Collins's ear on the problems
of policing—David Neligan and Eamon Broy. Both men had
experience in the ranks of the D M P and both served as
double agents for Collins while working in the G Division.

Surprisingly, however, in spite of the ready availability of
professional police advice, little or nothing was done to set
up a new force during the six months from July 1921 to February 1922. In early February, after much valuable time had
been lost, Collins hurriedly selected a number of his former
police agents, together with a group of army officers and asked
them to form an organising committee to draw up plans for a
new police. The committee, under the chairmanship of
Michael Staines, a Dáil T D, 1916 veteran and acting head
of the Republican Police, began work at once but found that
they had a bare three weeks to lay down the foundations
of the proposed police force before recruitment was to begin.
On 24 January 1922 at a meeting in the Colonial Office,

Collins and Greenwood had fixed 20 February as the official date for the disbandment of the R I C, and the Provisional Government agreed that enrolment in the new force should begin immediately the Royal Irish Constabulary ceased to be operational.

On 8 February Staines's group met in the Gresham Hotel in Dublin, together with a committee appointed by the Provisional Government, and a number of basic decisions were taken on the structure of the proposed police force. The chairman of the Provisional Government's committee was Richard Mulcahy, the Minister for Defence; present also were Eamon Duggan, the Minister for Home Affairs, under whose control the police would now come, a number of former R I C and D M P agents who had been working for Collins, and Collins himself, who sat apart from the committee and watched silently while they made their decisions. Staines's committee was expanded and instructed to work out more detailed proposals for the new force and the organising committee agreed to meet every day until the basic organisational groundwork would be complete.

The task of finding a replacement force for the R I C had undoubtedly been allowed to drift in the previous six months and that neglect did not end with the Gresham Hotel meeting. There was an extraordinary lack of awareness of the complexity of the problem of creating a new police force. Not only would it have to earn for itself the support and enthusiasm of the people but it would have to bury the ghost of the hated R I C, a task which was made infinitely more difficult as the country divided over the issue of the Treaty. Moreover, the roots of serious difficulties which were to emerge later in 1922 were firmly planted in the days after the Gresham Hotel meeting and Collins was to regret bitterly that he had not supervised the arrangements more closely himself or delegated responsibility for the police to one of the stronger men in his cabinet.

Much of the Provisional Government's neglect and indolence in the planning of the new police force was directly attributable to the growing tensions between the Irish leaders in the autumn and winter months of 1921. Throughout October and November, as the debate on the settlement with Britain raged, relations between the Collins-Griffith and the de Valera wings deteriorated. After the signature of the Treaty on 6 December the extent of the rift became apparent in the acrimonious debate which preceded the Dáil's ratification of the Treaty by a majority of only seven. On 9 January de Valera announced his resignation as President of Dáil Éireann. The split was now in the open and the primary concern of the Provisional Government which was to come into office later in the month was to prevent that split developing into open war.

Throughout January and February Collins and Griffith were moving constantly back and forth between Dublin and London working out the details of the takeover from the British. There were massive difficulties to be resolved, financial arrangements to be settled, army and civil service personnel to be replaced, and there was the continuing problem of public order. But there were two questions which over-shadowed all these and which were to occupy on their own the greater part of the energies and attention of Collins and Griffith in these weeks—the drafting of a constitution for the new Irish Free State and the settlement of its exact territorial limits.

The bulk of the work—in addition to the continuation of negotiations with the 'Republicans' (i.e., those who demanded complete autonomy for Ireland rather than the 'Free State' imposed by the Treaty)—fell ultimately on Michael Collins. The Provisional Government with which he began to operate in January was not as strong or as capable as he might have wished; its weakest link was probably Eamon Duggan, who as Minister for Home Affairs had direct responsibility for public order and the raising of the police for the new state. Some of the most capable men in the government of the Second Dáil, including Brugha and Gavan Duffy, had gone with de Valera, while Collins, as Chairman of the Provisional Government did not perhaps deploy the remaining talent to the best advantage. W. T. Cosgrave was placed in charge of the Department of Local Government–hardly a priority location. Kevin O'Higgins, still relatively unknown, was allowed to help out with the drafting of the constitution, but his energies were in the main directed into the Department of Economic Affairs. Ernest Blythe, capable and energetic and supremely efficient, did not become a member of the Provisional Government until August. Patrick McGilligan was acting as secretary to Kevin O'Higgins, a post in which his considerable talent was largely wasted; he was later created Minister for Industry and Commerce.

Eamon Duggan, who had succeeded Austin Stack as Minister for Home Affairs in the Dáil government earlier in January, became, in addition, Minister for Home Affairs in the Provisional Government, thereby in terms of strict precedence becoming Collins's deputy. In retrospect it is clear that it was not the right appointment. Duggan was fiercely loyal to Collins and Griffith but it is unlikely that he could have successfully coped with the organisational challenges which now lay ahead. Yet as Minister for Home Affairs, the primary responsibility for the restoration of order was his, as was responsibility for phasing out the old system of police and courts and replacing it with the new institutions of the Free State. It was a massive task and Duggan's qualities of loyalty alone could not have ensured that it would be successfully discharged.

In the event, much of the day-to-day running and all the important decisions at the Department of Home Affairs had to be taken by Collins himself, assisted later in the year by O'Higgins and Blythe. Thus the Provisional Government's supervision of the infant police organisation was fragmented and inadequate. Collins found himself, to an ever-increasing extent, relying upon the advice of his former R I C and D M P contacts, and once the basic decisions on the structure of the proposed force had been taken by Mulcahy's committee, there was little, if any, further thought to be given to the fundametals of police policy.

Collins's main concern was simply to get the new force out quickly. Recruitment began under the careful eyes of Collins and Staines by circularising the brigade intelligence officers of the I R A in certain selected areas in early February. These men in turn picked suitable recruits at local level and despatched them to Dublin. On 20 February Guard J. J. McInninney was formally attested as the first member. Meanwhile Duggan took over as minister responsible for the D M P, the disbanding R I C, the courts and the various record and registry offices. A proposal which Collins had made in the Dáil early in January to set up a committee of public safety representative of both Treaty and Anti-Treaty opinion had not materialised. Had it been followed through, the urgent necessity for speedily creating a new police would not have been as great and some of the difficulties which the new force was to encounter because of its hasty construction might have been avoided. But, as has been shown, the rate of violence continued to rise unabated in the early weeks of 1922. A single day's tally (20 January) included the shooting of an off-duty policeman in Dorset Street, the armed robbery of three premises in Dublin, the murder and robbery of a farmer in Dundrum, Co. Tipperary, and the serious wounding of three civilians in gunfights in Tralee, Co. Kerry. In addition to these, there were upwards of thirty other incidents involving the use of firearms throughout the country. Collins's sense of urgency was justified.

But probably the most important single cause of the Provisional Government's disjointed and ambivalent approach to the problem of setting up a new police was the opposition of the Anti-Treaty group to any moves which might give the appearance of undermining the authority of the Dáil government. Stack and Brugha made it clear that they would regard any attempt to create a new police force as a usurpation of the sovereign power of the Dáil. The only police force legally entitled to operate in Ireland, they argued, was the Republican Police of Dáil Éireann.

Stack had already made it clear to Griffith that he would

regard the creation of any such 'unauthorised' police force
as a provocation, and whether or not because of this consideration, it was not until the end of February 1922 that the first
public acknowledgement of the existence of plans for a new
force was made by Collins. Since the enlistment of Guards
had started on 20 February the matter can hardly have been
a secret after that date but it is clear that the Provisional
Government did not wish to publicise its intentions any
earlier than it had to. It was further significant that when
recruitment began there were no public announcements, nor
any advertisements in the press. Collins and Staines preferred
to rely on the recommendations of their I R A officer contacts.

On 9 February Sir Hamar Greenwood had told the House
of Commons that some police equipment had been left behind
in Ireland for use by the Free State government but he did
not elaborate on what plans, if any, had been drawn up for
replacing the Royal Irish Constabulary.

Yet Greenwood must have been aware that the two committees under Staines and Mulcahy had been sitting for some
time, for he had been visited by Collins only two days previously and such an important development in a situation of
growing disorder and violence would almost certainly have
been mentioned.

The Provisional Government's reticence concerning its
plans for the creation of the new police was just one facet of
Collins's and Griffith's low-key approach to the Republican side
during these weeks. Thus it was that the new force was brought
into being, if not in absolute secrecy, at least under a cloud
of uncertainty and apprehension. But by the end of February
there was no further possibility of keeping the police proposals
quiet. A general election was to be held in June and Griffith
and Collins would have to seek a mandate for all their policies
—including the new police.

On 28 February there were brief references in the Dáil
to a 'new police force' which the Provisional Government was
raising but government spokesmen did not elaborate. The
first indication of the model which the force was to follow was

not given until 5 March, when Michael Collins addressed an election meeting in College Green. He told the crowd: 'We want the support of the people now. We want your support for the police force which we are forming. It will be a people's guard for the protection of all classes and parties. Will our opponents hinder and obstruct that course? Will they go on making difficulties.' Collins did not specify the nature of the obstructions and difficulties which he was encountering in creating a new police but it is evident from the tone in which he spoke that the attitude of the Dáil towards the new police was not one of unanimous enthusiasm.

Meanwhile the organising committee had produced its report which was forwarded to the Provisional Government in the last week of February. Its suggestions were accepted without reservation. It proposed a unified, unarmed force with a maximum strength of 4,300 men, administered by a Commissioner who would be responsible to the government. The basic rank would have powers similar to and would be the equivalent of the British constable, and the force would be non-political in its administration and composition. It was to be called the Civic Guard.

With the vital exception that it was to be unarmed, the Civic Guard was to differ little in its construction from the Royal Irish Constabulary which had preceded it. The ranks system was to be an exact reproduction of the R I C with Chief Superintendents and Superintendents fulfilling the func- they go on making difficulties?' Collins did not specify the was to be a non-commissoned rank of Inspector corresponding to that of Head Constable in the R I C and the rigid distinction between officers, N C Os and men, which had distinguished the R I C from British police forces and the D M P, was to be continued. Pay was better in all ranks than it had been in R I C. The Commissioner, whose functions were exactly similar to those of the R I C Inspector-General, was to receive £1,300 a year plus a lodging allowance of £120; a Chief Superintendent was to receive £650 on appointment, rising to £800; a Superintendent was to receive £400 on appointment, rising to £600, and an Inspector was to start at £310, rising to £350. A sergeant was to draw £5 a week on appointment, rising to £5 12s. and a guard £3 10s., rising to £4 10s.

But what was to be really significant for the future development of the force and its relations with the various governments under which it was to serve was the recommendation of the committee that the Commissioner should be directly responsible to the government rather than to a police authority as was the case with British police forces. This recommendation meant that the Civic Guard was to occupy a status in relationship to the government which was identical with that of the R I C to the old Castle administration. The British police forces, with the exception of the London Metropolitan, were administered by watch committees or police authorities which operated in conjunction with the Home Office, thus ensuring that the day-to-day administration of the forces was kept at one remove from the influence of government. That principle, for obvious reasons, had never been applied to the R I C which had a clearly identifiable role as an arm of the Dublin Castle administration.

It was remarkable that none of the members of the Provisional Government were apparently troubled by the seeming contradiction between the avowed aim of setting up a police force which would protect 'all classes and parties' while at the same time retaining complete control of the force through a Commissioner who was to be a direct political appointee. The decision was all the more remarkable because of its contrast with the British system which, during the deliberations on the Mulcahy Report, was taken by several members of the Provisional Government as the ideal model upon which to base their new force.

This particular aspect of the force's constitution derived largely from the influence of the high-ranking ex-R I C men who provided professional police advice for the organising committee. There were no fewer than nine ex-R I C men on the committee including three District Inspectors and a Head

Constable. With the exception of Michael Staines, who had some amateur experience as head of the Republican Police, these were the only experienced police officers who were consulted by the Provisional Government. Their influence with Collins appears to have been considerable. This was to be vividly demonstrated at a later date when Collins threatened to disband the entire Civic Guard force rather than remove some R I C men whose appointment to senior ranks had been taken badly by the rank-and-file membership.

There is substantial evidence to suggest that at a very early stage of planning Collins had envisaged the new force almost as a direct replica of the R I C. Ideological and political differences apart, he had an intense admiration for the efficiency and tenacity of the force, and since none of his immediate advisors had any experience of any different policing systems, it was natural that the construction of the new Civic Guard should be heavily influenced by the model of its predecessor. Since no copy of the organising committee's report is known to have survived, it cannot be determined whether any consideration was ever given to the possibility of directing the Civic Guard through a police authority, but it does appear that at a very early stage there was considerable dissension as to whether the force should be armed in the manner of the old R I C.

In the very early stages of organisation new recruits were put through precisely the same training in musketry as had been the R I C. Colonel Paddy Brennan, one of the three brothers from Clare who were among Collins's most trusted military advisors in the War of Independence, was selected to act as Assistant Commissioner under Staines, and in late February he supervised the transfer of a substantial quantity of rifles, revolvers and grenades to the Guards' training quarters at the Royal Dublin Society grounds in Ballsbridge. These were primarily intended for defence of the training centre, but new recruits were simultaneously being put through the intensive firearms course based on the R I C training manual. Subsequently, when the Guards took possession of the Phoenix Park depot from the R I C, the weapons were stored away and firearms drill was reduced to a single day's training. Clearly there had been some change of policy, for the use and knowledge of the Lee-Enfield rifle and the Webley revolver had constituted a major element in the training of the very first Guards.

It may have been, on the other hand, that the first recruits were drilled in the use of firearms simply because their ex-R I C instructors were unable to train them in anything else at that stage. There were only a few R I C training manuals available in the first weeks and there were no trained lecturers to brief the recruits in police duties, criminal law or court procedure. As a result the emphasis was almost entirely on physical training—marching, drilling, athletics, boxing and wrestling. Nothing would have been more natural than for the former R I C men to train the recruit guards in the way they had themselves been trained; indeed, they knew no other way.

Michael Staines's young force found itself confronted with serious operational difficulties in the first weeks of its existence. There was no accommodation in any of the Dublin military barracks which were in the process of being evacuated by the British. Where any vacant space became available it was quickly acquired by the Provisional Government's army which was being put on a permanent footing by Collins and Mulcahy and whose ranks were being reinforced by thousands of recruits from around the country. Finally, in late February, the Guards got a temporary loan of the R D S grounds at Ballsbridge on condition that they would vacate them by the end of April to allow the society to prepare for its annual spring show. Staines and his staff moved to the R D S and the message went down the country, through the Republican Police system and under the careful screening of Collins's agents, to send up the recruits.

The first recruits, with the exception of the approximately fifty headquarters staff which Staines had recruited in Dublin, came from Clare, Galway and East Limerick. They were followed by men from Leitrim, West and North Limerick and

Laois and Offaly. Next came Kilkenny and Wexford, with the Corkmen and Kerrymen arriving in May. But the time the new force was due to evacuate the R D S, over 1,500 men had arrived from ten counties and the main hall of the Ballsbridge showgrounds had become a vast dormitory by night and a gymnasium by day.

An estimated 97 per cent of the recruits in these months were ex-I R A men and of these 30 per cent were actual 'column men', battle-hardened guerillas who had done their fighting in their native counties among the hills and bogs. They were all remarkably young. Of sixteen men who arrived from East Galway early in March, the eldest was twenty-one and several were below the minimum permitted age of nineteen. These last were sent off to the Free State Army until they came of age.

Many of the new recruits did not even know what they were joining until they arrived in Dublin. In many instances the local Republican Police officers did not go into any great detail beyond telling the eager young men that Mick Collins wanted them for a job in Dublin. The following account of his recruitment by a guard from West Clare was not untypical :

It was 2 a.m. in the morning and I had just delivered twin calves on my people's farm when the Brigade Police Officer arrived up at the house. I was sitting by the fire and he just knocked at the window and when I opened the door he told me I had to be at Kilrush railway station at half past eight in the morning. I had a fair idea we were wanted for something special in Dublin but I had no information beyond that.

At Kilrush station in the morning I found twelve more of the local boys and we all headed off to Kingsbridge station in the morning train. When we got there we were met by a fellow in a wagon who had been sent to pick us up and on the way to Ballsbridge he told us we were Civic Guards. I knew about the force but some of the boys didn't know what it was and they were all for jumping from the wagon and going home. This was on the 9th of March 1922.

Collins's screening process was thorough and in the event only a handful of the first 2,000 recruits were to go over to the Republican side in the Civil War which was to break out in the following June. Brigade police officers in a number of areas whose sympathies were not fully behind the Treaty were by-passed and instead Oriel House men were consulted in order to find suitable recruits from these districts. This was just one by-product of Collins's careful policy of placing one or two men from each of the thirty-two counties among the Oriel House C I D.

The recruits who arrived at the R D S in early and mid-March did not encounter any difficulties on the way but by the end of March, when the fact of recruitment had become common knowledge throughout the community, recruits in many areas met with violence and intimidation as they travelled to Dublin. At Limerick Junction throughout March and April government troops had to give protection to the recruits who were pulled from railway carriages and beaten. In East Cork, near Midleton and Mitchelstown, windows in homes which had sent recruits to the force were smashed and there were reports of intimidation from Galway, Westport and Athlone. In Dublin the R D S grounds were under almost constant sniper fire during the first two weeks of March. Finally, towards mid-March the Guards began to shoot back and eliminated one or two of their sniper antagonists, resulting in a noticeable reduction in the frequency and intensity of the nightly volleys.

Staines and Duggan estimated that the first Civic Guards would be out of training and among the people by mid-June, and accordingly plans went ahead to regularise the courts system which had all but broken down as the split between Treatyites and Anti-Treatyites had widened. The Republican courts which operated at district and parish level had limited usefulness inasmuch as their work could only be conducted on the principle of conciliation—with the consent of rival parties to abide by their decisions. Moreover, although this system functioned excellently in some districts, the standard of justice administration in others left much to be desired. Above all, it was evident that the principle of conciliation courts, while operable in the troubled years 1919–22, would not continue to be effective once a restoration of normal conditions would come about. Once the unifying influence of the common struggle against the British had passed, the Sinn Féin courts would lose much of their acceptability throughout the community.

The planning of a new system of justice to supersede the Sinn Féin courts and the old magistrates' courts was placed in the hands of Kevin O'Higgins and Hugh O'Kennedy, who held the position of Law Officer to the Provisional Government, an almost direct equivalent of the post of Attorney-General. O'Higgins, assisted by his secretary, Patrick McGilligan, spent almost the entire spring and summer of 1922 occupied variously with the drafting of the Free State constitution and the planning of new courts. The focal point of the courts system which finally emerged from their study was to be the creation of a new, permanent, professional magistracy for the courts of summary jurisdiction. It was further arranged that a commission under Lord Glenavy would investigate and advise on the organisation and administration of the higher courts.

The Glenavy Commission was not to report until June 1923 but the first of the new professional magistrates—known as District Justices—went out as early as November 1922 while the Civil War was still raging. Twelve District Justices had gone out by the end of November and they were followed in January 1923 by a further thirteen. The Republican courts, which had become disorganised and ineffective as a result of the split over the Treaty, were phased out in two stages. In July 1922 all courts outside Dublin, with the exception of the main district and parish courts, were suspended and in October the remaining Republican courts were abolished.

Initially the District Justices were obliged to operate under the Adaptation of Enactments Act which gave the Free State power to adapt British statutes for the administration of the

C

new state. Because most of the old magistrates' functions could not be exercised by less than two magistrates sitting together, it was necessary at first for the District Justices to work in pairs. In March 1923 the District Justices (Temporary Provisions) Act regularised the situation and a standardised and efficient administration of summary justice throughout the country was assured.

The Crown courts in their last weeks of existence had very naturally become the object of eleventh-hour retribution throughout the country. Most of them had long ceased to function effectively in any event, but this did not deter many patriots whose courage was of recent origin from making a final gesture against the old system. During April and May 1922 armed men descended on Crown courts in Offaly, Laois, Westmeath and Wexford and prevented them from sitting. In Dublin the City Commission and the police courts operated only under constant guard by troops and police who sealed off the courthouses with barbed wire and fixed bayonets.

Early in April the campaign of vengeance against the withdrawing agents of the Crown reached a peak. On 7 April the disbandment of the R I C was temporarily suspended for twenty-four hours and all men ordered to stand to on full alert as a wave of attacks on R I C barracks swept the country. On 3 April two retired R I C men had been shot dead in Ballyhaunis, Co. Mayo. On 6 April three constables were shot in Co. Clare. On 8 April Sergeant McManus was shot dead at Templemore, Co. Tipperary, while he visited his fiancée. On 18 April ex-Sergeant Dunne was shot in Ennis and on 26–29 April there was a series of sectarian killings in West Cork in which nine apparently innocent Protestants were shot in or near their homes by groups of armed men.

At Dunmanway a local solicitor, a retired draper and a retired pharmacist were shot dead in their homes. The Church of Ireland and Methodist ministers escaped only by taking to the fields in their nightclothes. At Clonakilty and Ballineen five people were shot including a Church of Ireland rector, the caretaker of a Masonic Hall and a youth of eighteen who was killed in his bed. On 29 April a Protestant farmer was shot dead as he worked in his fields near Bandon. The killings were intended by their misguided perpetrators as revenge for the murders of Catholics in Belfast, and Collins, de Valera and Griffith in turn issued condemnations. But the condemnations were not sufficient to allay the fears of the Protestants of West Cork and over a hundred families fled the district in the next forty-eight hours, some to Cork City, some to England and not a few to Belfast. Brigadier Commandant Tom Hales issued a proclamation from Bandon barracks warning all unauthorised holders of firearms to hand them in on pain of being shot, and the area was densely occupied by government troops.

Meanwhile the force which the Provisional Government had raised to police the new state was suffering from a multiplicity of ills and there was little likelihood that it would operate effectively anywhere within the period envisaged by Staines. Collins had become bogged down in the difficulties of the Border dispute and he had become exasperated in his attempts to reconcile the Treaty and Anti-Treaty factions in the Dáil. The organisation of the Civic Guard was understandably— but unfortunately—far down in his list of priorities and its development had been left in the indecisive hands of Eamon Duggan and his advisors.

But Staines and Duggan might on their own have been able to organise the force and get it out among the people, were it not for the explosive mixture which Collins had unwittingly left behind among the very foundations of the new police. His R I C protégés had now taken over the direction and training of the men from the columns and there had been a natural development of friction and resentment in the ranks in consequence. It was not long before the explosive mixture was to blow up in the faces of the Provisional Government.

4 From Mutiny to Civil War 1922

On 25 April 1922 the Civic Guards, now 1,500 strong, evacuated the Royal Dublin Society and marched through the city to Kingsbridge Station where they boarded trains for the town of Kildare, thirty miles away. There they were to take possession of another temporary training centre, the Artillery Barracks, part of which had been reserved on their behalf by the Dublin Rangers of the Free State Army as soon as the British had evacuated. Only the Dublin *Irish Independent* remarked on the first appearance in the streets of this new force of which little or nothing was known at the time. The *Irish Times* had indeed sent a reporter down to look at the 'Guardsmen' as he called them, who were in training at Ballsbridge and he had reported that they looked in every respect 'a splendid body of men'. But there was nothing unusual about formations of marching men in the Dublin of April 1922 and the un-uniformed Civic Guards marching in formation along the quays must have attracted no more than a passing glance from the population of the capital. There were far more interesting and colourful processions to watch all over the city. The British Army and the R I C were marching out, the Free State Army was marching in, and the Republicans who did not accept the Treaty of the previous December had begun to drill and march in the city streets as well. The British troops, the Black and Tans and the Auxiliaries cheered for the king as they evacuated their barracks and Dublin urchins jeered back 'Up the Republic!' as they passed out.

The Guards had sent an advance party to the Kildare barracks on 21 April and they had received a cool reception both from the Free State Army units which held one end of

Acting Sergeant, Mounted
Troop

District Inspector Service
Uniform 1

District Inspector Service
Uniform II

District Inspector Service
Uniform III

RIC Men c. 1900

1913 Lockout
Baton Charge following a meeting in Sackville Street
(now O'Connell Street).

Three police forces on duty at Earlsfort Terrace, Dublin, 1922 (l to r) A
member of the British Military Foot Police, two members of the IR
Police and a member of the DMP-holding up traffic during the sitting of
the Dáil.

The first Irish Police Force headed by Michael Staines. Gárdaí enter Dublin Castle 1922.

A typical station party of 1922. This one was at Cavan, arriving from temporary headquarters at Ship Street Depot in Dublin on September 26th 1922. Included are: Sergeant John Harnett and Guards John J Moore, Patrick Kelly, James J Kitson, Pat Moroney, Donat Hussey, Andrew Carey, Felix C Gibbons and John Hogan.

On the night of November 14th 1926, many Garda stations were
attacked by armed IRA groups. Sergeant James Fitzsimmons, St Luke's,
Cork was shot dead; Garda Hugh Ward, Hollyford, Co Tipperary, was
mortally wounded. A reorganisation of senior officers took place as part
of a Garda response and Commissioner O' Duffy held a series of regional
conferences. This photograph of young officers was taken after the southern regional conference, held at Union Quay, Cork, probably in
December 1926.

Seated: (l to r) Chief Supt Garret Brennan, Cork East; Commissioner
Eoin O'Duffy; Supt E Mansfield, Union Quay. Centre row: Supt JJ
Moore, Skibbereen; Supt W Burns, Listowel; Supt CC Brady (author's
father); Supt T Collins, Kinsale; Supt P Casey, Castlebar; Supt T
Noonan, Callan; Supt G Butler, McCurtain Street; Supt JD Curtin,
Killarney (murdered at Friarsfield, Tipperary, March 2nd 1931). Back
row: Supt C Heron, Dingle; Supt G Stack, Macroom; Supt P Doyle,
Monaghan; Supt T Heaphy, Clonakilty;Inspr P Kelly; Inspr WP Quinn
(later Commissioner); Chief Supt R Muldoon, Sligo; Supt E Reynolds,
Fermoy; Supt J Fleming, Bruff; Supt J Devine, Kanturk.

the barrack complex and from the British artillerymen who held the other.

The section of the barracks which the Guards were to occupy had been used as stables by the British. It was uninhabitable in the condition in which the Guards found it and for two nights Staines's advance party was obliged to sleep on the barrack square under their greatcoats. The air of the chilly April nights did little to improve their disposition and tempers finally snapped when it became apparent that the officer in charge of the Free State troops had placed sentries to keep an eye on these strange arrivals who described themselves as policemen of the new state. Finally the Guards loosed off a few rounds of .303 at the Free State sentries, who hastily withdrew.

Commissioner Staines, his headquarters staff and the remainder of the 1,500 men from the R D S arrived on the evening of the 25th, and began to settle into the cleaned, or at least disinfected, Artillery Barracks. But conditions were still appallingly bad and this added to the tensions which had grown up in the R D S between the ex-R I C and the men from the columns. One contemporary account describes the accommodation in the barracks :

The camp was divided into eight lines of 'huts' running parallel to each other, each company of a hundred men with a company to each line . . . We had no cookhouse, only a coffee bar where food was cooked as best you could, potatoes cooked in the open, dinner usually consisted of boiled beef, cups were few—usually disused bully beef tins.

The Guards had left the R D S at Ballsbridge under a cloud of recriminations. The headquarters staff had become isolated from the recruits and the officers were divided among themselves. The trouble had begun when an alleged former Black and Tan was discovered among the new recruits. The Claremen who had made this unhappy discovery did not bother to report their find to the Commissioner and decided to deal with the unwelcome recruit in their own way. Since orders at the camp perimeter directed that the gates would not be opened for anyone during the hours of darkness, it was decided that the departing recruit should go out over the fourteen-foot high gate in his night attire. Then with shots hitting the ground at his heels, he made off into the city. If Staines and his staff ever knew of the incident, they gave no sign and the evicted one was not heard of again.

But this episode was only a relatively harmless surface manifestation of a deep anger and resentment among the column men who watched virtually every rank above that of sergeant being handed over to their erstwhile enemies in the R I C. Apart from Staines, Brennan and, later, Eamonn Coogan, virtually the entire headquarters staff was made up of ex-R I C men, the most senior being John Kearney, a former District Inspector who was appointed as Deputy Commissioner, and Patrick Walsh, a former First Class District Inspector who was also to become a Deputy Commissioner. Brennan, as Assistant Commissioner, was junior to these.

During the month of April dissatisfaction began to build up in the ranks and Brennan, who no doubt was also dissatisfied with his relatively junior rank, passed on the men's views to Staines. Whatever may have been his personal views of his own headquarters staff, Staines did nothing to allay the complaints from the ranks. In this he was supported by Collins, who considered that these R I C men who had served the cause from within the ranks of the police during the war were entitled to their reward. Unfortunately, many of the recruits were not as sure of the R I C men's patriotic credentials as were Staines and Collins.

The first serious confrontation came when an advance party of Kerrymen recognised Deputy Commissioner Kearney, the man who, as Head Constable Kearney, had been in charge at Tralee barracks when Sir Roger Casement was arrested in April 1916. In the event, the Kerrymen misjudged the unfortunate Kearney because he had in fact befriended Casement in Tralee barracks and they had parted on mutually respectful terms. But the niceties of their encounter were not to be considered by the Kerrymen and the rumour that the betrayer of Casement was in the camp spread rapidly. Meetings were organised and statements prepared on behalf of the men. Finally, a demand for the removal of Kearney and all former R I C men who held commissioned ranks was sent to Staines through Brennan. Staines again refused to move and there was open talk of protest.

Whether Staines had consulted the government at this stage or whether his intransigence was entirely personal is unclear, but it is certain that Collins was supporting him in principle. Collins was adamant that the Guards should accept the leadership of the men whom he had used in his intelligence network. On the other hand, it was perhaps asking a lot of the men who had spent the previous two years fighting in the hills to accept without quibble that all these R I C men had in fact been on the side of the Republic all along. Some of them had been noted for their zeal in pursuing the struggle against the I R A, and the subtleties and intricacies of intelligence and counter-intelligence were lost on men who had survived rough and dangerous conditions during a vicious guerilla war. To the ordinary recruit the R I C men were Peelers who had refused to 'come out'. They were the arch-traitors.

Kearney's life at the R D S had become a misery and he spent most of his time in his office, guarded by armed sentries. Finally, in the middle of April he resigned and left for England. The story was put around the camp that he had had a nocturnal encounter with the ghost of Roger Casement, but it is likely that the causes of his passing were of more direct human origin.

The departure of Deputy Commissioner Kearney was a victory for the column men and there was a temporary relief of tension at the camp. Nevertheless, when the Guards arrived at Kildare barracks, resentment and anger were still high and after the promotion of five more R I C men was announced on 11 May 1922 they finally overflowed into open mutiny.

Brennan, together with Superintendent Seán Liddy and one

or two other former I R A men who held intermediate ranks in the camp, made a last desperate appeal to Staines and for three or four days they managed to hold the discontent of the men in check. But on the morning of 15 May, when parade was called, Staines and Deputy Commissioner Walsh appeared from the staff office, flanked by the five newly promoted R I C men. A small group of guards who had been appointed to act as spokesmen stepped forward and some words were exchanged. A murmur of conversation rippled through the ranks and Commandant Joe Ring called the men to attention. There was a hush as Staines faced the ranks and began to speak. He had spoken for about three minutes, eulogising the experience of the former R I C men and warning of the seriousness of mutiny. There was nothing in his address to indicate that the newly appointed officers had played any role in the struggle of the previous two years. Men began to heckle from the ranks and suddenly there was a surge forward. Staines moved back, calling for those who stood by him to move to his right. Joe Ring with about sixty men stood stock still. Another sixty moved to the right with Staines and Walsh, but the overwhelming majority of the 1,500 men on the square moved to the left. There was half a minute of tense silence and then Staines and his aides backed away to their offices.

For the rest of the day all was confusion in the Artillery Barracks. Staines and his staff remained locked in their offices, reportedly with drawn revolvers on the table. The recruits decided to keep on drilling and the committee which had been selected to negotiate with the Commissioner went into discussions with the few officers who remained on terms acceptable to both sides. Sometime that evening Staines and his senior officers slipped out of the camp and headed for Dublin where the news was broken to a horrified Provisional Government which already had enough trouble on its hands. Collins, Duggan and Staines spent the night discussing the mutiny and it was finally agreed that the Kildare camp would have to be split up and then occupied by the army.

It is difficult to understand the process of thought which led

Collins and the Provisional Government to this drastic decision. It was evident that the mutineers were firm in their loyalty to the Treaty and that their only quarrel was concerned with domination of the force by members of the Royal Irish Constabulary. Staines believed a plot was being worked out among the mutineers by Anti-Treaty elements and it seems likely that Collins accepted his evidence of this. Subsequent developments were to show that there was indeed such a plot among the new recruits but that it had nothing to do with the question of leadership in the new force.

Uppermost in the minds of the government must have been the fear of the mutiny spreading to the nearby army bases at the Curragh and Newbridge. As Commissioner Staines left Kildare barracks, Free State troops had begun to take over the Curragh base from the British and camp discipline had not yet become fully effective there. However, the army itself was rapidly splitting as the Anti-Treaty forces consolidated themselves. The Dublin Four Courts, the Dublin Port and Docks Board offices and the Kildare Street Club had already been occupied by Anti-Treaty units. In Limerick and Cork the Anti-Treaty forces had seized factories and public buildings, and since the ultimate loyalties of the troops in the Curragh-Newbridge area had yet to be established, the possibility of the mutiny spreading to the army must have appeared very real to the Provisional Government. Most of the Guards had relatives and friends in the army and many had earlier held ranks in the Volunteers which they might easily regain by popular acclaim of the men if not by commission from the government.

Moreover, Staines's officers had given it as their opinion to the government that the Guards would carry a lot of weight, perhaps even a decisive influence, with the army. Nonetheless, the government's decision to try to quell the mutiny by force rather than conciliation remains somewhat of a mystery. In retrospect, it can only be concluded that the government believed the issue to be a much wider one than the appointment of officers.

Collins regarded the Kildare mutiny as a trial of strength and a challenge to his personal judgement. He was sorely offended that the recruits to the new force saw fit to query his assessments of the R I C men whom he had picked to officer the force. Some indication of the government's thinking at the time was given in a speech in the Dáil by Kevin O'Higgins in the following October, after Collins's death. Expressing the hope that the unhappy beginnings of the Civic Guard would be forgotten, O'Higgins explained :

The late Chairman of the Provisional Government was Director of Intelligence during our conflict with the British. We accepted his information implicitly, we acted upon it to the advantage of the country, we did not ask where it came from or whether we were quite sure it was right.

We acted upon it implicitly and it is to be regretted that when certain members of the Royal Irish Constabulary were admitted into the Civic Guards with his endorsement, there was not the same implicit acceptance of his endorsement.

On the morning of 16 May information came to Kildare from an advance party of guards which had been posted at Newbridge barracks that units of the army were on the way to take over the Artillery Barracks and subdue the mutineers, by force if necessary. Immediately the Artillery Barracks came alive with activity. The armoury was emptied of its three hundred rifles and every available round of ammunition was distributed. Boxes of Mills bombs appeared mysteriously and no less mysteriously seemed to remain the monopoly of the Claremen for the rest of the day in spite of pleas from less fortunate contingents to be included in the lucky find. The entrances were blockaded and sandbagged and vantage points taken up by snipers at intervals along the main road from Dublin. Guards for whom there were no weapons were instructed to remain in barracks. By 10 a.m. the Kildare barracks was a fortified camp with three hundred armed men under the command of two sergeants, O'Meara and O'Brien, ready and willing to take on the Free State Army. The few remaining officers, under Brennan and Superintendent Seán Liddy, went into urgent conference to try to find a way of avoiding bloodshed.

At 3 p.m. an armoured car and two Lancia trucks packed with Free State soldiers roared down the hill towards the barrack gate from the direction of Dublin. They came to a sudden halt outside the gate and the turret of the armoured car traversed the walls of the barracks, the gates and the sandbagged fortifications. There was a heavy silence for five minutes while the army commander in the car considered the possibilities. He could see a few, but not all, of the three hundred rifles which were trained on his party.

Finally the hatch of the armoured car opened and the officer, Captain Dunne, put up his head. After another half minute Superintendent Liddy climbed down over the barricaded gate and walked up to the side of the armoured car. Dunne told Liddy he had instructions to take over the camp as it was in danger of falling into the hands of anti-government forces. He would give Liddy five minutes to surrender after which he would come through the gate one way or another. Liddy indicated the rifles behind and alongside the roadway and a guard, nonchalantly tossing a grenade from hand to hand, appeared from behind the barricaded gateway. Captain Dunne rapidly reconsidered the situation 'Can we discuss the matter?' he asked. And Civic Guard and Free State Army officer sat down on the mudguard of the Lancia while their men on either side faced each other down the barrels of their Lee-Enfields and Lewis guns.

Liddy was a Dáil member for his native Clare. He told the officer he had voted for the Treaty and stressed that there was no question of the camp being held for the Republicans. Dunne, after some hedging, conceded that he had been misled into thinking that the Guards had gone over to the Anti-Treaty forces. He would have to think about his orders, however, before he could decide what to do. The two men stood up, Dunne climbed back into the armoured car and Liddy was hauled back over the gate into the barracks. There was

another three-minute eternity of silence while Dunne conferred with his lieutenants in the armoured car. At any
second the heavy machine gun on the turret and the Lewis
guns mounted on the cabs of the Lancia trucks could open
up and nothing could then halt a costly and bloody gun
battle between police and soldiers of the new state.

Suddenly the engine of the armoured car roared into life
and the vehicle jerked into reverse, backing away onto the
roadway from the barrack gate. Followed by the two Lancias,
Dunne took his armoured car to the end of the Artillery
Barracks and then turned and made a fast run past the gates.
But instead of the anticipated hail of machine gun bullets
from the army vehicles the Guards got a resounding cheer
from the soldiers and a salute from the captain as the little
column vanished in a cloud of dust back along the road to
Dublin.

The mutineers now set about regularising the camp. The
committee, largely under the direction of O'Brien and
O'Meara, drew up a proclamation and issued routine orders
for the running of the camp. The proclamation was run off on
a typewriter left behind in Staines's office and posted up at the
gateway to the camp. It read :

Whereas five persons holding senior commissions in this depot
(disbanded and ex-members of the Royal Irish Constabulary)
were retained against the wishes of the members of the Civic
Guard, and whereas the presence of those five persons was not
conducive to the good order and discipline of the depot we
requested their expulsion and pending the decision of the
Provisional Government we found it necessary for the peace
and good order of the depot to take over temporary control.

We declare our loyalty and the loyalty of the members of the
Civic Guard to the Provisional Government and Dáil Éireann.
                                                By order of the Committee.

The committee, which had been elected by the men in each
of the eight companies which made up the camp, then selected
a new headquarters staff to take the place of Commissioner

Staines and his senior officers. Paddy Brennan was appointed as Commissioner, P. J. Haugh as Deputy Commissioner, Martin Lynch as Commandant and Seán Liddy as Adjutant. Training recommenced as normal—largely because there was nothing else to keep the men occupied—but the heavily barricaded gates and the outer perimeter of the barracks remained closed. Armed sentries patrolled the walls and look-out posts were located along the roads leading to Kildare town.

It is not known what reaction Captain Dunne received when he reported that the mutineers were still in control of the Artillery Barracks, but since no further attempts were made to subdue the mutineers by force, it must be assumed that his superiors believed he had taken the right course in avoiding open bloodshed. The Provisional Government then decided that the best tactic was to try to starve out the mutineers. Supplies were halted to the camp, pay was cut off and all future recruits were to be diverted from Kildare to a new head-quarters which Commissioner Staines was to open in Dublin. By these means, it was hoped, the mutineers would eventually be made to climb down on their demands or forced to evacuate the Artillery Barracks and disperse.

The new headquarters which Staines set up in Dublin almost immediately became a problem in itself to the govern-ment. No suitable accommodation could be found and the offices were moved from the Ormond Hotel to Henry Street, then to Little Denmark Street, and finally to Clonskeagh.

Thus for a two-month period, the new Civic Guard was divided into two rival groups, each with the full paraphernalia of a headquarters staff, a training centre and a recruitment office, one situated in Kildare under virtual siege by the government which had created it, the other moving around Dublin City, taking accommodation wherever it might for a week or two at a time. The real victims of the confusion were the new recruits who arrived from the country to find them-selves with a bewildering set of alternatives to choose from.

Most of the recruits in May and June came first to Kildare where, on being acquainted with the rather bizarre circumstances of the force, they either elected to join the majority in Kildare without pay or to move on to Dublin where they could—eventually—locate the other Civic Guard which was still offering pay. Many simply went home, a few went to join Michael Staines, but the majority climbed in over the barricades. A small number, viewing the prospect of a career in the Civic Guard with considerable suspicion, went on to Dublin and joined the Metropolitan Police which was opening a big recruitment drive.

There was also a third element of the Civic Guard, which, although supporting the mutineers, was in receipt of pay from Commissioner Staines. This group consisted of about forty guards who were employed as a security force at the Mansion House and the Treaty Rooms—the offices of the Provisional Government. They enjoyed the best of both worlds until they were finally brought into the reunified force in July.

By the end of May the Provisional Government had become greatly alarmed by the continuing existence of the mutinous force at Kildare. It was evident that the mutineers were not going to surrender without some concession to their demands and the policy of isolating them and recruiting a rival force in Dublin had not been successful. In the meantime the Anti-Treaty garrison which had occupied the Dublin Four Courts had presented the Provisional Government with an unavoidable challenge. Collins and Griffith were under pressure to move against the Four Courts rebels and that could only be done by open military confrontation which would shatter the last vestiges of peace. A showdown with the men in the Four Courts appeared inevitable and it was evident that it would result in a general outbreak of hostilities throughout the country. In that event the force of 1,500 trained and partially armed men in the Kildare barracks would be an important factor and they would certainly be a welcome addition to one side or the other. Over and above these considerations, the British government had become aware that

the new police had mutinied against the Provisional Government and assurances had to be sent to Churchill that the
matter would be sorted out quickly. Accordingly, on 22 May
the government made oblique overtures to the Kildare mutineers through an intermediary and Brennan and Liddy were
invited to meet Collins and Duggan.

The first attempt at reconciliation did not bring the parties
much closer together. The meeting took place in the City
Hall and Collins and Liddy immediately came to grips. Collins
opened the conversation by shouting out: 'Liddy, you should
know as well as I do what the country owes these R I C men.'
Liddy answered that he did not. 'It would be interesting to
hear what your solution would be,' Collins said. Liddy's reply
may have been deliberately provocative: 'I'd give them their
thirty pieces of silver and call it a deal.' Collins stood up,
banged the table and shouted at him: 'By God, if I smash the
country with it, these men will remain in the force.' He
stormed out of the room and Duggan quietly closed the
meeting.

The next attempt at reconciliation was not made until
nearly a fortnight later when Liddy and Brennan (who was
also a Dáil deputy) attended a meeting of Pro-Treaty deputies
in Earlsfort Terrace. Staines was also present at the meeting, as
were Collins, Griffith and Duggan. The mutiny was on the
agenda for discussion and Staines opened the subject by describ-
ing the men in the Kildare barracks as mutineers and ruffians.
When Staines had finished, Collins queried Brennan: 'I
suppose they'll have to be disbanded?' Brennan and Liddy replied that if the men were disbanded, they would ask to be
disbanded along with them. That was their trump card, for
they were both influential T Ds and their votes—any votes—
would be of crucial importance in the Dáil when the Provisional Government would finally move against the Anti-Treaty
forces in the Four Courts.

After the meeting Collins, Liddy and Brennan had a private
discussion about the wider implications of the mutiny. Collins
explained in detail that he had obligations to meet towards

ex R I C members in the Kildare barracks, who had not only risked their lives in the cause of Irish freedom but by reason of the undercover role they had played in its achievement had also earned the odium and wrath of their fellow-countrymen. The nature of their usefulness to the struggle was such that their true loyalties had to be hidden during the period of warfare with the British, and if the members of the Civic Guard could not accept his word on that, it was too bad.

It appears that some indication of the government's intention to move soon against the Four Courts was given and the discussion turned to the role which the Guards would have to play in the event of a protracted civil war situation. It was agreed in principle that the force should not be asked to undertake any offensive military role and Liddy and Brennan assured Collins that there was no question of the garrison going over to the side of the Anti-Treatyites. Finally Collins was prevailed upon to accompany Brennan and Liddy to the Kildare camp to meet the committee and to iron out their differences.

Collins visited the camp four times in a period of ten days and a compromise arrangement was worked out whereby the R I C men were to be re-employed as civilian advisors and training instructors. Operational ranks were, in the main, to be given to men selected from the ordinary recruits. But before these arrangements could be put into effect, the last link in the chain of events which led up to the battle of the Four Courts had been forged and the entire development of the Civic Guard was to be temporarily suspended.

On the night of 17–18 June the small Anti-Treaty element in the Kildare barracks surfaced and made their first and only endeavour to bring the Civic Guard over to the side of the Republic. The attempt involved about a dozen recruits, mainly from North Tipperary, under the direction of Sergeant O'Brien who had already been active in the camp committee which took over on the departure of Commissioner Staines and his staff.

On the pretext of collecting some men from the Mansion

House guard, O'Brien left the camp at around 11 p.m. on the night of the 17th, with his hand-picked supporters in a couple of Crossley tenders. The Camp Commandant, Martin Lynch, went with them. Once the party had passed Naas, O'Brien's plans went into operation. An armoured car and several lorries filled with troops from the Four Courts were waiting in a wooded lay-by. The party was led by Rory O'Connor, the commanding officer of the Four Courts garrison, and he was accompanied by Major-General Ernie O'Malley and Commandant-General Tom Barry. The encounter had been carefully planned, and Lynch was hauled from his tender and left under armed guard in a small wood off the roadway. O'Brien, followed now by a convoy of four trucks and an armoured car, returned to the Kildare barracks, announced to the guards that the soldiers in the trucks and the armoured car had been sent for the protection of the camp and, once inside the compound, emptied the contents of the armoury into the trucks. Two hours later the convoy roared out through the gates again and made for Dublin, pausing only to pick up the men who were holding Commandant Lynch and to release him, unarmed and without transport, in the open countryside.

To compound the disaster, the few rifles which the Four Courts raiding party had missed disappeared the following morning from the former R I C barracks in Kildare town which was being held by a party of guards under Sergeant Foster. While his station party were at Mass Foster loaded the guns and ammunition into two cars and drove them, accompanied by two guards, to the headquarters of the Anti-Treaty forces in Co. Laois.

Whether through a realisation of how close the Anti-Treatyites came to taking over the Kildare barracks or through fear that things were becoming more dangerous as the dispute dragged on, Collins speedily concluded his terms with the mutineers after the arms raid. It was not a moment too soon, for morale in the camp was low and boredom had set in. The men had worn out their boots with constant drilling, and the long marches through the Kildare countryside which had passed the first weeks of the mutiny were no longer practicable. Since there had been no pay, entertainment was out of the question, beyond whatever the Guards had been able to provide themselves in the camp. Food had become a serious problem, and local traders who had been happy to supply the national police force on credit were beginning to have misgivings. The enforced co-existence of 1,500 men in bad conditions, with bad food and cramped space had begun to tell on their nerves. Tensions rose and altercations became common.

Pay arrived three days after the arms raid and there were wild nights as the 1,500 young recruits made up for lost time and worked off the tensions of a six-week seige. But the discipline had become slack; one recruit, Guard Farrell Liddy from Leitrim, was shot dead in circumstances which had as much misplaced exuberance as malice about them. The R I C instructors had not yet been reinstated and there was little real training going on.

As the crisis of the Four Courts grew nearer, Collins and Brennan made firm arrangements for the use of the Guards in a limited defensive role in protecting vital installations along the main roads into and out of Dublin. Both Collins and Brennan were reconciled to the fact that conditions would not allow the Guards to go out of their stations for some time yet, but it was fortunate for the subsequent development of the force that the temptation to mobilise the Guards as a fighting unit for the coming confrontation was avoided.

On 24 June after the general election in which the Treatyite group won 58 of the 128 seats, compared with only 35 for the Anti-Treatyites, Collins expanded and strengthened his cabinet. Blythe and Mulcahy were brought in and Kevin O'Higgins travelled to Kildare, addressed the men on the barrack square and told them that the government were prepared to forget about the unfortunate events of the previous two months. A new Commissioner was being appointed, he said, and an enquiry was being set up to look into the causes of the discontent. Finally, he gave an undertaking that no guard would be victimised as a result of the enquiry.

In fact the enquiry, which was being conducted by two senior administrators in the Provisional Government, Kevin O'Sheil and Michael MacAuliffe, had been at work for some time when O'Higgins visited Kildare, even though it was not officially appointed until 12 July. O'Sheil and MacAuliffe had been authorised by Griffith to conduct negotiations with Brennan and Liddy earlier in June and several of their meetings had also been attended by Eóin O'Duffy. Both Liddy and Brennan guessed rightly that it was he who was to replace Staines. Nevertheless, in spite of O'Higgins's announcement to the Guards at Kildare that a new Commissioner was to be appointed, Staines was to continue in office until the end of August.

Three days after O'Higgins's conciliatory visit to the Kildare camp, the long threatening battle of the Four Courts began. The incident which finally sparked off the fighting was the kidnapping of J. J. ('Ginger') O'Connell, Deputy Chief of Staff of the Free State Army by Anti-Treaty supporters as a reprisal for the arrest of a Republican who had commandeered £9,000 worth of motor cars. An ultimatum which was delivered to the Four Courts garrison was ignored and at 4 a.m. on the morning of 28 June government forces, using three eighteen-pound field guns supplied by the British Army, commenced the shelling of the Four Courts.

The bombardment of the Four Courts lasted two days but for a further week there was fierce fighting throughout the centre of Dublin. It was Easter 1916 all over again but with little of the colour and gallantry of that encounter, and with the added tragedy of Irishman fighting Irishman. Huge sections of the city centre were razed to the ground and O'Connell Street was gutted for the second time in six years. In a matter of days fighting and violence had spread all over the country.

Within six weeks the Provisional Government, now committed to a final struggle with the Anti-Treatyites, was shattered by the sudden death of Arthur Griffith on 12 August.

Disaster was mounting upon disaster and worse was yet to come with the death of Michael Collins in an ambush in his native Cork on 22 August.

But the Civic Guards had been reconciled in time, and already the force had begun to assume the stability which was to be its key characteristic and one of the vital influences in the construction of the new state in the months ahead. On 17 August the remaining members of the R I C headquarters staff had withdrawn from the Castle and the Guards had marched in, led by Commissioner Staines and Chief Superintendent McCarthy. In spite of the reconciliation at Kildare, Staines had not returned and he had taken office at Ship Street at the rear of the Castle. Now, at last, the force was at least to have the dignity of a permanent headquarters.

But the Guards were not to have the doubtful pleasure of taking over the Castle directly from the R I C. At 8 a.m. on the morning of the 17th the last R I C man left the Lower Castle Yard and left the ancient stronghold in the charge of a detachment of the King's Shropshire Light Infantry, under the command of Major Torin. At 1.30 p.m. the Guards marched up to the Castle gate and were received by Torin, accompanied by the Assistant Under-Secretary, Alfred Cope. There was no undue ceremony, just an exchange of salutes, and the Guards' column, 380 strong but with only sixty-five men in uniform (a mistake had been made in the specifications) passed through into the heart of the Castle. Three hundred of the guards had come from Kildare and Newbridge that morning and joined the eighty members of Staines's headquarters staff. They had marched through the city together, along the quays, down Westmoreland Street, through College Green and up Dame Street into the Castle. A few of the disbanded R I C men in plain clothes, together with some uniformed officers of the D M P, had come to watch the ceremony and made their own salute as the new police marched in.

Meanwhile, Brennan's guards at the Kildare barracks had been content on the whole to stay out of the fight. Early in

July they were again visited by O'Higgins who addressed them on parade and warned them that the time was coming when they would have to go among the people, a people still divided by the conflict which was taking place. To gain the goodwill and confidence of the public as a whole the police would have to remain aloof from the struggle over the Treaty. Not all the Guards were prepared to accept that absolutely and there was a constant, if small, flow of men leaving the barracks to take up with one side or the other. Some of Collins's senior police advisors, such as Broy and Neligan, had gone into the army as soon as the Four Courts shelling began and Paddy Brennan himself was to leave the Guards in September to become Deputy O/C of First Western Command.

In the early months of the Civil War the Guards were organised into protective units which were spread out through the counties of Kildare, Carlow, Laois and parts of western and southern Co. Dublin. Heavily armed with Lee-Enfields, Webley revolvers, Mills bombs and the occasional Lewis gun, the Guards patrolled the railway lines and the main roads and stood guard over bridges, reservoirs and signal boxes. A permanent force was posted to guard the railway viaduct at Monasterevin which was an obvious and tempting target for the Anti-Treaty forces. However, the only engagements in which the Guards participated were one or two brief gun-fights with small Anti-Treaty parties which roamed the area of Ballysax at the southern end of the Curragh and no casualties were recorded in these encounters.

By late July recruitment had begun again in earnest and Newbridge barracks began to fill with young men who knew nothing of the Kildare mutiny or the many difficulties which had almost smothered the new force at birth. Staines and his small staff continued to work in the Castle, planning the basic structures upon which to build the force once the time came to send the Guards out among the community. On 24 August the Civic Guards, now uniformed, drilled and at least looking like policemen, made their first public appearance since the takeover of the Castle. But they came on the streets

of Dublin with drooping banners and muffled drums, marching in pride of place behind the coffin in the funeral cortège of
Michael Collins.

5 O'Duffy leads the Guards

THE new Minister for Home Affairs, Kevin O'Higgins, who succeeded Duggan in June, was, if anything, more anxious than Collins had been to get the Civic Guards out among the people. He saw the restoration of normal policing in the community which had grown accustomed to the role of the gun in three years as the first and most important step towards a return to normality. Collins on his last tour through the South, just a week before his death, was struck by the lawless condition of the towns and countryside. The stability and balance which had characterised rural Irish life had been overwhelmed by the tide of violence and bitterness, but Collins was convinced that it had not been buried very deep and merely required the restoration of a measure of order and trust to allow it to re-emerge. The Civic Guard was the instrument by which that order was to be achieved. Collins's last communication from Limerick, before he set off on the tour of inspection on which he was to meet his death, referred to the complete flouting of the law even under the noses of the army, and he had stressed the urgency of getting the Civic Guard into the district as soon as possible.

But for the time being it was impossible even to consider civil policing in any but a few areas outside of the immediate environs of Dublin and these were occupied by 'Guardsmen' —as the press had begun to refer to the members of the new force—during late August and early September, the first station being at Swords, Co. Dublin. But beyond these areas the Free State troops had hardly begun to move seriously against the Anti-Treaty forces, and there was no point in sending out unarmed policemen until the military had completed their task. In a sense the delay was fortuitous for it enabled the final sores of the Kildare mutiny to heal and it gave the new head of the force, Eóin O'Duffy, a chance to impart at least some professional police training to his men.

O'Duffy had succeeded Staines as Commissioner at the end of August 1922 and the brief and unorthodox leadership of Paddy Brennan came to an end. The MacAuliffe-O'Sheil enquiry reported to the government in the middle of August and although its findings were not published, it had evidently recommended a fresh start and a complete clean-out at the top of the organisation. Brennan was happy enough to go and join his brothers Austin and Michael whom, he reckoned, were engaged in much more productive combat against the Anti-Treaty forces with their army units. Before he left Kildare he was presented with a Wolseley motor car by the men, which cost them £750—a substantial sum by contemporary reckoning. On 10 September, Paddy Brennan, the only man with the unique distinction of being elected Commissioner of an Irish police force by the members thereof, transferred to the army. In the subsequent weeks most of the R I C officers who had been the cause of the Kildare mutiny were brought back as civilian advisors on O'Duffy's headquarters staff.

Contrary to long-held belief, Eóin O'Duffy was not the Cosgrave government's first choice for the post of Commissioner of the Gárda. The post was first offered to Commandant Seán Ó Muirthile, a relatively unknown officer in the Free State Army. Ó Muirthile refused the job and O'Higgins was assigned by the cabinet to approach Eóin O'Duffy. O'Higgins explained to O'Duffy that there would be a vital job to be done with the Guards long after the country had returned to peace conditions.

O'Duffy was sensitive to many of the things O'Higgins was passionately concerned for in the new state and the challenge and the opportunity was irresistible to a man of his character. He agreed to become the second—if one excludes Paddy Brennan—Commissioner of the Civic Guard.

Eóin O'Duffy at thirty years of age was precisely the man to organise and direct the novel and ambitious undertaking of creating an unarmed native civil police for a country whose experience of justice administration had been the contrary of this ideal. He had a natural flair for organisation and imagination. He shared with O'Higgins a boundless energy which could range from one problem to another as quickly as the situation demanded it. In addition, he had a keenly developed sense of nationalism and idealism. The ideal of giving the Irish people their own unarmed police which would be 'Irish in thought and action' appealed to that sense. If anybody could give the Guards zeal and purposefulness, it would be O'Duffy.

But there was more than flamboyant idealism to O'Duffy. As O/C of Northern Command of the I R A he had acquired a good reputation as a man of decisive and effective action. His fighting career against the British was a distinguished one, and while acting as liaison officer in Belfast during the truce period he had shown an aptitude for handling delicate situations with discretion and firmness. But he had as many faults as virtues and, like his virtues, his faults were big ones. He was vain, domineering, constantly in search of publicity, intolerant of the shortcomings of others and slow to credit their virtues. But his talents were ideally suited to the crisis days of 1922, and it was not until much later that the governments of the Cosgrave era were to realise just how difficult a man Eóin O'Duffy could be.

On the understanding from O'Higgins that he would have complete administrative autonomy over the force, O'Duffy immediately began to put his programme into effect. The aim—in the short term—was swiftly to fashion a police machine which, with a basic training and a reasonably good organisation, could go unarmed among the community at the . earliest possible opportunity. In the long term it was O'Duffy's aim to construct a force which would be a model reflection of his ideals, a perfect microcosm of the healthy, free and Catholic nation which Ireland was to become and which he was later to aim at through his Blueshirt organisation. Happily, the Civic Guard and its construction was not to be marked by the same excesses which were to characterise O'Duffy's subsequent political career.

In the autumn of 1922 the odds hardly favoured the success of either aim. The Kildare mutiny had left a serious discipline problem and O'Duffy immediately addressed himself to the task of setting up a proper rank system within the force. His senior deputy was now Eamon Coogan, a highly capable, if somewhat erratic administrator and his junior deputy was Paddy Walsh, a former District Inspector of the R I C, a close friend and confidant of both Collins and O'Higgins and coincidentally a distant relative of O'Duffy's. Walsh was set to work to draw up a strict disciplinary code for the force which, not unnaturally, emerged virtually as a transcript of the R I C code. Coogan was allocated the more difficult task of supervising the distribution of the force and in the meantime he was also given responsibility for crime investigation. It was a huge brief because of the sheer difficulty of getting men and materials into remote country areas and more so, once having got them there, to keep in contact with them. Nevertheless, Coogan and Walsh coped well, and it was in his own task of selecting and appointing middle-grade officers that the new Commissioner came up against his first serious problem.

The old R I C ranks of County Inspector, District Inspector and Head Constable were to be replaced by Civic Guard ranks of Chief Superintendent, Superintendent and Inspector. O'Duffy had to find, all told, just short of two hundred men to fill these all-important posts. Once the Guards went out into the country their direction at local level would be almost entirely dependent on these officers. In fact, for the first few months the entire system would pivot on the performance of local officers, for communications with headquarters would be non-existent. The selection and training of suitable officers from among his recruits—ex-column men and volunteers— was to create a recurring dilemma for O'Duffy in the early years of his commissionership.

A cadet scheme providing full training for intermediate

posts was to be instituted in 1923, but because the problem was so urgent in the autumn of 1922 a number of appointments had to be made immediately from among the existing recruits. Because the intermediate ranks carried with them functions which would require a good level of education and ability—prosecuting cases in the courts, administering the police strength of whole counties, and heading the investigation of all serious crime—O'Duffy had to be certain that he was getting the right men. He therefore picked officers who were, on the whole, a little older than the average recruit—about twenty-five or twenty-six years of age—and where he could he selected men who had been interrupted in the course of some form of higher education by the War of Independence. There were medical students, prospective solicitors, trainee teachers, engineers, a pharmacist or two. What they lacked in professional police training they were expected to make up for in initiative and intelligence. Above all, in O'Duffy's scale of values they were to be beyond all whisper of reproach in their discipline and in the conduct of their personal lives.

At the same time O'Duffy began to weed out some of the more truculent elements behind the Kildare mutiny. About a score of the tougher mountain men disappeared quietly over a six-week period from the end of August to early October, mostly into the army. Another larger group of perhaps forty or fifty men were taken aside, one by one, by O'Duffy or Coogan and told that strict discipline was now being imposed and that they could take it or leave it. Probably less as a precautionary measure against a repeat of the mutiny than as an indication of their unarmed status, the Civic Guards' armoury at Kildare was left behind when headquarters was transferred to Collinstown in October 1922 and the extensive course in musketry was abolished.

O'Duffy and O'Higgins shared an ideal for the role of the new Civic Guard in Irish society and together they began to hammer out a coherent philosophy for the force. They agreed that if the Guards were to be truly successful they would have to be given a sense of purpose, an ideal above and beyond the simple enforcement of the statutes in a community which, though torn by violence, was still basically stable and law-abiding. For O'Higgins this ideal took the form of a firm belief that the Civic Guard should serve the Irish people and the law rather than any party in power. It was to him a vital canon in his philosophy of government for the people by the people.

An impartial and non-political police, drawn from the people and fully answerable to them through their elected representatives was for O'Higgins a key element in his envisaged scheme of reconstruction for the Irish nation. It was a theme which was to preoccupy him during the difficult and dangerous months of 1922 and which was never to be far from his mind in the five years from then until his death in 1927.

O'Higgins was, however, to a great extent alone among the Provisional Government and Cumann na nGaedheal administration in his priority view of the new police force. Nobody disagreed with him that the Civic Guard was a vital element in the building of the state but few, if any, of his cabinet colleagues appear to have shared fully his sensitivity to the concept of an unarmed force, executing the people's laws precisely as the people saw fit to direct them through Dáil Éireann. The contrast with the R I C which in the last analysis was merely the mailed fist of the Castle administration was clear enough, and the concept of the unarmed policeman dependent upon the moral support of the community rather than on the force of arms had a universal appeal to the members of the early cabinets of the Free State, who regarded it, in Ernest Blythe's words, as 'a very civilised idea'. Perhaps they failed to share O'Higgins's unbridled enthusiasm because they were more realistically aware that the ideal could not be maintained indefinitely. No matter how much the Minister for Home Affairs might explain his doctrine of accountability to the people through their elected representatives, one still had to reckon with the fact that there was a very large minority of the population who did not accept the legitimacy of the parliament in which they sat and who denied both the right of the Free State government to legislate on their behalf and the authority vested in the Civic Guard to enforce those laws.

Moreover, O'Higgins's preoccupation at government meetings with the problems of the new police was to cause some tension in the crowded first months of the existence of the Free State. On one occasion when O'Higgins expressed mild annoyance because some problem concerning the police had been placed down the agenda, one or two members of the government present pointed out that they too had problems in their own departments. O'Higgins retorted emphatically : 'If the Guards lose, we all lose. If the Guards don't succeed, we might as well all give up.'

O'Duffy worked hard to get the Civic Guard out among the people, and early in September the first groups of guards had left the Collinstown barracks to occupy nineteen stations scattered the length of the country from Letterkenny to Limerick. The far South—Cork, Kerry, Tipperary and Waterford—was still the scene of bitter fighting and could not be policed. The first guards went in relatively large groups of either twenty or twenty-five men. The first stations and their strengths were as follows : Limerick (20 men); Bruff (20 men); Ennis (25 men); Wicklow (25 men); Clones (20 men); Galway (25 men); Ballinasloe (20 men); Monaghan (25 men); Cavan (25 men); Roscrea (20 men); Maryborough (Port-laoise) (25 men); Kilkenny (25 men); Naas (25 men); Mullingar (25 men); Longford (25 men); Athlone (25 men); Granard (20 men); Letterkenny (25 men); Buncrana (25 men). By early October these first detachments, about 500 men in all, had been augmented by a further 1,000 guards, the total force occupying just over 80 stations. By the end of the year there were 2,000 guards occupying 190 stations, a countrywide network, but still far short of the projected target of 4,500 men and over 800 stations.

O'Duffy took it upon himself personally to inspect and address every party before they left for the country and to exhort them to uphold the principals which he had reiterated on numerous occasions on the barrack square. 'We paraded before General O'Duffy at 7 a.m.' one recruit recorded. 'He inspected us to see that we had all our equipment and that we were neat and clean. Then he told us we were going out to do the most difficult job of our lives and that the whole Irish nation would have their eyes on us. He warned us against the evils of drink and then finally spoke a few short words of Irish. He saluted and left us.'

Much as the Guards feared the anger of O'Duffy's tongue and the severity of his discipline, they trusted absolutely in him as a leader whom they could depend upon always to be on their side. He infused them with a vital confidence and sense of mission and they followed his basic instructions to the letter.

O'Duffy outlined a strategy of passive resistance for the Guards to follow when confronted by the force of arms. It worked well but it depended upon the exercising of supreme discipline and confidence on the part of every guard faced with the necessity of putting it into effect.

When confronted with the threat of armed force, O'Duffy instructed, a guard was not to be deterred from the task in hand. He was to continue to perform his duty as if the gunman were not there. If he found an opportunity to disarm and arrest the gunman, so much the better, but no blame whatever would attach to a guard who chose not to take that risk. No member could be expected to put his life completely at risk with the odds so heavily weighed against him. If instructed to hand over his uniform the guard should refuse, thereby obliging the assailant to take it from him. If ordered to leave his station, the guard should refuse and force the assailants to carry him out if necessary. If ordered to put up his hands, he should refuse and simply carry on with whatever he was doing. In short, the gunman was to be ignored wherever that was at all possible. If resistance were necessary, it should be passive unless the guard thought he had a reasonable chance of effecting an arrest. When his station was burned out, he was to find another, and if that were burned out, he was to find yet a third. If necessary, he was to camp by the roadside but he was not to be driven from his designated district.

In most areas local people had no foreknowledge of the arrival of these first contingents of Civic Guards and there was initially confusion and mystification in many areas at the appearance of the strange young men in the blue uniforms. But reaction varied very much from place to place. In Waterford the Guards were received by a local delegation headed by the mayor who made a speech of welcome. In nearby Co. Wexford, however, guards in a number of stations had great difficulty in getting anyone even to speak to them for some weeks after their arrival. In Monaghan the Guards woke on their first morning in the station to find a group of towns-people, headed by a piper, outside on the street to make them welcome. They had brought gifts of food and bedding which were gratefully accepted on loan since the station party had been despatched with only scanty supplies. By contrast in nearby Co. Leitrim, Civic Guards' parties were greeted with volleys of shots through their station windows and arson attempts on several stations. In Ballyhaunis, Co. Mayo, things took an ironic turn when the soldiers of the Free State Army, resentful of the Civic Guards' threat to their local supremacy, shot up the station with a machine gun. In Rathmore, Co. Kerry, when the newcomers arrived at the church to attend Mass on their first Sunday morning, a young girl stepped from the congregation and spat in their faces.

But the overall reaction was good. Where the Guards were met with violence it was rarely from the ordinary people but from the extreme Anti-Treaty section of the population which, of course, was to be found throughout the whole country, varying in strength and activity from place to place. In many places local people came to the assistance of guards who had been robbed or whose stations had been burned. At Elphin, Co. Roscommon, the station party having been burned out of three different buildings, the local people finally prevailed on a publican to give the unfortunate guards a room over his premises in the main street. At Glasslough, Co. Monaghan, the

Orange Order turned over the local Orange Hall for the use of the Guards after their station was destroyed by armed men.

On 20 November in the presence of the Irish and international press—carefully prearranged by O'Duffy—the new Commissioner made his first public address to the force. There was in fact little in it that the guards who had gone down the country had not heard already in personal lectures from O'Duffy, but in this instance the ideal of the unarmed guard for the people was propounded to a much wider audience than the six hundred recruits who paraded to hear the general's words and to witness the raising of the first Civic Guard flag. O'Duffy began to explain his principles for the new police force, and the reporters' pencils began to work hurriedly as their owners gradually realised that O'Duffy was outlining something as yet unheard of in the entire Irish experience of law administration. The Civic Guard was to be strictly non-political, he told them. It was a police force for the people, for all the people and not for any one section of the people. Each guard before going to the country had specific instructions that he was to carry out his duties with absolute impartiality. It was not their business how the people thought politically; everyone was entitled to his own opinions, whatever they might be. In O'Duffy's words,

They are prohibited from taking part in politics, or from associating with one side more than another. They will serve whatever government the people of Ireland put into office and, as far as they can, they will protect the lives and property of all the people, irrespective of whether they support the government in office for the time being or not.

Later in the same address, O'Duffy picked up the theme which was to become his preoccupation in the years ahead— the unarmed guard; and characteristically he expounded a standard of performance which was at once utterly impracticable and supremely idealistic :

I trust that when you go to your stations you will not let down the Civic Guard and the people by abandonment of your post at the behest of any armed coward who would shirk from meeting you in combat on an equal footing. Far better the grave than dishonour. Don't be alarmed at the sound of a shot. You have heard it before and you were not subdued because you had right on your side and gunmen had only might.

It was hardly the most reassuring or encouraging message to give to young men about to travel unarmed in small groups to remote areas of the country where they were themselves unknown and knew nobody. (Walsh's disciplinary regulations, as did those of the R I C, prohibited a policeman from service within thirty miles of his native place.) And already one young guard, Harry Phelan, had died at Mullinahone, Co. Tipperary. He had separated from his companions for a few minutes to buy a hurley ball in a shop when he was set upon by three armed men. Two held him to the floor while a third put a .303 rifle to his head and shot him dead. It was callous and unprovoked killing, inexplicable even in the insane political situation of the day.

Phelan was barely twenty years old, he was in plain clothes and off duty in an eara where the Guards had hitherto enjoyed reasonable success with the people. The incident augured badly for the force and yet, incredibly, Guard Phelan was the only member of the Civic Guards to die violently throughout the course of the Civil War. Many guards were injured, some quite badly, but it was not until December 1923 that the next fatal casualty was recorded.

Nevertheless, the young recruits who listened to O'Duffy at Collinstown and subsequently in the Phoenix Park were not in a position to know that Harry Phelan was to be the only fatal casualty of the war. For them the Mullinahone killing only served to confirm their worst fears—that their unarmed and non-combatant status was to be ignored by the Anti-Treaty forces.

The young guards did not know, nor does it appear that any attempt was made to inform them, that in a directive from

D

Liam Lynch, the Chief of Staff of the Anti-Treaty forces, the Republicans had been instructed not to inflict physical injuries on the members of the new force. They were to be an approved target for intimidation, they were to be driven from the countryside, their barracks were to be destroyed, their property commandeered and their uniforms removed, but the Guards themselves were not to be harmed.

There were, of course, breaches of this directive by members of the Anti-Treaty forces and there were instances where the vigorous resistance of guards caused members of the Anti-Treaty forces to panic and open fire. But on the whole it was well observed. Had it not been, there would have been a fearful casualty toll among the force which by the end of November had begun to occupy small isolated stations. Had the Anti-Treaty forces adopted a more murderous policy, there would have been no easier target than the Civic Guard.

There was no single reason for the decision by the Republicans to grant immunity from their guns to the members of the new police force. Unarmed Dáil deputies and other supporters of the Treaty were regarded as legitimate targets—especially after a number of Republicans had been shot out of hand in Dublin—presumably either by Oriel House men or members of the Free State Army. Yet the Civic Guards who, after all, were by definition Free Staters, were not included in the list of persons suitable for liquidation circulated by Liam Lynch at the end of November to the Republican forces. In part, no doubt, Lynch must have been influenced by the fact that the police had been deliberately kept out of the fighting during the months of the summer and autumn of 1922. Furthermore, their unarmed and therefore non-combatant status was clearly apparent, and they were completely isolated and exposed as they performed their strictly civil police duties in small pockets around the countryside. They were not, on the whole, fair game for the gunmen.

Excepting the Civic Guards from their campaign of terror against the Free State was to cost the Republicans dear. The Guards were the first element in the process of normalisation envisaged by O'Higgins. Where they succeeded the other component parts of the new state's administration would follow. If they did not succeed, normal government would be impossible. They were the one device which could make rural Ireland governable for the Free State. If they could hold on and enforce some kind of order, social life and commercial trade might begin again. If they were driven out, commercial life and business would stand still, economic hardship would tighten its grip, crime would increase as a result, and the vicious circle would spread its dimensions wider and wider across a community which had already indicated its weariness of fighting and a desire for a return to peace.

The Republicans' error in their reaction to the Civic Guard was that they only terrorised them slightly. They inflicted sufficient casualties and damage to make the new police a *cause célèbre*, to gain the sympathy of the public and to supply O'Duffy and O'Higgins with sufficient material to give the force a public image of courage, determination and purpose in the face of gunmen and violence. It is tempting to speculate what might have been the ultimate effect on the Civic Guards if the Republicans had gunned down the first pioneers, unarmed and defenceless, in cold blood. One thing is certain : the ideal of the unarmed guard would not have survived very long.

Quite apart from the I R A attacks on a number of stations, the first Guards faced serious problems of accommodation. Over half the 1,200 R I C barracks which were spread throughout the area of the Free State had been destroyed in the War of Independence or during the truce, and of the remainder, many were in such a condition that their occupation was in itself a health hazard. Many stations which the R I C had evacuated were stripped of roofs, doors and windows and by the time these were replaced, the wind and rain and storm of three winters had already done their worst.

In many instances local people offered their services and even their money to assist in repairing the buildings, but too often Civic Guard detachments arrived in towns and villages to

find the R I C barracks burned down and no other suitable
accommodation available. It was a desperate situation and in
early 1923 O'Higgins was obliged to ask the Dáil to pass
a temporary bill enabling the Commissioner to take over
suitable premises for the use of the force. The passage of the
bill through the Dáil was long and bitter, although both
government and opposition agreed on the necessity of finding
accommodation for the Guards. Provision was made for the
compensation of landlords whose property was commandeered
in this way and, in fairness to the government, the act was
only used in cases of absolute necessity.

The Guards themselves would have been happy to see it
used more widely, for many of the premises they were obliged
to use were unfit for any kind of habitation. Even in 1929 bad
and unhealthy housing was still an issue which caused tensions
between the Guards and the government. Burnfoot station in
Co. Donegal became a celebrated case and the favourite
instance of the Guards' Representative Body of the wretched
conditions in which its members were forced to live. A resolution at its annual general meeting in December 1929 condemned the conditions at Burnfoot, pointing out: 'Sergeant
Maguire fell into bad health, Guard Tiernan had to be advised
to resign and travel abroad to recuperate. Gardaí McCabe
and Hannon were sent home on sick leave and died shortly
afterwards. Gardaí Mullen, MacEneany and Murphy applied
for transfers on health grounds and Guard Cosgrave was sent
to the depot hospital for treatment. Guard McKearnan arrived
in seemingly good health and had to undergo an operation.'

Burnfoot station was, of course, like many other stations
throughout the country, a breeding ground for tuberculosis.
Walls, floors, roof and fittings were filled with damp and rot-
tenness, and sanitary conditions were primitive. Many of
the young guards, in spite of their selection initially on grounds
strong physique, had been weakened by months of active
service with their I R A units on the hillsides and in the bogs,
and their continued and enforced habitation of sub-standard
buildings had the effect of finally breaking their health either

through pneumonia, tuberculosis or other respiratory illnesses.

Where a good R I C station was still standing and where its contents had been kept reasonably intact the lot of the inexperienced guard was a much happier one. Apart from the obvious advantages of having a sound roof over his head and a stout door he could lock against his enemies, he could also make the old station records his textbooks of police training and knowledge. Most of the station parties sent out up to mid-1923 had no training in the little disciplines which are an indispensable element in the work of a rural policeman anywhere. They had no knowledge of the basics of crime investigation, they had no idea how to begin writing a report or drawing up a case for presentation in the courts. They had no knowledge of filing systems or methods of recording information. Many a station party was to be eternally grateful for the meticulous book-work of some departed Peeler who had carefully written in all that pertained to the keeping of the peace in the best black Stationery Office ink.

Because of the necessity of sending out the Guards swiftly and because of the disruption of training—if training it could be called—by the mutiny, O'Duffy had reconciled himself to the fact that he would have, at first at any rate, a police force which knew little or nothing of professional police duties. Accordingly, he devised a system whereby police instructions, legal notes and the basic guidelines to crime investigation could be circulated to every station by post—or by hand where necessary. Early in 1923 a semi-official journal, *Iris an Ghárda* (later re-entitled the *Gárda Review*), was set up and for a time O'Duffy's police orders were incorporated in the *Review*. Each guard was instructed to buy a copy of the magazine and there were strict orders that it should be filed for reference in the station. In addition to O'Duffy's police duty section, the *Review* contained a magazine section which dealt with police affairs and it carried a continuous series of lessons in the Irish language. It was to become a factor of considerable importance in the formative years of the force.

But in spite of the undoubted enthusiasm of the Guards at

local level and in spite of the effectiveness of his little paper, the force still laboured under numerous disadvantages. O'Duffy's command structure was still grossly inadequate. Few stations had telephones, hardly any had regular postal services; and where such services did exist, their security and regularity of operation could not be guaranteed. Moreover, whole districts were often physically isolated as bridges were blown up and roads blocked and destroyed. There was too large a gap between each sergeant and his little party of guards and the depot headquarters in Dublin and it was clear that intermediate ranks were going to have to be reinforced and strengthened. Even in February 1923 most stations outside the bigger towns which had been occupied by Civic Guards since the previous autumn had never seen a superintendent or an inspector. As far as headquarters was concerned, many station parties might as well have vanished as soon as they were despatched—as indeed had happened to one or two.

In February 1923 O'Duffy received instructions from O'Higgins to set up a temporary cadet system. Thirty vacancies were advertised for the cadetships which were to be filled by persons with a good record in the national movement. A six-month training period was to follow for the successful candidates, after which they would be appointed with the rank of Superintendent. In fact, over half those selected came from within the ranks of the force itself and in August fifteen cadets were selected from among the officer corps of the army. The six-month training course covered every aspect of police work, including the laws of evidence, court procedure, crime investigation, administration and physical training. Meanwhile O'Duffy stepped up the process of accelerated promotion from the ranks for suitable candidates. At the end of 1923 the first fully trained officers of the Civic Guard began to take up their duties.

The temporary adoption of a system of cadet promotions might well have been a sensitive issue within a force which still smarted over the promotions issues raised in the Kildare mutiny. Yet there was little, if any, discontent over the appointments—perhaps due to the fact that they were open to the ranks as well. The system worked reasonably well and with a few outrageous exceptions the new officers were energetic, intelligent and capable. But O'Duffy was prepared to pay well for good material and the rewards for a young officer were not inconsiderable.

A Deputy Commissioner's salary was to be £900 a year plus a lodging allowance of £80. A Chief Superintendent's salary ranged from £650 to £800 with generous travel allowance and he was provided with an official driver. A Superintendent's salary began at £400 and progressed to £600 and he too became eligible for generous transport allowances which were tantamount to a free motor car.

For a bright young man in his twenties, whose alternative five years previously might have been the emigrant boat, the lower ranks of the Castle civil service or the humdrum existence of a small school or business house, the opportunities were very good. These were the days, furthermore, when every person who owned a motor car was thereby known and noted in the district and when the finest house in the suburbs of Dublin could be had for £1,000.

Almost 3,000 recruits had joined by the end of 1922 and most of the other 1,500 which made up the authorised strength came in during the first half of 1923. Relative to the pay of the officers, the lot of the sergeant and guard was not particularly good, but the job offered what was very difficult to find in the Ireland of the 1920s—security, the chance of promotion and a degree of esteem in the public eye. The recruits came from every one of the thirty-two counties of Ireland and a handful from Great Britain.

Up to 1928, three years after the force's amalgamation with the Dublin Metropolitan Police, the total number of recruits by counties of origin was as follows :

Cork 701; Kerry 598; Mayo 560; Galway 533; Clare 447; Dublin (including city) 430; Limerick 405; Roscommon 352; Tipperary 318; Donegal 312; Leitrim 279; Sligo 258; Monaghan 257; Kilkenny 243; Laois 209; Longford 191;

Cavan 185; Wexford 177; Offaly 141; Carlow 138; Kildare 130; Meath 121; Westmeath 113; Wicklow 111; Fermanagh 103; Tyrone 91; Waterford 88; Antrim (including Belfast) 87; Derry 63; Louth 62; Down 45; Armagh 44; Great Britain 36; Total 7, 838.

6 The Security of the State 1922-23

By the late autumn of 1922 the Civil War had been carried out of Dublin into the Irish countryside. In military strength and organisation the forces of the Provisional Government clearly had the upper hand and Free State troops were already in control of provincial areas such as Cork and Kerry where Republican activity had been greatest. It could now only be a matter of time before the remaining enclaves of Anti-Treatyite resistance would be stamped out. But guerilla fighters are notoriously difficult to subdue, and an ugly and protracted campaign of squalid ambushes and skirmishes ensued as the government troops pursued the Irregulars among their remote fastnesses in the mountains and bogs. Atrocity was followed by counter-atrocity, and violent and brutal crime, often disguised as part of either side's war effort, was rampant. Each day brought its tally of innocent victims, shot down, often without provocation, sometimes by common criminals, sometimes by Republican or Free State soldiers.

Civil war is also notorious for the legacy of bitterness and hatred which it leaves behind in the community, often for generations. (The spectre of the Civil War still haunts the political and socical life of Ireland.) To President Cosgrave and his colleagues it was only too evident that, even after the official cessation of hostilities had been declared, they would be faced with an immense problem of law and order for some time to come. While the Civil War drew near to its inevitable conclusion, the search for civil peace had hardly begun.

It was scarcely the ideal atmosphere in which to put into practice the concept of an unarmed, non-political police force. O'Duffy and the government were both aware that conditions in the country in the autumn of 1922 were such that the guards would not be able to carry out normal policing on their own. Open fighting was still in progress in many areas even as the Guards occupied their stations, and groups of armed criminals, many of them disbanded or deserted members of the two armies, were operating throughout the country. Moreover, even where criminals did not actually resort to the use of firearms in the furtherance of crime, no unarmed guard could follow them without great risk to himself. It was clear that where the unarmed guard could not have the assistance of the military in dealing with armed criminals, his police role was going to be severely limited for some time to come.

It was this situation which made it necessary for the government to direct the Guards to concern themselves strictly with civil duties, leaving the conduct of the war and the suppression of armed crime to the military. It was a difficult and dangerous task, for violence had become almost part of everyday life in the Irish countryside and the likelihood was that, except within the larger towns and villages, the unarmed guard would often encounter armed men. But on the whole the Guards did their best to follow the government's instructions, and their success in doing so was later to stand them in good stead with the population at large.

However, in late 1922 it was obvious that for better or worse the as yet untried Civic Guard was going to be regarded as yet another extension of the Free State administration, an R I C administered by Irishmen on behalf of Britain, their uniform and claim to authority a usurpation of the powers of the Republic as passed on by the Second Dáil. It was evident even at this stage that the force's biggest problem would be the establishment of its own legitimacy in the eyes of the people rather than its simple physical survival in a war situation. The attitude of the Republicans towards the institutions of the new state—and thereby the attitude which the Guards could expect from the Anti-Treaty section of the population—was set out by de Valera in an interview with the political correspondent of the *Daily Mail* in November: 'We are in arms against and resisting now exactly what the whole nation resisted in 1919–21,' he said. 'The only difference is that in the earlier period England was maintaining her claims directly. Now she is maintaining them indirectly through Irishmen.'

De Valera's absolute claim to continuing leadership of the 1919–21 struggle left very little ground for compromise with the Provisional Government, whose attitude was set out repeatedly in the Dáil and elsewhere by Kevin O'Higgins. The people had given their acceptance of the Treaty at the ballot box and their will was to prevail, backed up if necessary by the iron hand of the state. The conflict of these two principles, each passionately supported by their own followers, resulted in fearful atrocities as each side sought to impose their legitimacy upon the other. In August Free State intelligence officers dragged two young Republicans from a car at Drumcondra, Dublin, placed them against the piers of a gate and shot them dead in full public view. Significantly, Staines, who was at this time still Commissioner of the Civic Guards, made a point of turning up at the inquest to stress that the Civic Guards had no connection with Oriel House or Free State intelligence. He did not know who had been responsible for the killings, he told the inquest, but there was a possibility, he thought, that it might have been members of the army, Oriel House or of the Irregular forces.

On 4 October two young supporters of the Treaty were taken from their homes near White's Cross in Cork, tied together in a turnip field and shot dead. On 7 October two young Republicans were found shot dead at the Red Cow, Clondalkin, just outside Dublin. A third died later of his wounds. On 10 October three warders and a prisoner were killed in a riot at Mountjoy Prison.

In September the Provisional Government conferred drastic emergency powers of search, detention and execution on the army, and the war entered on a new phase of authorised and legalised executions. Three of the attacking party which had attemped to bomb Oriel House were executed in mid-November. But perhaps the most fearful example of the use of these new arbitrary powers occurred after an attack on two Pro-Treaty members of the Dáil, Seán Hales and Pádraic Ó Maille who were shot as they left the Ormond Hotel on the Dublin quays on 7 December. Hales was killed and Ó Maille gravely wounded. As a reprisal, four of the Anti-Treaty leaders who had been in prison since the capture of the Four Courts were shot by order of the Executive Council the following morning.

It was perhaps the most dangerous and ominous incident of the entire Civil War. Both sides had descended to institutionalised killing—murder with a legal face on it. The Republicans viewed Hales and Ó Maille as traitors to the nation and thus deserving of their fate. The Provisional Government regarded the four men executed on 8 December as armed rebels who had taken arms against the majority will of the Irish people. In this light they too saw their victims as deserving to die.

The executions of 8 December can be seen as marking the nadir of the Provisional Government. What appalled even the most fervent supporters of the government was not that the men had been shot but that they had been killed without any vestige of statutory or legal authority. The four prisoners, whatever their sympathies, could have had no connection with the shooting of Hales and Ó Maille, for they had been in custody since the previous July. Deputy Gerald Fitzgibbon, later to become a judge of the Supreme Court, summarised the sense of outrage which was felt even by supporters of the government :

Let the Executive Council come here and get authority for any form of drastic action they please against the people who have been concerned in the rebellion against organised government here. I confess that it seems to me that the men who suffered this morning were treated with extraordinary leniency in being allowed to live so long . . . They . . . particularly deserved their fate as much as many men who have been executed in this country during the past fortnight or so, but they deserved their fate for something they did not do yesterday, but something they did weeks or, it may be, months ago.

But throughout November, December and January, reprisal and injury were countered by more violence and punishment. The death toll mounted and the campaign became more vicious and inhuman as the Anti-Treaty forces were split into smaller and smaller groups by the government troops. A total of seventy-seven men were executed by the government, seventy-three of them under the powers conferred on the army in September. They included Erskine Childers who was shot on 24 November for being in possession of a small pistol given him by Michael Collins. In the field too there were atrocities. A favourite device of Anti-Treaty stragglers was to open fire on a Free State detachment and then surrender before they sustained any casualties themselves. In at least one instance the Free State troops had simply shot their captives out of hand. In another instance when a party of Free State soldiers had been blown to pieces by a bomb at Macroom, their companions had refused to take the assailants prisoner and one was shot dead before an officer intervened.

At Ballyseedy, Co. Kerry, on 7 March 1923 eight Anti-Treaty prisoners were killed while roped together at a road-block which had been rigged with a landmine. The government forces claimed that the men had been instructed to clear the block as an alternative to risking the lives of Free State troops. The Anti-Treaty side claimed that the prisoners were tied with their hands behind their backs and that the mine was exploded deliberately. On the same day four prisoners were killed under even more obscure circumstances at Countess Bridge near Killarney where a mine had also been rigged. On 12 March there was another incident at Cahirciveen, Co. Kerry, when five more men died in a similar explosion.

Nor were the Civic Guards immune from attack. While Anti-Treatyites generally adhered to their policy of not shooting unarmed policemen, the use of almost every other form of intimidation was widespread. Between September 1922 and September 1923 there were almost two hundred attacks on Civic Guard stations with bombs, fire and bullets. More than sixty stations were destroyed—many suffering the same fate several times. Moreover, almost four hundred members of the force were physically beaten, stripped of their uniforms, publicly humiliated or robbed of both personal and official belongings.

The *Gárda Review* of 5 March 1923, covering what might have been a fairly typical fortnight reported three attacks on stations, at Granard, Co. Longford, Inistogue, Co. Kilkenny, and Ahascragh, Co. Galway. At Ahascragh, the *Review* reported 'five guards under Sergeant Rodgers have since occupied temporary premises and were visited again on Thursday night by twenty armed men who seized all their private property. A bomb was also thrown at the Guards' quarters early in the week without doing any damage.' Drawing a moral for its readers, the *Review*, however, pointed out : 'On the occasion of their last visit, the raiders gave the Guards orders to clear out of the district, a request, however, which the Guards do not intend to comply with.'

At Inistogue, the *Review* reported, the raiders seized 'articles of public property, burned same and took away the bicycles.' The same issue also reported that Inspector Doyle and his group of three guards were fired at in Kells while returning from a raid on a licensed premises—showing that not quite all the violence was politically inspired !

Not all the Guards were disciplined enough to withstand the tension and strain of living unarmed and unprotected, perhaps thirty miles away from the next police station, among a people who seemed friendly enough in the day-time but from whose numbers armed raiders would come at night. One guard, burned out repeatedly in a little station in Connemara, wrote to O'Duffy in pleading terms : 'How long more am I going to be left in this God-forsaken place. Am I like Dumas's prisoner in the Bastille, to be left here to rot and grow grey in the service, surrounded by squalor and poverty, rocks and bogs, cut adrift from all social amenities and the things that make life worth living?' In some instances Guards simply took off for England, America or some other refuge, often after repeated pleas to headquarters for some improvement or other in their conditions had gone unheeded. In at least one instance an entire station party disappeared, leaving books and station records behind, neatly balanced with a final entry noting their departure for the United States. At Elphin, Co. Roscommon, the local sergeant had been burned out so often that when O'Duffy called on a surprise inspection in August 1923 the station party could not find the books and official records: they had been hidden so that they would not be captured by the raiders the next time they struck.

Survival with dignity was an inordinately difficult task in this situation for young men who had been used to the feel of firearms and knew how to use them. There was a constant danger that the young members of the force might become disillusioned and frustrated. It is easy to understand and sympathise with such feelings. They were obliged to stand at gunpoint while their stations were burned, their property looted and their very role and function held up to ridicule by the men with the firearms. They needed all the sense of purpose which O'Duffy and their own officers could give them.

But by early 1923 the struggle for the Republic was weakening. On 29 January Liam Deasy, the Deputy Chief of Staff of the Anti-Treaty forces, who had been captured, issued an appeal to the other Republican leaders to surrender, and on 8 February the government offered an amnesty to any who handed in their arms and surrendered. On 7 April Dan Breen was captured. On 10 April the Anti-Treaty Chief of Staff, Liam Lynch, was captured in the Knockmealdown Mountains and died shortly afterwards of wounds received in the skirmish. Finally, on 27 April 1923, Eamon de Valera ordered a cease-fire by the Anti-Treaty forces.

But the peace which the spring of 1923 was to bring—if peace it could be called—gave nobody victory. It was the peace of exhaustion and indecisiveness which has always followed civil war anywhere when both sides realise that they cannot convert each other and yet have to live side by side, sharing the same country. The negotiations which followed the April cease-fire were inconclusive and it was this inconclusiveness which was to a large extent to be responsible for the continuation of the hardline security policy by the Free State government in the years after 1923.

At the end of April two members of the Free State Senate, James Douglas and Andrew Jameson, received letters from de Valera asking whether they would be prepared to act as intermediaries for peace dicussions with the government. They agreed and a series of proposals was put forward by the government for de Valera's consideration through this channel. The terms provided for a recognition by 'every party in the state' that 'all political issues, whether now existing or in the future arising shall be decided by the majority vote of the elected representatives of the people' and that all weapons in the country should be under the effective control of the government responsible to the people through their representatives. Prisoners were to be released conditional upon their individual subscription to these principles. The government further agreed to facilitate de Valera and his supporters in contesting the next election provided they undertook to adhere strictly to constitutional action.

De Valera issued a set of counter-proposals which were unacceptable, if only on one count—his extraordinary plans for the storage of arms. De Valera did not accept the government's implied demand that all arms be handed over to it; instead he formulated a proposal for the storage of Republican arms in specially selected provincial depots under the care of pledged Republican troops. These arms would be distributed among their owners or disposed of in whatever way would be decided by the government which would come to power after the next election. The Cosgrave government did not, of course, accept these proposals and the communications between the two sides, via Senators Douglas and Jameson, came to an end. Shortly afterwards, de Valera in effect brought the Civil War to an end. On 24 May he issued his celebrated 'Legion of the Rearguard' proclamation.

TO ALL RANKS, FROM THE PRESIDENT

Soldiers of Liberty! Legion of the Rearguard! The Republic can no longer be defended successfully by your arms. Further sacrifices on your part would now be in vain, and continuance of the struggle in arms unwise in the national interest. Military victory must be allowed for the moment to rest with those who have destroyed the Republic.

Do not let your sorrow overwhelm you. Your efforts and the sacrifices of your dead comrades in this forlorn hope will surely bear fruit. They have even already borne fruit. Much that you set out to accomplish has been achieved. You have saved the nation's honour, preserved the sacred national tradition and kept open the road of independence. You have demonstrated in a way there is no mistaking that we are not a nation of willing bondslaves . . . May God guard every one of you and give to our country in all times of need sons who will love her as dearly and devotedly as you.

But de Valera had not surrendered his principles and had therefore not resolved the differences which had brought about the Civil War: his declaration and the accompanying message from the Chief of Staff, Frank Aiken, was was no more than an order to dump arms. Perhaps very skilfully, perhaps unwittingly, he had presented the Free State government with a political and moral dilemma which it could not overcome and which over the years was going to erode its majority in the Dáil and among the people. Confronted with a situation which was not peace and yet not war, opposed by a party which refused to relinquish its weapons and which reserved the right to use unconstitutional means to achieve power, the successive governments of W. T. Cosgrave were to seek to defend themselves by an almost endless succession of Special Powers Acts and Public Safety Acts. All de Valera had to do was wait.

And with the moral onus thrown on the shoulders of the

Cosgrave government, it was only a matter of weeks after the cease-fire before the first pressures of the dilemma became apparent. The first major issue was the question of political prisoners. An estimated 12,000 men and women were in prisons and camps throughout the country when de Valera issued his proclamation. Conditions were appalling, as much through ineptitude on the part of the military and prison authorities as through malevolence. Food was bad and supplies of medicines were irregular and intermittent, sanitary facilities were primitive and medical attention was limited. Moreover, security was brutally effective, sentries and warders being liable to the most severe disciplinary punishments if prisoners escaped. Predictably, the atmosphere in the camps was explosive and often marked by violence. Trigger-happy sentries killed or seriously wounded over a dozen prisoners and four prison guards were killed and half a dozen wounded.

The existence of these 12,000 prisoners in Free State jails and prison camps was perhaps the most urgent manifestation of the difficult situation in which the Cosgrave government now found itself. By de Valera's declaration of cease-fire a state of war might be deemed to have concluded and yet it was evident that large quantities of arms and ammunition were still accessible to the Anti-Treaty forces throughout the country. If prisoners were released in large numbers, there was a danger of a resumption of hostilities, but much more realistically there was the danger that small groups with access to local arsenals might decide to continue in armed opposition in spite of de Valera's proclamation.

The problem of the prisoners preoccupied O'Higgins and his security heads, including O'Duffy, not only on humanitarian grounds but also for operational reasons. The Army Emergency Resolution, whereby military executions and imprisonments had been authorised during the war, was now in jeopardy as a result of the cease-fire, and as soon the courts would hold that a state of war no longer existed, Habeas Corpus would again become effective and the prisoners would automatically have to be set free. O'Duffy was of the belief that he needed until the summer of 1923 to consolidate his police system and if the hardline gunmen could be kept out of the way until then, the Guards would have stabilised the state of affairs in the countryside sufficiently for the released prisoners to be quietly absorbed back into the community. Nevertheless, O'Duffy did not press for the continued detention of the prisoners beyond the point where he considered it absolutely necessary. In this he was supported by Pat Moynihan and Peter Ennis, the two chiefs of Oriel House, who believed that with proper selectivity and surveillance of suspects, it should be possible to release large numbers of prisoners. Even army intelligence, a body not noted for its liberal views towards the Irregulars reckoned by June 1923 that conditions had vastly improved and that a return to normal conditions was imminent.

Cosgrave and O'Higgins were not satisfied. In O'Higgins's own words to the Dáil, there was not going to be a draw in the Civil War 'with a replay in the autumn'. Whether a gesture of generosity and trust in the form of a general release of prisoners would have turned back the tide of public support in favour of the government is now an academic point. For better or worse, a policy of ultra-cautious, stern and rigid security administration had been adopted and it was in time to cost the Cosgrave government their hard-won victory among the people.

The hardline policy of the government was not, as tradition and myth would have it, the sole creation of Kevin O'Higgins. Terence de Vere White, in his definitive biography of Kevin O'Higgins, points out that when the four reprisal executions were being considered in December 1922 by the government, O'Higgins was one of the last two members of the Executive Council to agree to the shootings. The Provisional Government and the subsequent Cumann na nGaedheal governments of W. T. Cosgrave were made up of stern men. Apart from O'Higgins, there was Mulcahy, Minister for Defence and Commander-in-Chief of the army, possibly the strongest advocate of firm measures against those Anti-Treatyites who took up arms against the Free State; there was Blythe, a tenacious and principled Northern Protestant, but equally a man of unshakeable determination to use force where force was necessary; there was Eóin MacNéill, similarly principled and determined and no less strong-minded in his willingness to apply the iron hand where he thought it appropriate. If they had a failing collectively as a government, it was their reluctance to trust sufficiently in the people, for from the day they came to power until the day they fell they were to follow a security policy which was narrow, ungenerous, unimaginative and, in the long term, one of the main factors in their ultimate rejection by the people on whose behalf they had carried it out. Perhaps the only exception to that undistinguished record was to be the creation of an unarmed, non-political, national police.

Three applications for Habeas Corpus during the month of June 1923 were turned down by the Master of the Rolls and on 15 June, when it had become evident that very shortly the courts were going to direct the government to release their prisoners, O'Higgins introduced in the Dáil a Public Safety Bill which would give the government power to keep and take more prisoners without trial. The bill was passed by the Dáil and went to the Senate in the third week of July where it was the subject of severe criticism on several counts, mainly in that it placed on the shoulders of the Civic Guard responsibility for detention orders which should properly have been carried by the Minister for Home Affairs. If the powers were abused, a number of senators pointed out, they could not vote the Civic Guard out of office but they could vote the minister out of office. Senator Douglas put it succinctly : 'What I want to avoid if possible is bringing in these new forces, particularly the Civic Guard and mixing them up with this bill in the eyes of the public. I should like it to be made quite clear that if an officer of the Civic Guard arrests a man, he brings him forward in the ordinary courts for trial. But if, in the meantime, under the bill, the minister interferes and interns him, the public cannot blame the Civic Guard officer.' Senator W. B. Yeats concurred : 'The principle is that the minister can be changed if he does an unpopular act. He can go away taking the bitterness he had raised with him. But the Civic Guard cannot be changed.' Nonetheless, O'Higgins was intransigent. It was perhaps the first instance of grave inconsistency in the government's attitude towards the new police. On the one hand, they were heralded as the servants of all the nation. On the other they were held in tightly under the wing of Cumann na nGaedheal as if they were the government's personal property.

On 31 July 1923 the Court of Appeal issued its long-expected decision that the state of war in the Free State had come to an end. The further detention of internees was therefore illegal. The government immediately called into operation the provisions of the Public Safety Act, and detention without trial was thus continued. Oriel House had been directed to begin a screening of prisoners in custody to determine who could be safely released and who should be detained. By the end of July the report was with O'Higgins, but instead of making large-scale releases, prisoners were only set free in small batches. Over a thousand men still remained in jails and camps, the proportion of those convicted before the courts as compared with those interned being in the approximate ratio of one to three. There was considerable disquiet throughout the country over the government's action, and by November the Roman Catholic Primate, Cardinal Logue, departed from the Church's traditional standpoint of unreserved support for the government to express, rather pointedly, the hope that the last of the prisoners might be out by Christmas. Within days of the Cardinal's statement, two hunger-striking Republicans, Denis Barry and Andrew Sullivan, had died in prison and on 23 November the remaining hunger-strikers in Kilmainham ended their protest which they had maintained over several weeks. Immediately the government, taking advantage of the opportunity of not appearing to be bowing to pressure, began to release the prisoners in great numbers until there was only a handful left, including de Valera and some of his lieutenants who had been arrested by the Free

State Army during the general election campaign in August 1923 under the Public Safety Act.

The development of the Civic Guard in these formative months was greatly influenced by the government's emphasis on cautious conservatism and by its near obsession with security. O'Higgins and the government, while allowing Eóin O'Duffy considerable freedom of manoeuvre in the management of the force, never had any intention of granting it the completely non-political status which, as a civil police, it should have had and which the Labour Party called for repeatedly in the Dáil. The principle, long accepted in Britain, that the police forces should not be identified with central government, was ignored. O'Higgins's rationale was his classic, inflexible and not entirely valid (in the Free State context) theory of democracy. The Civic Guards were the people's police, he agreed. But the people controlled them through the government they had elected and the police were answerable to the people through the minister responsible for their administration. In a message to the force, delivered through the medium of the *Gárda Review*, O'Higgins told its members:

Drawn from the people, it is your proud duty to see that the laws and regulations which, through their elected representatives, they enact for the better ordering of their lives, are obeyed by all. There is no law in operation in Ireland now that has not been either sanctioned and adopted or actually initiated and passed by the elected representatives of the people. If the people require the amendment or repeal of a particular law, the machinery is their disposal. No law prevails or can prevail which lacks the great seal of their endorsement. No government can hold power, no policy can be pursued which has not the sanction and approval of the majority of the people of Ireland. You are therefore in the fullest and truest sense the people's servants, the guardians of the people's peace.

O'Higgins was being at best unrealistic, at worst less than honest. The laws which the Guards were to enforce were, in the main, approved of by the people—being the normal body of civil and criminal regulations which exist in any society. But there were also on the statute book many regulations inherited from the British administration which the people and their elected representatives had had no chance as of yet even to consider. Many of these were subsequently found to be impracticable or unworkable and had to be repealed. But of infinitely more consequence was the very real fact, blandly overlooked by O'Higgins and indeed by O'Duffy in their exhortations to the Guards, that a huge proportion of the population—perhaps as much as forty per cent—did not accept the right of the Free State government to rule the country. The normal processes of democracy did not run smooth in Ireland and there was not the same consensus in Irish politics as in British. However much O'Higgins might have liked to believe it, each individual Civic Guard in his everyday work among the people was not going to have the same acceptance and implicit trust as his counterpart in the villages and towns of rural England; rather than a closer identification with central authority, the Irish policeman needed to be given an independent status, answerable to law and not to government.

O'Higgins and O'Duffy did accept, of course, that while the Guards would always be fully accountable to the Free State government, that government might not always be a Cumann na nGaedheal one. At least the Guards were told repeatedly that their loyalty was to whatever government was in power —though it is arguable that in these years the prospect of a constitutional takeover by any other party was so slight as not to bear serious consideration. At Collinstown barracks in February 1923 O'Higgins told a parade of recruits:

The internal politics and political controversies of the country are not your concern. You will serve, with the same imperturbable discipline and increasing efficiency, any government which has the support of the majority of the people's elected representatives. Party will no doubt succeed party in the ebb and flow of the political tide. New issues will arise and the landmarks of today will disappear but you will remain steadfast and devoted in the service of the people and of any government which it may please the people to return to power.

O'Duffy echoed the principles in his parade-ground lectures. The Guards were to be the unarmed guardian of the people's peace 'raised by the people themselves as their breastplate and helmet of protection . . . The Gárda do not rule. They are simply the medium through which the people rule.'

But for all his protestations about the people's police, O'Higgins was reluctant to give the people much of a say in the manner in which the force should be conducted. In July 1923 he introduced in the Dáil a Civic Guard Bill to authorise the permanent implementation of the force which had been drawn up on the basis of General Mulcahy's organising committee report of February 1922 and which had hitherto operated under the Adaptation of Enactments Act and a section of the District Justices Act. There were to be no departures from the basic principles drawn up in Mulcahy's report—an unarmed, non-political force, responsible to the government through its Commissioner, who, together with all the commissioned officers of the force (all ranks above and including Superintendent), would be appointed by and removable by the government. In proposing the bill, O'Higgins told the house : 'It is felt that to preserve strictly the theory that all executive power and authority wielded in this country is, in fact, the delegated power and authority of the people, that commissions in this police force should be given by and on behalf of the Executive Council and it is clear that commissions can only be withdrawn by the body which gives them.' He did make the concession of assuring the house that the Executive Council would 'act through well defined channels and will in fact act on the recommendations of the person who is placed at the head of the force'.

The opposition Labour Party was not, however convinced that this was the only or ideal way to run a police force. Cathal O'Shannon pointed out from the opposition benches that there could be different conceptions of the nature of a permanent police force in Ireland. The bill provided for one kind of police force, but, he added, 'The strength of arguments may well be in favour of that particular kind—that is a strongly centralised police force at the moment—and until such time as things in Ireland become somewhat more normal. But undoubtedly if we were in more normal times there would be a great strength of feeling in favour of a different and perhaps more localised police force. That is not possible under this bill.' The leader of the Labour Party, Tom Johnson, then suggested that instead of passing the bill as a permanent measure the house might pass it as a temporary one, renewable in 1924, with amendments at that stage if necessary. O'Higgins agreed to accept the amendment and the bill was designated as a temporary measure, though when it came to be renewed the following year there was still to be no departure from the highly centralised government-controlled force of Mulcahy's committee. On 31 July in the committee stage of the temporary bill, O'Shannon moved an amendment that the name of the force be changed from the Civic Guard to Gárda Síochána, a rough Irish equivalent for the words 'Guardians of the Peace', and the legend already in use on the force's crest and badges. The amendment was accepted. It was the last meaningful intervention the opposition was allowed to make in the construction of the force.

The relationship between the Gárda Síochána and the government of the Irish Free State in these early, turbulent years of their existence was the clearest vindication of the adage that the political health of any society can be judged by the way its police behave. The Free State governments of 1922–32 were to be highly principled, scrupulously honest and self-demanding but arrogant, conservative and inward-looking. So too was the direction of the Gárda Síochána. The force had to win its acceptance at local level almost in spite of the Cosgrave administration.

7 The People's Peace 1923-25

In the summer of 1923 Ireland was undergoing the painful transition from civil war to uneasy peace. Full-scale military engagements between the opposing forces had ceased, yet sporadic violence and disorder were still rife and the country had by no means returned to normal peace-time conditions. For the early months of their existence the Civic Guards found themselves in the unenviable position of trying to maintain a reasonable standard of order in the day-to-day affairs of the Irish countryside. The government's rigid insistence that, in the continuing presence of the Free State Army and disbanded Irregulars, the pursuit of armed criminals was strictly the province of the military meant that the Guards were often obliged to stand helpless in the face of provocation and intimidation. But this very limitation of their duties had the effect of bringing the Guards into close contact with the rural population and, eventually, of winning their acceptance. Within a surprisingly short time the new police gained the respect of the majority of the people by their energetic attempt to bring a degree of security into their lives. After three years of chaos and almost total lawlessness there was plenty for them to do.

Although the level of recorded crime in the community was extraordinarily high in the years 1922–23, there was little the unarmed Civic Guards could do immediately and directly to bring it down. But it was O'Duffy's intention, by restoring a measure of normality in the lives of ordinary members of the community, to isolate the criminal and the gunman from the safe havens and retreats he had readily found during the Civil War. In the atmosphere of conflict in the previous three years no Irish home was likely to close its doors to a man on the run and whether he was a patriot or a common criminal mattered little. If one had to have proof of the bona fides of one's guest's, one might as well not offer one's hospitality and shelter in the first place.

But the war was now over and the clearest way of bringing the fact home to the people was by enforcing once again the normal regulations of a society in times of peace. There had been a complete breakdown in social and commercial life since the withdrawal of the Royal Irish Constabulary. Trade and commerce had all but ended in many districts. Unemployment and vicious worker-owner confrontation had occurred on a widespread scale—in Drogheda, Limerick, Wicklow, Wexford, Cork, Kilkenny and, in particular, in Waterford. In small communities many shopkeepers and traders who had refused to supply goods on credit were being intimidated. Farmers who thought they had been left short in the land distribution acts of the previous decades were taking the opportunity to settle what they considered to be justifiable scores. All the many feuds and tensions of a rural society which had been regulated and kept in line for many years by the firm hand of the R I C had surfaced, often under a thin guise of nationalism, and were now manifesting themselves in violence and intimidation. The final touch of chaos stemmed from the total breakdown of the administration of civil as well as criminal law. Debts could not be collected, court orders could not be enforced and summonses could not be served.

One problem, in particular, had come to the fore as a huge social evil in the three years since the beginning of the Civil War—the growth in the poteen trade. The illegal and potent spirit, long confined to its traditional manufacturing area of the south and west coast, had spread right across the country to areas where it had never been known before. It spread into Dublin itself, where a thriving and highly organised poteen business was being conducted by one of the city's main criminal gangs. The still was eventually discovered two years later in the suburb of Rathmines from where its produce was distributed in fast cars throughout the counties of the east coast. Poteen, as much through economic necessity as through alcoholic indulgence, had become the staple industry of the counties of the western seaboard by the end of 1922. Manufactured from a grain base or occasionally from potatoes, it contained a highly potent, almost raw, alcohol. Conditions and ingredients, however, were often unhygienic or of low quality and the result was often fearful physical damage or even death for the consumer. Moreover, the product of the little pot, being highly addictive if taken in excess, had become a threat to the welfare of many small communities. Perpetual drunkenness had become the norm for the menfolk of many western areas and the attendant evils of violence, poverty and mental deterioration were widespread.

Apart from the massive scale of illicit alcohol manufacture and consumption, excessive drinking of legitimate products had also become a problem in many areas. Licensing laws were openly flouted—indeed many publicans who sought to observe them were often forced to reopen their premises at gunpoint by the Free State Army. Licences were not renewed, opening hours were meaningless, and in some places the worst type of poteen was being sold across the counter in the place of regular commercial whiskey.

By the time the Civic Guards were about to occupy their first stations, the stamping out of the 'drink evil', as the *Gárda Review* referred to it, had become a priority with the clergy of rural Ireland and with the government. O'Duffy and O'Higgins were bombarded with letters from priests in remote rural areas who spoke of whole villages and communities under the influence of the poteen maker and the shebeen men. Reports from dispensary doctors confirmed their claims that a huge health problem was being created by drink. Inter-family and faction quarrels, often accompanied by extreme violence, had become an everyday problem for the local clergy—in the absence of any police. O'Higgins was determined to put down the poteen trade. He spoke in the Dáil of villages in the West of Ireland where children 'going to and coming from school were reeling around the road drunk' and O'Duffy hammered into the Guards the message that drink was evil, exhorting them, by their own example, to show the communities of which they were to become a part that it could be done without: 'Once you allow yourselves to give way to drunkenness or any of the evils that follow in its train,' he told the recruits at Collinstown, 'you will go from bad to worse until your future career will be blasted.'

The fact that it was the clampdown by the Guards on the poteen trade which first gained for them the respect and acceptance of many communities in the West and South gives an idea of the extent to which the problem was affecting the daily lives of the people. Almost immediately they arrived in their stations, guards began to find themselves in receipt of information about the poteen trade. Breaches of the licensing laws were—incredibly—more often reported by the public than actually discovered by members of the force. Local councils and other authorities began to pass resolutions applauding the work the Guards were doing and officers were able to report to O'Duffy that initial reactions to the new force were favourable.

In 1923, the first year for which figures are available, there were almost 10,000 prosecutions outside the Dublin Metropolitan Area for offences connected with the licensed trade and the manufacture of illegal spirits. In 1924, armed with the provisions of a new Intoxicating Liquor Act which made possession of the ingredients for poteen an offence, the Gárda undertook 12,400 prosecutions, and by 1925 the trade had been driven back into the most remote districts of the western seaboard and a few islands off the Mayo, Galway and Donegal coast.

Massive co-ordinated swoops on the poteen trade were not to come, however, until the network of stations was sufficiently widespread to allow the Guards to operate in reasonably large numbers against poteen makers and shebeen owners. Meanwhile the Guards had begun to sort out local problems—land disputes, labour troubles, allegations of overcharging by traders and counter-allegations of failure by customers to pay accounts. The ordinary law-abiding people took to the Guards immediately, turning to them with their local difficulties. They were in demand for every kind of minor problem, their youth and inexperience quite overlooked in people's enthusiasm for the reintroduction of a measure of order and day-to-day security.

O'Duffy was delighted. His reports to the government contained glowing accounts of young guards sorting out the most delicate and intricate problems of little communities. The *Gárda Review* became a favourite vehicle for publicising expressions of gratitude and admiration from local authorities, clergymen and any other dignitaries who had something complimentary to say about the new force. In retrospect, the practice perhaps seems somewhat fatuous but in the reality of the times O'Duffy felt, rightly or wrongly, that the Guards out in the country needed every bit of encouragment they could get.

O'Duffy's influence was that of a welding force on the new Civic Guard. He was likely to appear in the day room of a three-man station in Tipperary as on the depot square at any given time. He repeatedly told the Guards that they were the finest of the Irish race and the finest police force in the world. He drew freely on a great store of superlatives in putting his message across to the force. At the end of 1923 he returned from the International Police Conference in New York and told the headquarters force, specially assembled on the depot square, how the police chiefs of Japan and Honduras had begged him for an opportunity to come to Ireland to see at first hand its famous new police force. And in characteristically pompous fashion he related how the traffic in New York was stopped to get him to his ship and how the American navy had provided the vessel with an escort of destroyers for twelve miles out to sea. But O'Duffy gave the Guards an unshakeable sense of mission. They were, he told them, the very foundation of orderly and civilised government in the emerging state. Everything depended on them. And they in turn worshipped

him for his confidence and enthusiasm. 'The General' was the
guiding light of the force, a remote untouchable figure but yet
the personification of order, discipline and righteousness which
every guard was to be. He was eulogised in speeches at conferences and public meetings wherever the Guards were involved. He was lauded in the *Gárda Review* and even the
amateur poets of the force dedicated their stanzas to him. In
late 1923 some unknown scribe in the *Review* wrote of
O'Duffy:

> The Chief of the Force is not sleeping tonight,
> He's awake!
> A phone's at his side and a map's on the wall,
> And his look is intense as he answers a call—
> The General's awake, yes awake! . . .
>
> So I stand and I think, then I walk up and down,
> On my beat,
> And the night passes on and the little stars peep,
> Yet the General works on in the silences deep,
> Alert and awake, wide awake.

The ideal and spirit of the force was also a common theme
for poets writing in the *Gárda Review*. A glimpse of the
enthusiasm and fervour with which the Guards took up
O'Duffy's ideals can be seen in the following acrostic verses,
submitted to the *Review* in 1923 by an anonymous 'Depot
Sentry'.

> C   hildlike force, with manly vigour,
> I   n our country's peace we strive.
> V   ieing hard with one another,
> I   reland's soul still to preserve,
> C   ontended, pure and free.
>
> G   uide our efforts, God we pray Thee,
> U   nder Thy protecting hand,
> A   nd instil into our actions
> R   everence for our motherland,
> D   istracted long in strife.

Through the *Review* and through a constant visitation of stations throughout the country O'Duffy sought in these crucial months to hold the infant force together. The smallest success anywhere by the Guards was lauded generously in the *Review* and in official circulars. The arrest of two itinerant housebreakers in Swinford, Co. Mayo, evoked the declaration from the *Review* : 'Since their coming to Mayo the Civic Guard have been ceaseless in tracing crime and tracking down criminals. Not only are they combating the poteen evil in the remotest parts of the county but their activities in apprehending midnight marauders has won for them the wholehearted appreciation of the people . . . As the members of the Guard left the town with their prisoners they were loudly cheered by the people who were supposed to be hostile.'

By the end of 1923 the gradual withdrawal of the Free State Army from the countryside had begun and it was no longer always available to the Guards as a force to fall back upon. The Guards were now obliged to adapt to a situation in which, as a properly constituted police force, they were expected to deal with armed criminals. The big Anti-Treaty units had split up and in many instances were operating locally in small groups. The dimensions of the problem of public order were now therefore much more suited to a policeman's approach than a soldier's. The bands of armed robbers or arsonists were now much more likely to run into an unarmed guard than an armed unit of Free State troops, and with astonishing frequency the unarmed Guards (supported by the armed detective branch organised by David Neligan in 1923 to replace the old Oriel House C I D) sought to make arrests and very often succeeded.

The most serious security problem faced by the Civic Guards in the immediate post-Civil War period was, as might have been expected, caused by the release of the Republican internees and prisoners. The salient provisions of the Public Safety Act were re-introduced in 1924 when the act itself was due to expire, but by May 1924 the number of political prisoners had fallen to just over six hundred, comprising roughly equal proportions of convicted prisoners and detainees. By the autumn there were just over two hundred, and by early 1925 only a handful of them—almost exclusively men who had been convicted and sentenced—remained.

No sooner were the prisoners back among their own friends in their native districts than they recommenced drilling and training. In some areas there was a noticeable upsurge again in crime, as much perhaps due to economic necessity as ideological conviction. Many of the internees had lost their means of livelihood and many found their families in straitened circumstances. The temptation to make one swift swoop on a bank or post office with some of the weaponry which abounded in every townland was very great. These were indeed the exceptional cases but nevertheless they did occur. More often than not the Guards merely had to contend with drilling, marching and the occasional verbal outburst against the Free Staters. The Guards themselves became the focal point for the anger of Republicans in many areas. Stations were still coming under frequent attack and guards patrolling in remote areas still ran a serious risk of physical assault or of being relieved of their uniforms and equipment.

The ordinary guards were now in a dilemma. Government policy was clearly to release as many internees as was possible, and if every possible prosecution had been taken against released internees, most of them would have been back in jail in a matter of weeks. Thus it became standing practice for the police to ignore relatively harmless manifestations of anti-Free State sentiment. This was the essence of the policeman's right of discretion but it was only workable where the Republicans themselves were prepared to adopt a policy of live and let live with the Guards. Where the Republicans insisted on denying the Guards' authority in the district, trouble was sure to follow, and O'Higgins and O'Duffy agreed that where a basic challenge to the Guards' legitimacy was laid down it should be taken up with full vigour.

Where the recently released internees failed to come to terms with the fact that the Guards were with them to stay,

E

the Guards almost inevitably retaliated by making arrests under one or other of the Public Safety Acts. More often than not there would be punch-ups, baton charges, violence and counter-violence.

Nevertheless, the Guards, with the help of the detective branch, were on the whole successful in regulating the process of normalisation throughout the country which O'Higgins set in train by a gradual scaling down on internment. The crime statistics showed that the situation was gradually being brought under control. By the autumn of 1924 armed robberies in the Dublin area had dropped to 14 a month, compared with 33 a month in the previous year. By the summer of 1925 that figure had dropped to 5 a month. In Dublin too the figures for murder had dropped dramatically—from 23 in 1922 to 16 in 1923 and to 2 in 1924. Outside of Dublin, however, the drop was less marked—for there was no detective branch here : offences against property with violence decreased from 2,726 in 1923 to 1,961 in 1924 and to 1,879 in 1925, but offences against the person actually showed a slight increase from 359 in 1923 to 448 in 1924 and to 502 in 1925.

But police casualties were high. By early 1924 another four guards had died, three quite unarmed, the fourth—Guard Patrick O'Halloran of Baltinglass—looking helplessly at a pistol which a well-intentioned shopkeeper had thrust into his hand as he went to arrest two men robbing a bank in the town. In December 1923 Guard Jim Woods of Scartaglen, Co. Cork, was shot dead in his own station when he tried to disarm a raider who had ordered him to put up his hands. In May 1924 Sergeant Tom Griffin and Guard John Murrin of Cregg, Co. Tipperary, were shot dead when they tried to arrest a man armed with a Colt revolver.

Unfortunately, discipline did not always stand the test. Guards in a number of areas armed themselves clandestinely. In Macroom, Co. Cork, in 1924 Chief Superintendent Burke received reports that shooting had been heard in the rear of the Gárda station in the town. On investigation he found that two local sergeants had equipped themselves with .45 Webleys and were busy at target practice while awaiting the return of some local bloods who had been giving trouble in the form of midnight forays against the station.

Of infinitely more serious consequence, however, was the development from about the end of 1923 onwards, of the problem of maltreatment of prisoners. In Wicklow, Waterford, Cork and Tipperary and later in Clare there were allegations of severe ill-treatment of prisoners in custody, many of whom were never even charged. O'Duffy was later to confess in 1929 that the problem had been serious. When power was given to men it could not be expected that all would resist the temptation to abuse it, he wrote in the *Gárda Review*. But he did admit that there had been 'a few instances of such abuse in the Gárda during its seven years of existence'. 'On a few occasions, following the murder or attempted murder of their comrades,' he went on, 'some individual members had not sufficient strength of character, will-power and moral courage to control their tempers and to display that restraint and moderation so essential in the disciplined and thoughtful policeman.'

O'Duffy warned: 'All ranks now understand that the fullest vigour of the code and of the law will be enforced for trans-gressions of this nature, that no plea of extenuating circum-stances, over-zealousness in the discharge of duty, or meritori-ous past service will be considered, and while the Gárda is protected by law in all authorised acts, if they overstep the legal boundary of their duty in the slightest degree, they are then answerable to the law, both civil and criminal.'

The issue of Gárda violence was in 1926 to bring O'Duffy and the government as near as they had ever come to an open row. But the celebrated stormy exchange of views be-tween the Commissioner and O'Higgins related to the brutal reprisal attacks on prisoners convicted of crimes which were essentially *political* in origin. In direct contrast, the limited use of physical-force methods on a *social* level often helped the Guards to enjoy a better relationship and understanding with the people among whom they worked. In small rural communities the local family feud or land agitation could often be settled by a young agile guard taking the village tough down a laneway for a good thrashing, and respect for the law was often attained through the heavy hand of a Gárda boxing or athletics champion. Moreover, the long-term ignominy and bad feeling generated by a prison sentence could be avoided in this way. Above all, this rough justice took account of the economic factor. A farm worker or small tradesman who went to jail almost inevitably left his family and dependants in very straitened financial circumstances, and in the rural Ireland of the 1920s there was a bleak outlook for a family which was to lose its breadwinner for three, six or twelve months.

Very frequently where local problems could be sorted out without recourse to the courts, the Guards could settle a troublesome situation with a few thumps on the appropriate skulls and a certain element of physical violence thus came to be an accepted part of the relationship between police and people. It was one of the vital differences between the R I C and the Guards. The R I C rarely withdrew a prosecution if they had one, for their system of ranks and their administrative structure saw to it that due process was always followed on the English model. This had ensured that the R I C was an efficient police force but hardly a popular one. The majesty of the law was a concept which had reasonable acceptance among the population of rural England but it was not suitable for transplanting to rural Ireland, there to be administered by inspectors of the Royal Irish Constabulary who had been educated and trained in England. Rural Ireland had been conditioned to be 'agin the law' and the signing of the Treaty had not changed that.

The Civic Guard, drawn from the people and, above all, officered and directed by men drawn from the people, understood that attitude. Nothing would destroy the Civic Guard more swiftly than petty officiousness, bringing in the courts and the full legal process to deal with the smallest disturbances in a community which neither understood nor respected those

Garda Officers acted as pallbearers at the funeral of Kevin O'Higgins, murdered in 1927

Large parties of uniformed and detective Gardai had to be assembled in the years of the Blueshirt disturbances. This was "The Squad" which drew members from Cork and Tipperary to police large gatherings and to conduct raids and searches.

General Eoin O' Duffy addresses a Blueshirt meeting at Bandon.

Guards caution 600 Blueshirts before a march to Bluebell cemetery, Inchicore, County Dublin, 30 November 1933. The Blueshirts put on overcoats over their uniforms and the march proceeds. . . . .

...at the cemetery, following an oration over the grave of a volunteer killed thirteen years earlier, Blueshirts give the fascist salute.

processes. There were of course exceptions—like the sergeant who prosecuted an unfortunate man in Longford for lighting a bonfire to celebrate the anniversary of Easter Week or the superintendent who always made a point of instructing guards to show their batons and handcuffs when he met them on duty at a fair or race-meeting, often in the presence of women and children.

O'Duffy had a keenly developed sensitivity to the mood of the people of rural Ireland in the early 1920s and he was well aware that if the Civic Guards did not accord with that mood they would find it difficult—perhaps impossible—to win the acceptance of the people. There was a real danger that the new force would simply come to be regarded as a continuation of the old R I C with a change of uniform. From the beginning, he stipulated it was to be the keynote of the Civic Guard that it should identify in every way at local level with the people whom it served. Moreover, O'Duffy had among his headquarters staff and his officer corps a strong body of men of like mind—young men who during the years of the struggle had been prominent in the various aspects of revived Irish nationalism—sport, the language, Irish music and dancing.

Almost as soon as the Guards had gone out to their stations, O'Duffy and his staff were organising them into Gaelic football and hurling teams, Irish language discussion groups, and committees of one sort or another. The Guards were to be 'Irish in Thought and Action', he told them through the medium of the *Review*. And with their sporting prowess they were to 'play their way into the hearts of the people'.

The response from members of the young force and from the people themselves was good. All over the country the young men in the Gárda stations became involved in organising Gaelic clubs. Many were already accomplished sportsmen in the national games, the preponderance of their numbers coming as they did from counties which were strongholds of hurling, Gaelic football and handball—Cork, Kerry, Tipperary, Galway, Clare and Mayo. The Guards brought their sporting skill to the youth of towns and villages which had never heard the clash of hurleys, seen the speed and flash of Gaelic football or watched the fascinating dexterity of a good handballer. Hundreds of new local teams were raised under the coaching of Gárda sportsmen, and the Guards themselves attained the status of local celebrities as selections for county teams. Particular encouragement was given by O'Duffy for the construction of handball alleys against the back walls of suitable police stations. These were usually built by joint efforts of police and people and then became meeting places for the guards and young people of the neighbourhood.

But it was in athletics—and especially in boxing and tug-of-war—that the Guards really excelled. Divisional sports were organised annually throughout the country. In Dublin an annual Gárda sports drew attendances of up to 10,000 people. Even in the country divisions there were large attendances. At Mallow, Co. Cork, in 1929 hundreds of people had to be turned away because they could not get transport to the Gárda sports on the packed buses and trains which were serving the town for the day.

The Guards dominated the field events—hammer-throwing, javelin, discus, pole vault, high jump and long jump, and at one time or another each national record in these events was held by members of the force. Gárda boxers too captured Irish, British and European titles and, as a result, the Guards came to be in popular demand at local level as coaches and trainers for boxing clubs.

Simultaneous with O'Duffy's propagation of sport among the Guards, the new Commissioner of the Metropolitan Police, General W. R. E. Murphy, whom O'Higgins had appointed in 1922, also began a campaign of developing sport within his force. His *forte* was also in boxing. His men, like the Gárda boxers, held European titles, and in 1924 his tug-of-war team won the world championship.

Later, when it was clear that the Guards' role as sports coaches and trainers had become fully established, O'Duffy turned more seriously to the possibilities of using the force as a medium for organising discussion and tuition groups in the

Irish language. In many areas the Guards had already organised special classes for themselves which were open to the public. O'Duffy organised the distribution of linguaphone record sets and gramophones to each station as an aid to the furtherance of the language, and in many districts Irish debating societies under the auspices of the local guards resulted.

O'Duffy's methods of integrating the Guards and the people had been entirely successful, and as the level of actual crime in the community dropped, they bore even more fruit. The Guards themselves were delighted and the people were happy. The government—in particular Kevin O'Higgins— was satisfied. But this happy state of affairs was not to last indefinitely. As the hard bitter years of the 1930s approached, the relationship between the Guards and the government was to become strained. O'Duffy and the government were frequently to be set at loggerheads, with a great deal of bitter feeling on both sides, and the brief period of perfect integration between police and people was to be largely clouded over.

From September 1922 until about mid-1924 the Gárda Síochána had been accountable primarily to the people who lived around them. The demands of the Superintendent and Chief Superintendent and the demands of the government were largely secondary. What counted was the way the guard behaved among his neighbours. If he did not please them, he was in real trouble.

But by 1924 the security situation had stabilised to the extent that the government decided it was now time to use the civil police as the first line of defence against the enemies of the state. The political and economic welfare of the country demanded that the Free State should stand on its own feet without the dubious assistance of internment without trial, a massive army garrison and intensive police surveillance of its political enemies. It was an understandable decision but one which was to cost the Gárda Síochána dear for it was to take from the police for many years their well-established non-political and impartial status. They ceased to be primarily the guardians of the people's peace and became instead part of a highly centralised bureaucracy and the Cumann na nGaedheal government's listening-posts among the people.

O'Higgins was particularly concerned at the continuing presence of the army spread throughout scores of small provincial towns. Either the Free State was a reality or it was not, he pointed out in the cabinet, and if it needed to have armed troops posted in every town and village, then it had not been a success. Already the government had made a beginning with the disbandment of large numbers of troops. In March 1924 the demobilising of 2,000 officers and 35,000 men had been ordered—representing something over half the standing army of 60,000 officers and men. A mutiny by senior officers, partly inspired by discontent at the mass demobilisation and partly by I R B influences within the officer corps, temporarily delayed the disbandment. O'Higgins, who was acting head of the government during the illness of President Cosgrave, asked for the resignation of several senior officers, and the Minister for Defence, General Mulcahy, also resigned. There were echoes of the crisis in the Dáil and eight deputies resigned in sympathy with the army men. Nevertheless, by the end of 1924 the matter had been satisfactorily settled and the loyalty of the army was guaranteed, Eóin O'Duffy having been sent in temporarily to exercise the joint functions of Gárda Commissioner and Chief of Staff of the army.

During the last three months of 1924 and the first three months of 1925 the government began to pull back the remaining army garrisons from towns throughout the country which they had held since the Civil War. The government was in agreement that soldiers could not be left there indefinitely and O'Duffy was anxious to see how the Gárda Síochána would manage on its own. Once the troops pulled out, the maintenance of order would rest entirely on the shoulders of the unarmed police and their true effectiveness and the attitude of the people towards the force would be put to the ultimate test.

The result was far from happy. Some districts remained
peaceful after the military had been withdrawn, but huge
areas of Cork, Kerry, Tipperary, Clare and the Border
country immediately became open territory not only for the
remaining active bands of Republicans who could find very
good reasons to rob banks on behalf of the Republic but
also groups of ordinary armed bandits. There was, furthermore,
a mushrooming problem of disbanded Free State troops turning to violent crime. Donegal, Tipperary, Waterford and
Limerick were the main areas of operation for these ex-soldiers
and they were in competition with Republicans and ordinary
criminals in parts of Counties Leitrim, Cavan and Monaghan.
Within weeks of the troops being pulled back it became evident
that the unarmed Civic Guards were unable to cope on their
own in a community where familiarity with and access to
weapons was still a common feature of everyday life.

The government's policy of normalisation included a
decision not to renew the Public Safety Act when it expired
in 1925. In its place, O'Higgins considered, there should be a
permanent act, giving limited but permanent powers for the
government and security forces and providing exceptionally
severe punishments for crimes against the state. The Treasonable Offences Act, as the new legislation was to be entitled,
passed through the Dáil only with great difficulty late in 1924.
It provided the death sentence for levying war against the
state and provided very severe penalties for intimidation and
usurpation of state functions. The formation of armies or police
forces was a misdeameanour punishable by lengthy terms of
imprisonment, with or without severe fines in addition.
Corporal punishment was to be provided for certain scheduled
offences. O'Higgins was determined that the state would
stand on the Treasonable Offences Act—the 'Whipping Bill'
as its opponents called it—a permanent piece of legislation
which would be there for the use of any government that
came to power. The army was to be withdrawn to a few main
centres and scaled down in numbers, but as these developments were put into effect, it was to become apparent to

O'Higgins and O'Duffy that the exisiting police structures would also have to be strengthened if they were successfully to carry the entire burden of state security in a situation which was still far from fully stabilised. This strengthening took the form of two highly significant changes in police organisation introduced in the year 1925 : the amalgamation of the Gárda Síochána and the Dublin Metropolitan Police, and the creation, as part of this unified body, of a new armed detective squad —'Special Branch'.

8 The Birth of Special Branch

THE Civic Guard, dispersed among the towns and villages of Ireland by the end of 1922, was not the only police force with which the government hoped to foster the security of the infant Free State. Two other separate and independently operating agencies were in existence in 1922—the Dublin Metropolitan Police and the Oriel House C I D—and both of these, particularly the latter, constituted major problems for Kevin O'Higgins from the earliest days of his period of office. These problems were partly due to the badly defined threefold division of duties: the Guards had no authority in the metropolitan area, while the D M P had only limited powers in the counties adjoining the city and county of Dublin; Oriel House, which had begun as an armed sub-division of military intelligence reporting directly to Collins, performed quasi-police functions both within and outside the Metropolitan Area; it was responsible to the Minister for Defence until September 1922 when it was transferred to the control of the Minister for Home Affairs. As early as September 1922, therefore, O'Higgins had indicated his intention of unifying this anomalous distribution of police responsibilities.

On 1 April 1922, in accordance with Article 10 of the Treaty, the D M P—or rather what remained of it—came under the control of the Provisional Government. It was not in the healthiest condition. It had become demoralised and ineffective during the War of Independence and it had become largely an object of ridicule in the context of the struggle. It had simply ceased to be a factor in the contest between the I R A and the Crown forces and its members had learned that in the violent and unpredictable conditions of urban

guerilla warfare, the best steps for an unarmed civil policeman to take were short and slow ones. Downes's pub in Haw-
kins Street, behind Brunswick Street station, became an obliga-
tory halt for any D M P man directed to attend at the scene
of any serious crime. With any luck, by the time he emerged
the Black and Tans or the Auxiliaries would have things
under control again.

As soon as Article 10 became effective, almost half the
force's 1,200 men elected to resign under the favourable terms
which the settlement offered by adding twelve years to their
actual length of service in reckoning pensions. In addition,
over two hundred members of the force were due to retire in
the normal course of events. Thus the new government, in
addition to recruiting for the Civic Guards had to find
another eight hundred men to bring the D M P back up to
authorised strength. Moreover, there was the problem of
finding somebody to head the force. The existing Commissioner, Colonel Edgeworth Johnston, had understandably
decided to relinquish his post when the Provisional Government takeover came about. In the following April O'Higgins
appointed a new Commissioner, William R. E. Murphy, a
native of Co. Wexford who had served with great distinction
in the British Army and afterwards as second in command to
O'Duffy in the South-western Command during the Civil
War. He later became Director of Training and Operations
in the Free State Army. Murphy was both brilliant and skilful
as a soldier and administrator.

Murphy was the ideal man to lead the D M P. With experience in the service both of Great Britain and the Free State,
he had a foot in both camps and he could lead the residue
of the old Castle D M P as well as the recruits of the new
generation. 'Nonetheless, Murphy's appointment was made
initially with reservations by some senior cabinet members.
His performance in time was to prove their doubts unfounded'.

As soon as the D M P had passed into the hands of the
Provisional Government, Collins had ordered a handful of his

Oriel House men to take over the detective branch of the force, the infamous G Division of political detectives which had been one of the primary targets of Collins's 'squad' three years earlier. Joe Kinsella was awarded the doubtful pleasure of taking control of the department which six months earlier would have thrown a lavish party had they been able to kill him. But with the G men tied down under a reliable officer, there was little harm that any malcontents in the D M P could do to the Provisional Government.

But Oriel House itself was already becoming an embarrassment to the government. Things which could be tolerated by Michael Collins the guerilla chief could not be countenanced by Michael Collins the head of the Provisional Government—at least not openly. And Oriel House and its methods were rapidly becoming counter-productive as far as the government was concerned. Rightly or wrongly, Oriel House had been suspected of responsibility for the murder of the two young Republicans who were shot at Yellow Lane in Drumcondra in August 1922 and of complicity in the death of Noel Lemass who was taken into custody in Dublin in July and whose body was found in the Dublin mountains in October. Later, indeed, evidence was to come to light of the severe maltreatment of prisoners by members of the Oriel House force and members of the government were to claim, rather inadequately, that they knew nothing about such methods at the time. Ironically, the allegations of ill-treatment by the C I D were not to come from Republicans but from members of the Free State Army who had been subjected to severe brutality during the investigations of relatively trivial offences. Allegations were made that prisoners were physically beaten and psychologically tortured by having guns fired behind their heads and by being deprived of sleep and food.

By the end of 1922, however, even the hardline elements within Cumann na nGaedheal had become aware that Oriel House was doing the cause of the Free State more harm than good. Moreover, its claims to legitimacy were somewhat tenuous: its statutory basis under the Department of Home Affairs has never been fully explained and its existence appears to have been justified on the principle *'salus populi suprema lex'*. The uneasy feelings aroused by the C I D came into the open in May 1923 when O'Higgins introduced the C I D estimates in the Dáil. He came in for heavy criticism, particularly from Charles Gavan Duffy, who spoke out explicitly what many deputies felt privately:

I have a good deal of sympathy with the normal decent detective as such because he has a very unpleasant job to do and a very unpleasant task. But I cannot help feeling that a section of the present detective force has not been recruited in the right place or from the right source. Comparing some of your men with the Civic Guard you will see what I mean. We should have as fine a force in Oriel House as the force which commands universal respect under General O'Duffy—but we have not. One of these C I D men the other day put it very frankly: 'There are', he said 'two hundred of us, natural gunmen.' One has to make a great deal of allowance for propaganda in these times and I make every allowance for it but there is no man in the Dáil but is well aware that the conduct of certain members of the detective forces has been exceedingly reprehensible.

O'Higgins made no attempt to refute the specific charges which had been made repeatedly against Oriel House in the previous months but he hit back at Gavan Duffy's blanket condemnation of the C I D. Collins had rushed three or four score men into Oriel House under people whom he considered particularly trustworthy and reliable, he told the Dáil, and Oriel House had started out as a semi-military body.

'We may take it that the three or four score men were not selected according to any drawing-room standards,' O'Higgins went on in his inimitable vein of haughty sarcasm. 'We may take it that the establishment of that institution was something of a gesture, if you wish, something of a threat to those who were planning very dark and very violent enterprises. Putting it baldly, it was the Provisional Government's Four Courts.'

Admitting that there had been a certain amount of in-discipline 'as in every aspect of the state', O'Higgins continued: 'I claim that that little bunch of men down there in that building have done great work for this state, that they got after this criminal conspiracy here in Dublin in an energetic manner, day in, day out, night in and night out, with the maximum of risk and the minimum of ease. They have been doing valuable work for the infant state and it is not a right or a creditable thing that a deputy should come in here and brand them as natural born gunmen.' And then with characteristic acidity he lashed into Gavan Duffy: 'They may not handle a cup of tea as gracefully as the deputy but they have saved this state at a time when the deputy's efforts were in a rather contrary direction. Kipling said "Single men in barracks ain't exactly plaster saints." Those men were not plaster saints.'

It was not untypical of O'Higgins's benevolent autocracy towards the police forces that he should not have given the members of the Dáil any indication of dissatisfaction within the government at the manner in which Oriel House was being run. O'Higgins had already expressed to David Neligan his anxiety to scale down the operation of Oriel House and to integrate its personnel either with the D M P or the Gárda Síochána. But undoubtedly he felt a certain debt of gratitude towards the members of the force, and there was the cardinal rule of politics that no government can afford to ignore the interests of the men whom it calls upon to do its dirty work.

Moreover, a number of the Oriel House detectives had already been killed in the execution of their duty. Detective Officer Tony Deane was killed in September 1922 as he held off with his revolver a party of Anti-Treaty supporters who tried to rush the building in Westland Row. On 29 December Inspector Matt Daly was shot dead at Ellis Quay as he pursued a group of armed men, and in October 1923 another detective from the unit, Tom Fitzgerald, was shot dead at Ashbourne, Co. Meath, while pursuing a party of armed robbers who had raided a candle factory and grabbed the payroll. His assailant, William Downes, who was executed at Mountjoy Prison on 29 November, earned for himself the unenviable distinction of being the first man to die by hanging in the Irish Free State.

The fall-off in violence following the Republican cease-fire order of May 1923 brought the general security situation within rather more manageable proportions. Armed crime in the Dublin area however, had diminished only slightly since the cease-fire. Armed robberies alone in the city averaged thirty-three a month during the period between October and December 1923. In addition, there were countless instances of intimidation, reprisal raids and inexplicable sporadic violence.

The future of Oriel House became an increasingly frequent topic of discussion between O'Higgins, Mulcahy and O'Duffy. In September O'Higgins asked Neligan, now acting as the army's Director of Intelligence with the rank of colonel, to draw up a report and a set of proposals for the future deployment of Oriel House. Neligan suggested that the best of the CID should be transferred to the detective branch of the DMP to serve as the nucleus of a professionally trained special branch which would be at the disposal of the Free State government. Of the remainder, he proposed, a proportion should be drafted into the Protective Corps, a small unit under the control of the Minister for Defence which was concerned with the protection and surveillance of government buildings and public officials and politicians. The expanded DMP detective branch which Neligan thus envisaged would be centred in Dublin but it would be able to operate as required throughout the country.

Perhaps not unexpectedly, O'Higgins asked Neligan to take charge of the new unified detective branch, with Inspector Billy O'Connell as second in command. Neligan agreed, and in October the disbandment of Oriel House was begun, thirty-one members being transferred to the new detective branch. These were to augment the existing strength of the DMP's G Division, which at the time totalled twenty-three men. The full strength of the new unit, including Neligan, therefore came to fifty-five.

Neligan himself was the ideal choice as leader of the unit. Tough, resourceful and deceptively casual in his manner, he had all the Southerner's native shrewdness and perspicacity. He had, moreover, a celebrated sense of humour which ensured his popularity with his own men and which came through at its best when the going was roughest. Neligan had joined the D M P at eighteen years of age and resigned in protest after a year of the War of Independence. He was contacted by Collins who immediately ordered him back into the force with instructions to join the secret service if he could. The transfer having been accomplished, he was then exhorted by his secret service chief to join the I R A if he could do so, and for two years he led the bizarre life of a double agent but with his loyalties in the last analysis on the side of the Republic. For those two years Neligan was probably Collins's most reliable and valuable contact in the Castle and so good was his cover that when the British administration was evacuating, Neligan was called aside by the Assistant Under-Secretary, Alfred Cope, and advised to get out while he could as he would certainly be marked for elimination by the Sinn Féiners.

Neligan immediately set about organising the detective branch, and his department began to lay down the network of a classic urban C I D operation. Police agents—creatures operating on the fringes of the underworld—were recruited to act as paid informers. Small criminals were offered deals if they could hand in bigger criminals. Agents were planted and very swiftly information began to flow into the detective branch. Six weeks after the setting up of the new department, Neligan's men made their first big coup when they caught a gang of armed robbers as they waylaid a bakery payroll van at Ballsbridge in the Dublin suburbs. The fortuitous coincidence by which an armed C I D patrol had passed the spot as the robbery was taking place was a source of great amazement to the Dublin newspapers and Neligan did not bother to contradict the reports which viewed his coup as an indication of the omnipresence of the new detective branch.

The methods of Neligan's detectives were not, however, always as orthodox. There was only a certain amount which could be achieved by conventional police tactics of crime anticipation and investigation. The I R A cease-fire had not meant a complete end to acts of war against the Free State government and its forces. Maverick units of Republicans were still likely to attack police stations, banks or persons whom, for one reason or another, they considered hostile to their interests. Early in March 1924 a number of detectives in the Dublin area took it upon themselves to make a house-to house visitation of known Republicans in the city to make their positions clear to them. Gerry Boland, then in charge of the Dublin Brigade of the I R A, was confronted with the simple proposition that it was in the detectives' and the I R A's interests to tolerate each other but that if any member of the police or detective branch were killed, he, Boland, would be peremptorily shot! Similar exhortations were made by other detective branch officers throughout the city and excursions were made into the provinces to convey the same message to leaders of the Republican movement elsewhere.

It was a vicious, dirty fight between policemen and the armed opponents of the state—both criminal and political —which raged during the next two years. Intimidation on both sides was common and there was much violence—though they were to become even more common in the late 1930s and 1940s when de Valera was directing the unified Gárda Síochána and D M P against the I R A.

But whatever criticisms were to be levelled at Neligan's C I D between the years 1923 and 1925, there could be no doubting its efficiency: for a short but crucial period in the development of the state this small handful of men ranged themselves against a wave of violent crime which threatened to paralyse the normal life of the country and succeeded in keeping it within reasonably manageable proportions.

Meanwhile O'Higgins had become increasingly conscious of the advantages of amalgamating the Gárda Síochána and the D M P. He was opposed by both O'Duffy and Murphy. But there were sound economic reasons for the reform : it would avoid duplication of training facilities, headquarters departments and administration. There were even better operational police reasons : Neligan's detectives were not always receiving as much co-operation as they wanted from the Guards in the provinces and there were great difficulties in maintaining adequate liaison between the two forces in joint operations. O'Higgins's mind was finally made up by an incident which occurred in the town of Baltinglass, Co. Wicklow, in January 1924.

On the morning of 28 January 1924 Guard Patrick O'Halloran was attracted by a commotion outside the local branch of the Bank of Ireland as he walked towards the Gárda station in the main street of Baltinglass. Running towards the bank he was confronted by two armed men who had just robbed the manager of £800. As they ran towards a waiting car a local trader pressed an automatic pistol in O'Halloran's hand. One of the men, seeing the uniformed guard with the gun, fired at him, hitting him in the chest. O'Halloran was taken to the Curragh military hospital but died the next day. Meanwhile the two bandits—demobilised Free State Army officers—had made their way back down the Wicklow mountains into Dublin. Baltinglass station had been unable to contact the Gárda stations at Rathfarnham and Tallaght, which blocked the bandits' escape routes, because they had no telephones, and by the time a message had got through to the Dublin Metropolitan Police office the two men were safely back in the city.

O'Higgins was furious at the inadequacy of communications and co-operation between the two forces, but worse was yet to come.

Neligan's detective branch learned through one of their agents that the two men had commandeered a taxi to get to Baltinglass for the robbery. The driver was traced and he was able to identify the two men who were already known to the

detective branch. By this time information had also come to
light that they had fled to Monaghan where a sister of one of
the men lived. Neligan and Superintendent Finion O'Driscoll,
an ex-Oriel House man, set out for Monaghan to make their
arrests but found the local guards unco-operative. The Inspector, whom the detectives asked to see, sent down a message that he was in bed and would not get up. But by the time
his two visitors had identified themselves and their mission his
mood for co-operation had improved considerably. An arrest
party was organised and one of the men was captured. The
other was subsequently arrested by one of Neligan's agents
in Liverpool. But O'Higgins needed no further convincing.
He was appalled at the fact that the two criminals had
managed to remain at liberty for so long and he decided that
nothing less than total amalgamation would suffice.

The Dáil debate on the Police Forces Amalgamation Bill
in February 1925 provides one of the best examples of the
entrenched illiberal attitude of the government towards the
role and functions of the police. Outlining the reasons for
amalgamation, O'Higgins explained that the method of
financing the D M P from the city rates would be gradually
phased out over an eight-year period. Major Bryan Cooper,
influenced partly by the principle that the ratepayers who
financed the police should have some say as to how it was run,
and partly by the idea that the police should be accountable
directly as well as indirectly to public opinion, proposed the
setting up of an advisory watch committee, drawn from the
local authorities, which would have consultative rights—
nothing more—with the Commissioner of the amalgamated
forces. Cooper proposed a Police Advisory Council for the
Dublin area, comprising twelve nominated members from
Dublin Corporation, the local authorities of Rathmines,
Blackrock, Dún Laoghaire, Dalkey and Killiney, and from the
Dublin Chamber of Commerce and the Dublin Workers
Council. The terms of reference he proposed were for this
council to 'advise and assist the Commissioner of the amalgam-
ated force in connection with any matter in relation to the

public order and security of the Dublin Metropolitan Area'.

Cooper ended his proposal with a gentle plea : 'I know that there is a certain dislike in the minds of members of the government towards doing anything which may detract from responsibility. The Consultative Council does not detract from responsibility. It is a device advocated by ministers in many cases during the last year, though I admit that the ministers usually maintain the right of nominating their own councils.'

Cooper's suggestion was a harmless one which had a great potential for good. Certainly it posed no threat to the government's control of the police and it did go some way towards establishing the principle that the police services should not be viewed as an arm of government but that their primary responsibility was to law and to the people, irrespective of government. However, O'Higgins's response was uncompromising and scathing : police problems could not be shared out between a police officer and a body of thirteen laymen, he retorted—'thirteen civilians elected haphazardly by half a dozen local authorities. It sounds nice. It is the kind of thing one can enthuse about, the right of public bodies to express opinions and so on. But in practice it would be almost incapable of smooth administration. I disapprove of it. I feel that if he [Cooper] were Minister for Justice he would also disapprove of it. He would probably disapprove of it a little more strongly after six or twelve months' experience of it in operation. I am not accepting the amendment.'

Tom Johnson demolished O'Higgins's reply with the swift retort that every person in such a position as the Commissioner of the Gárda would disapprove of any suggestion about receiving advice from anyone. But he picked up once again his theme of the accountability of the police at local level, pointing out that the country was not yet in a position to devolve upon local authorities the power for the maintenance of order locally : 'But I do look forward to the time when the police forces of this country will not be controlled centrally and will in fact be controlled locally with whatever co-ordinating national authority there may be.'

Stressing the desirability of associating locally elected authorities with the administration of the police forces, Johnson went on: 'The minister assumes that the Commissioner of Police will be sufficiently in touch with the needs of the community. It is possible that that may be so. A benevolent autocrat is very often looked upon as the most idealistic form of government, if you can find a benevolent autocrat and be sure that the one you get will be sufficiently benevolent to govern rightly. . . But we are not sure of our Commissioners of Police, we are not sure of our Ministers for Justice. When the minister refers to the idea of a local authority having at least the right of approach to the Commissioner of Police with regard to the keeping of order in the locality which it represents as if it were something new, has he never heard of police committees of public bodies, corporations, county councils and the like?'

But O'Higgins was not be to pinned down. In a somewhat abrupt manner he took the attitude that if these suggestions were to be considered at all, then the whole Gárda Síochána Act should be repealed and the government should divest itself of responsibility for policing the country. A local police system was one conception, he told the house, 'and if it were considered the wisest thing for the country and that we would get the best results in that way, we really ought to repeal the Gárda Síochána Act, divest ourselves of the responsibility for the policing of the country and place it in watch committees set up here and there in Ennis, Tralee, Galway and other towns.'

As an answer to a genuine and potentially fruitful alternative suggestion, O'Higgins reply was certainly ungracious and evasive of the question of principle which was raised. The Labour Party was not simply flying an opposition kite. Their suggestion of a system of locally controlled police forces dated back to the Treaty negotiations, when they put it forward as a major element in their proposals for a settlement. But Kevin O'Higgins can be said to have had a blind spot when it came to the actual implementation of his policy of police for the people. It was a principle to which the entire Cosgrave government subscribed—provided the interpretation of what the people wanted from their police was left in their hands.

The amalgamation, however, provided the opportunity for which O'Higgins had been waiting to put a bit of stiffening, as he described it, into the Gárda Síochána's role in combating armed crime. Since the withdrawal of the army, O'Duffy had reported, the Guards were simply not able to cope. Armed crime had again become a daily occurrence and guards were being held at gun point while banks were robbed, traders burned out and post offices and business premises emptied of everything of value. The Guards were being publicly humiliated and held up to ridicule by men who knew there was no power in the locality which could bring them to justice. In December 1924 O'Duffy told O'Higgins that he could no longer guarantee the discipline of the force or the enforcement of the law unless the Guards were given some support.

O'Higgins consulted Neligan on the feasibility of extending the detective branch throughout the country on a permanent basis. Neligan was enthusiastic and O'Duffy, after some initial reservations, agreed it was the only alternative to a widespread re-deployment of the army. Neligan suggested the formation of mobile detective units, each one consisting of about a dozen men equipped with a individually-held .45 revolvers; where necessary, units were to be equipped with Thompson sub-machine guns or Lee-Enfield rifles. Each unit was to have its own transport—a Ford car—and while accountable at local level to the District Superintendent for pay, discipline and administration, it would be accountable operationally in the first instance to Neligan in Dublin.

The proposal was thrashed out at length between O'Higgins, O'Duffy, Neligan and Murphy. Clearly the new units would detract somewhat from the ideal of the unarmed guard but that difficulty was overcome by O'Higgins's suggestion that the new detective should be regarded as an extension of the D M P detective system into the provinces rather than as an armed section of the Gárda Síochána. The only alternative was to make arms available to the uniformed guards or to invest certain units of the army with a police role for as long as necessary.

O'Higgins regarded this reinforcement of the Gárda Síochána as an indispensable element in his programme of normalisation. The time for emergency powers acts and using the military to control what was essentially a civil problem was long past. The Free State had to show that it could survive without them, but to leave the enforcement of the new Treasonable Offences Act in the hands of an unarmed police force would be ludicrous. The armed policeman had to return—at least in a limited role—if the Free State government wanted to break the unhappy traditions of repressive legislation on which it had come into being.

It was thus, in a sense as an alternative to continuing emergency legislation, that O'Higgins agreed to go ahead with the formation of an armed detective branch. But he was determined that it was not going to be another Oriel House. He wanted the best men selected from the Civic Guards and, where necessary, there was to be recruitment from the Free State Army officer corps. There was method in that latter stipulation too : it was a question of setting a thief to catch a thief, for much of the violent crime in the country was being committed by disbanded Free State Army personnel. A total strength of just over two hundred men was finally decided upon for the new detective branch, these to be divided into parties of ten or twelve men who would be posted to the headquarters of the twenty Gárda divisions outside the Dublin Metropolitan Area. A six-month training course was arranged for the new detectives at Kevin Street station in Dublin and at the Gárda depot in the Phoenix Park. It covered criminal law and police procedure, ballistic and forensic evidence and the advanced use of firearms and self-defence methods. By September 1925 the necessary administrative changes were arranged and Neligan's department had been officially divided into two sections—Crime Ordinary, for non-political crime, and Crime Special, for political offences. Special Branch, as it was to be known, was born.

The first area selected for introduction to the new detective branch was Co. Leitrim. Of all the twenty-six counties of the Free State, Leitrim was the most notorious, as O'Higgins had found out during a political rally there some months previously. The thin lines distinguishing political agitation from ordinary crime had become long blurred. I R A maverick groups operating from the Arigna Hills would descend on the towns and villages, stocking up with goods, provisions and money, sometimes giving receipts to the victims in the name of the Republic. O'Higgins's visit to the county in January 1925 was punctuated with violence and shooting. Finally, at a rally in Drumshambo, in spite of the best endeavours of a force of about fifty guards, O'Higgins was toppled off a platform erected in the main street. As he went down in a confusion of boots, batons and miscellaneous missiles he is reported to have shouted at the mob : 'I'll send men down here who'll be as quick on the draw as any gun-toting bully.'

One contemporary account of crime in the Leitrim area, written by a Gárda inspector, leaves little doubt as to the state of the county :

In Ballinamore. . .the Gárda barracks was raided by armed men, their entire property looted and stolen while public property entrusted to their charge was collected and burned. . . The same thing happened at Carrigallen, Cloone and Crumkerin. . . Uniformed Gárdaí were actually kidnapped at Cloone while on more than one occasion they were ordered off the street at rifle-point. A bank robbery took place in every town in South Leitrim where a bank is situated. . . Owing to the wholesale robberies of sub-post offices by armed raiders in South Leitrim, the system of paying pensions had to be altered and old age pensioners had to travel upwards of twenty miles from remote parts of South Leitrim once a month to draw their old age pensions in Carrick-on-Shannon. The law had to be amended to permit the service of jurors' summonses by registered post as a uniformed Gárda could only penetrate remote rural areas at his peril. I remember the cruel murder of Dr Muldoon at Mohill; of young Brien at Gowel; of Keville at Curraghcramp;

of Mulvey at Augacashel and of Reynolds at Clooneagh, all within a period of two years and all in South Leitrim. . . [The Guards] . . . were unable to cope.

In March 1925 twenty members of the new detective branch —or S Branch as they were now known in the force—arrived under the charge of Finion O'Driscoll at Drumshambo. The operation had been carefully planned under the personal supervision of O'Duffy and Neligan. A special meeting of Chief Superintendents and Superintendents from the adjoining counties had been chaired by the Secretary of the Department of Justice, Henry Frighil, at Carrick-on-Shannon a week previously. Local army commanders were called in and State Solicitors and District Justices were notified of the arrival of the new detective unit.

O'Driscoll's men arrived in Drumshambo with their Ford car, their .45 Webleys, half a dozen Lee-Enfield rifles and a writ under the Gárda Síochána (Acquisition of Premises) Act authorising them to take possession of a local bank for use as their headquarters. Within weeks of their arrival over two dozen arrests had been made throughout the county and charges were brought on a number of serious crimes which had hitherto been filed as unsolved. At Ballinamore, within a month of the detectives' arrival, a party of bank-raiders ran into a carefully prepared trap and in the ensuing skirmish one raider was killed and another wounded. By July 1925 the Arigna mountain fastnesses had been emptied and Co. Leitrim was no longer a safe refuge for the gunman.

Similar operations were effected throughout the rest of the country during the remainder of 1925 by other S Branch units. As a general rule they operated at divisional level, each unit covering one large or two small counties. In some instances, however, units subdivided, spreading themselves between several towns, while in other cases units from adjoining divisions came together for large scale operations. Units from Kildare/Carlow, Wicklow and the Metropolitan Area came together to carry out patrols and sweeps of the Wicklow Hills. A permanent Special Branch post was later established as Killakee on the Dublin side of the mountains.

The effectiveness of the S Branch swiftly manifested itself on the crime sheets. Offences against property with violence which totalled 1,879 in 1925 outside the Dublin area dropped to 1,610 in 1926 and to 1,241 in 1927. By 1930 they had dropped to 854. Offences against the person were more slow to show a reduction and actually increased slightly between 1925 (502 offences) and 1926 (525 offences). But in 1927 offences against the person dropped to 460, rising slightly in 1928 to 475 and reducing again in 1929 to 411. But what was of much more importance was the incalculable improvement in the morale of the unarmed Civic Guards. They were no longer open to intimidation and the threat of the gun in the normal execution of their duty. They retained the essential characteristics of an unarmed police force with the backing, where necessary, of colleagues trained and competent in the use of firearms.

O'Higgins was aware of the danger of mixing armed policemen with unarmed guards. There was a real difficulty that it might prejudice the relative immunity which the unarmed guard had hitherto enjoyed. The Guards had succeeded in the divided community of rural Ireland simply because they did not have the capacity to side with one group or the other as an armed force. In the Dáil in December 1925 O'Higgins went to some length to explain the safeguards which he was building into the scheme of detective units :

It is now probably generally recognised that the unarmed and uniformed force which operates in the country requires some stiffening and falling back, *vide* the performance of a criminal who resorts to arms in his crime. It is also recognised that it is not a proper state of affairs that the only stiffening and falling back should be the army. It is, I submit, very bad for the army and bad for the people that the army should be called on to intervene frequently in what is substantially a peace situation and it is wrong that the military machine would be called on to move

every time some thug holds up a bank or post office or perpe-
trates some robbery with arms in a rural area. The charge of
enabling the detective branch of the Metropolitan Police to
operate in the country in cases of the more serious form of crime
will tend to diminish the occasions on which the military will be
called on to intervene in the ordinary life of the country.

O'Higgins went on to explain his own apprehension about
the scheme:

I would like to assure deputies that there is a very full appreciation of the fact that when you put arms into the possession of
men who do not wear uniforms and when you put arms into the
hands of men who do not have a badge or insignia to distinguish
them from ordinary civilians, you take on a responsibility with
regard to the personnel of such a branch or organisation which
is even greater than that which you must accept with regard
to your uniformed forces. I recognise fully the necessity for that
but I recognise also and I ask deputies to recognise that one
cannot expect the Gárda Síochána to continue facing with their
bare hands, so to speak, the armed criminal, the man who uses
arms in the performance of his crime. I hope that the supple-
menting of the uniformed force with plain-clothes detectives
who will carry and use arms where necessary will have a good
reaction on the peace of the country.

O'Duffy went a little further. As an added precaution against
prejudicing the safety and standing of the unarmed guards,
he suggested to O'Higgins that the new S Branch units should
occupy separate premises from the ordinary guards. O'Higgins
agreed. The S Branch men, wherever practicable, were given
their own stations, and to preserve the myth that they were not
really Civic Guards but members of the D M P detective
branch they were entitled 'detective officers' as had been their
predecessors in the capital.

The Special Branch of the Gárda Síochána as it developed
during the remaining seven years of the Cosgrave administration in Ireland was to become perhaps the most controversial

element in the security policy of the state. Its members were to be regarded on the one hand by government supporters as the saviours of democracy and order, a terror to evildoers, good men performing a thankless and dirty task; conversely, they were to become the object of vilification and hatred by the large dissident minority which still opposed the Free State and everything it stood for.

But they did not set the pace of Republican-Free State confrontation during these years. It was a revival of I R A activity, bitter and vicious, as de Valera entered constitutional party politics, which dictated the pattern of attack and counter-attack during the latter half of the decade. The period was to be marked by the murders of several more members of the unarmed Gárda Síochána and by the brutal assassination of the man who had done most to guide the force's destinies during the early crucial phase of its existence.

By the end of 1925 the pathways of Eamon de Valera and the IRA had parted to the extent that de Valera was prepared to indicate his willingness to enter the Dáil if the Oath of Allegiance were to be removed. In March 1926 he resigned as President of Sinn Féin and in May, at the La Scala theatre in Dublin, he launched his new political party, Fianna Fáil—the Warriors of Destiny. With him he took most of the abler members of the old Sinn Féin party, Frank Aiken, Séan T. O'Kelly, Seán Lemass, Seán MacEntee, P. J. Ruttledge and James Ryan. The cleavage between de Valera and the hard-line Sinn Féin which still refused to recognise the legitimacy of the Free State was now complete, for however much he decried the institutions and performance of the new state, de Valera was nevertheless prepared to work the system and to gain control of it, if possible, as a way of attaining power.

The constitutional path which de Valera and his followers embarked upon at the La Scala meeting was to lead him first into the Dáil in August 1927, only weeks after the death of Kevin O'Higgins, and finally into government in March 1932. Behind him he left an embittered and increasingly inward-looking Sinn Féin party and an IRA which suddenly found itself cut adrift from the mainstream of Irish politics, without a coherent aim and without a leadership of any stature—by contrast with the previous years when de Valera and his senior lieutenants directed its fortunes.

Apart from the freelance activities of the splinter groups in a number of areas, active Republican operations had almost entirely ceased by the time de Valera and his followers decided to take the constitutional path. The IRA was intact on paper with a parade strength of perhaps 25,000 and there was still a plentiful supply of weapons stacked away throughout the country as a result of the dump arms order of May 1923 and there was a steady trickle of weapons coming in from the United States where Joe McGarrity, almost single-handed, was conducting the affairs of Clan na Gael.

The I R A still retained within its ranks many well-known, respected and capable Republicans, Tom Barry, Ernie O'Malley, Seán MacBride, Seán Russell and Moss Twomey. The new Chief of Staff was Andy Cooney, with Twomey as his second in command. But in spite of the survival of these men and in spite of the ready supply of weapons, the striking power of the I R A had effectively vanished—as much through loss of internal impetus as by the effects of Neligan's S Branch and the Gárda Síochána. Its activities over the next few years were to be mainly dictated by the necessity of keeping up morale and of giving the constantly drilling and marching young men a chance of some real action. In the main this action was to take the form of vendettas against local guards, arms and intelligence raids against Free State agencies and sympathisers, and the lending of armed support, where it was considered necessary, to the political struggle against the Free State and the renegade followers of de Valera. By no stretch of the imagination could I R A activity during these years be graced with the status and dimensions of a military campaign. It was a period of bloody and vindictive aimlessness for the organisation, not sufficiently serious to warrant the attentions of the Free State Army but posing for the Gárda Síochána policing problems of an inordinately difficult and delicate kind.

The Gárda-I R A conflict was to increase in bitterness and viciousness during the remaining years of the Cosgrave administration. The first serious incident occurred in November 1926 when I R A units throughout the country attacked a dozen small Gárda stations for reasons which still remain obscure. Certainly the objective of the raids cannot have been to capture arms, for none were stored in the stations. Nor

does it appear plausible that the raids were conducted, as
the Army Council of the I R A was later to claim, for intelligence purposes. Any political information which came into
the possession of the Guards was immediately passed on to S
Branch and it had long been part of Neligan's security policy
to ensure that as little classified information as possible should
be left under the control of the ordinary uniformed guards.
The most likely explanation for the November raids was an
attempt by Twomey to break the monotony of drilling and
endless training for the rank and file of the I R A by directing
their energies against the police. Local units were allowed to
pick their own targets and to employ their own tactics in
attacking the Gárda stations, with the result that in most areas
the raids never came off.

But in two of the raids which were successful there were
fatal consequences. In St Lukes in Cork and in Hollyford, Co.
Tipperary, things went badly wrong when the station parties
refused to co-operate with the raiders and resisted their
attempts to take over the stations. Sergeant Jim Fitzsimons
was shot dead in the public office of St Lukes station and
Guard Hugh Ward was killed in the hallway of Hollyford
station as he tried to bar the door against the attackers. Both
the dead men were, of course, unarmed.

Within hours of the attacks uniformed police and S Branch
men were hitting back at Republicans in several areas. Nearly
the entire headquarters staff of the I R A was arrested in
Dublin, and in many other centres—Cork, Tipperary, Kerry
and Waterford—local officers were rounded up for questioning.

The killing of Fitzsimons and Ward sent a wave of anger
through the force and triggered off a release of resentment and
bitterness which had developed in the force over four years of
constant tension between the police and the Republicans.
Neither of the dead guards had been in any way involved in
the pursuit or prosecution of political offences. They were
ordinary village policemen with whom the I R A had no
quarrel. If the I R A had a point to make, the police reasoned,
they should have made it with the Special Branch men who

were at least their equal in terms of firepower. Suspects were treated none too gently in a number of areas, but in Waterford a party of guards abandoned all controls of discipline. Republican prisoners who were in custody on totally unconnected charges were set upon in cells when news of the shootings came through and beaten by relays of uniformed guards and detectives for several hours. Later it was to be pleaded by the guards that some of the prisoners had jeered at the news of the deaths of Sergeant Fitzsimons and Guard Ward.

The Waterford affair became a *cause célèbre* for the Republicans and brought O'Duffy and O'Higgins into open confrontation over the whole question of the extent to which third-degree police methods could be sanctioned. Such a crisis was, perhaps, inevitable. The I R A's widespread use of violence and intimidation had led to the emergence from 1925 onwards of an unofficial, but equally determined Gárda policy of harassment and counter-intimidation. It was to become the standard police approach towards extremist Republican groups and it was to be accepted with varying degrees of tolerance by the chiefs of the Gárda, the Department of Justice, by the Cosgrave government as a whole, and by Kevin O'Higgins as Minister for Justice. It was the lack of any rigidly defined general directive on the subject that caused the serious difference of opinion between O'Duffy and O'Higgins.

Immediately the ill-treatment of the Waterford prisoners became known O'Duffy ordered the suspension of the men involved and began a sworn enquiry into the allegations. O'Higgins, who was in London for the imperial conference, was kept fully informed. He was enraged at what he was later to describe as 'this excess of and abuse of authority on the part of the servants of the people'.

There was little doubt in the mind of either man as to what would be the findings of the Waterford enquiry and both agreed that the guards responsible should be punished, but there was to be a significant divergence of views when it came to fixing a penalty.

F

O'Duffy pointed out that there were extenuating circumstances surrounding the incident. The Guards locally had been under more or less constant attack, physical and psychological, from a section of the population for several years. Their service records were good and they were, after all, merely victims of a situation in which a degree of violence and intimidation had to be allowed for in police policy towards militant organisations like the I R A. The Guards had put up with immense provocation at the hands of Republicans everywhere and the occasional lapse was inevitable. It hardly seemed to be fair to impose the maximum punishment on men who had, in these circumstances, been merely executing what had come to be accepted as normal Gárda policy but had gone too far. O'Higgins viewed things differently. Surveillance and harassment of subversive elements he could accept, and indeed support, as a necessary part of the police task in an impossible security situation. But deliberate brutality towards prisoners in custody went beyond all his limits. The Guards could no longer be regarded as pitiable, unarmed policemen at the mercy of every bloody-minded thug or gunman. They had got their 'stiffening' in the form of the Special Branch and they had the legal power and the physical strength necessary to take the appropriate steps against their gunmen opponents. O'Higgins insisted on the dismissal of the Guards involved.

O'Duffy was adamant that as Commissioner, discipline was his prerogative, and a trial of strength between the two men began. O'Duffy was summoned before the cabinet, where the government's views were made known to him. Either he dismissed the guards involved or a new Commissioner who would be prepared to do so would replace him. O'Duffy threatened to resign if he did not get his own way and O'Higgins shouted at him to go ahead and resign if he felt he had to. There was a barely concealed joy in the cabinet when O'Duffy tendered his resignation, for the vain, self-centred Commissioner had long lost most of his friends in the government, the only exception being O'Higgins himself.

In the end neither man got his own way and they were obliged to compromise : O'Duffy withdrew his resignation and the guards concerned in the Waterford incident were made to pay a portion of the costs awarded to the injured men. In spite of the angry exchanges between the Commissioner and the Minister for Justice, the affair did not create between them a rift of the dimensions which are sometimes drawn by proponents of the theory that O'Higgins was assassinated by disgruntled policemen, angered over his tough line with the Waterford guards. Such commentators overlooked the fundamental and deep-rooted convictions shared by the two men on the role and functions of the Guards. O'Duffy was too devoted to O'Higgins and to the ideals on which they had together built up the Civic Guard for him to abandon it so readily, while O'Higgins, for his part, was well aware that he would never find another Commissioner of O'Duffy's dedication and efficiency. Normal relations between the two men were, in fact, restored within a matter of days.

The real difference was one of emphasis in their two approaches to the problems of the Gárda which would undoubtedly have led to long-term difficulties had O'Higgins survived. Instead O'Duffy had to continue his fight for stronger legislative measures with O'Higgins's successor, James Fitzgerald-Kenney. O'Higgins and O'Duffy had balanced each other reasonably well but Fitzgerald-Kenney was no match for the indefatigable general and in that unequal contest O'Duffy became even more of an embarrassment to the government. Even if a Cumann na nGaedheal administration had remained in power throughout the 1930s, it is doubtful whether O'Duffy would have retained his commissionership for long after 1932; indeed, he possibly survived a little longer under de Valera than he would have done under Cosgrave.

The chain of events triggered off by the shooting of Sergeant Fitzsimons and Guard Ward was the first episode in a vicious circle of events which was to be repeated over and over again in the next six years. I R A activity, sometimes directed against the Guards and sometimes not, was countered by arrests,

swoops, intimidation and S Branch harassment, resulting in
I R A reprisals against the police and yet more counter-action
by the police against the Republicans. In the West, where
Peader O'Donnell had organised a campaign against the
payment of land annunities, there was almost constant confrontation between Guards and Special Branch men on the
one side and Republicans on the other. The I R A's sporadic
campaign of violence against the Free State and its agents
was maintained throughout the late 1920s. There were raids
on Gárda stations, bank robberies and hostile treatment of
persons and institutions considered to be loyal to the British
connection.

An even more ominous feature of these years was the
growing tension between the police and the community at
large. As the Guards sought desperately to cope with an extraordinarily difficult situation, the methods which they were
forced to employ were to alienate an ever-increasing section
of the community. In certain parts of the country, notably in
Co. Clare, resentment against the Guards was rapidly assuming extremely dangerous proportions. Criticisms in the Dáil
and Senate became more frequent, newspaper eulogies of the
Gárda Síochána became a thing of the past, and local bodies
and representatives became increasingly concerned at what
they considered to be the employment of the police in the
wrong manner and on the wrong problems. The wheel came
full circle when Leitrim County Council—where the full
effectiveness of the Special Branch was first felt—passed a
resolution calling for the immediate disbandment of the
detective branch of the Gárda Síochána 'in the interests of
peace'.

Matters only worsened after Kevin O'Higgins was ruthlessly
shot dead as he walked to Mass at Booterstown on the morning
of Sunday, 10 July 1927. The event had an immediate and
traumatic effect on the government. A new Public Safety Act
was passed, becoming law on 12 August. Habeas Corpus was
temporarily suspended in certain circumstances and the right
of trial by jury was also qualified. These measures offered a

temporary weapon to the police and were eagerly availed of during the next six months. Arrests and detentions were stepped up, but the massive investigations into the death of O'Higgins produced no arrests. Detectives worked almost continuously on the case for the next three years. A number of charges were considered against various individuals. Some charges were actually preferred and later withdrawn. Investigation teams travelled to Britain to interview suspects. There were the inevitable 'confessions' from deranged persons but the killers remained at large.

The assassination had the longer-term effect of entrenching the Cosgrave government even more firmly in its defensive and repressive conservatism—and not perhaps without reason. The gunman had shown that he could strike right into the heart of government if he so wished and special legislation, Civic Guards and Special Branch could not prevent him. Nevertheless, O'Higgins's death had the effect of spurring on the police to even greater efforts against the I R A, and taking advantage of the government's mood of increased severity, the S Branch began to hit back hard in South Tipperary, Cork and, most of all, in Clare.

Leading members of the I R A were picked up here and there, some imprisoned for brief periods, some released. The endless round of arrests, interrogations, allegations and counter-allegations went on unabated with the active support of the Cosgrave government.

A good illustration of the government's attitude towards the police effort came out of the attempted killing in Dublin in January 1928 of Seán Harling, one of Neligan's police agents. As a result of information supplied by Harling, the S Branch in Dublin had seized a large quantity of French ammunition which Seán MacBride had brought in for use by the I R A. The ammunition was seized by detectives as it was transferred to an I R A camp at Glasnevin in Dublin but Harling's cover was not as good as he believed it to be. It soon became clear that he was regarded as a marked man by the I R A and he was given a police escort to his home every evening and a personal revolver was issued to him for his own protection by Neligan. On 28 January when his police escort dropped him at his home in Dartry Road in Dublin, two men with their right hands stuffed conspicuously in their pockets approached him. Harling jumped behind a gate-post and as the first of his would-be assailants came by, he fired his revolver, killing the man. When the Guards arrived nothing was immediately evident and the circumstances of the man's death could not be easily explained. He was identified as Anthony Coughlan, a known Republican from Inchicore, but this was not to become common knowledge for some days. In the meantime, as far as the newspapers were concerned, it was a mystery killing. Was it an I R A vendetta, they asked, or a police revenge operation, or were members of the Special Branch again taking their duties beyond the permissible bounds of discipline?

On the day after the shooting Cosgrave sent for O'Duffy and Neligan and demanded an explanation of the strange events in Dartry Road. He had had enough, he explained to the two police chiefs, of complaints and allegations against the detective branch and the Gárda Síochána. There were limits beyond which the government were not prepared to allow them to go in dealing with the I R A. Neligan began to explain that Harling was in fact a bona fide police agent who had been merely defending himself—as he was entitled to do—and who had fortunately shot his prospective assassin before he himself had been shot. 'Do you mean we have nothing to hide?' asked Cosgrave, taken aback. 'Not a thing,' replied Neligan. 'Splendid,' said Cosgrave joyfully. 'In that case we'll have an enquiry.'

An enquiry was indeed held which lasted for several weeks and investigated the incident in great detail. It eventually exonerated the police and Harling himself. Shortly afterwards he left for America with some assistance from the Secret Service vote.

The year 1928 was also to see a sinister development in the relentless warfare waged by the I R A against the Free

State. Until that time the I R A's activities, though not without effect, had been largely uncontrolled and without any carefully planned objective; in 1928, however, its leaders came to a deliberate decision to sabotage the processes of law through threats, violence and, where necessary, through murder. A widespread campaign of intimidation against jurors' panels was devised and put into operation, resulting early in 1929 in the armed attack on two members of a jury which had convicted a young man named Healy for shooting at guards.

The campaign confronted the Guards with a new and extremely serious problem. Increasingly throughout the country the Guards and S Branch detectives found that conventional police methods and the ordinary processes of law were no longer effective. Apart from a period of just over a year after the killing of Kevin O'Higgins in July 1927, there were no emergency powers, no Public Safety Bills and no police powers of arrest and no detention beyond the normal processes of common law. The existing civil powers simply could not withstand large-scale organised intimidation and subversion. Witnesses could not be relied upon to give evidence, juries could not be relied upon to convict. Even victims of violence and intimidation could not be counted upon to sustain their allegations in the few cases where suspects could be brought to trial. The full normalisation which O'Higgins had sought for the processes of justice had not been attained—nor could it ever be attained as long as the police, detective branch and the very courts themselves were the objects of violence and direct terror. Later in 1931 O'Duffy sought to explain the Civic Guards' helplessness in the face of ruthless intimidation and violence which was directed not only at the police but at innocent members of the public who were called upon to act as jurors or witnesses. The ordinary processes of law, he told the cabinet, were not feasible where the safety of those who had recourse to them could not be guaranteed.

Explaining the inadequacy of the ordinary civil and criminal law in the Guards' endeavours to control the I R A,

O'Duffy told the government that all his men could do was to hamper and hinder the movement of the criminal as much as possible– 'to make them suffer, make their lives a burden, apply an unremitting surveillance to their every movement and generally make their connection with conspiracy and murder a non-paying proposition.'

O'Duffy's views had been ratified by the opinions of nearly all his officers at district and divisional headquarters throughout the country. He held regular conferences of his Chief Superintendents at the depot in Dublin and began to make increasingly frequent tours throughout the divisions to see the problems which his officers referred to at first hand. Everywhere the story was the same. Witnesses were being menaced, jurors were receiving bullets in the post. In some instances members of the uniformed force themselves had been threatened in this way.

The government attempted to ameliorate the situation by pushing a Juries Protection Bill through the Dáil in 1929. But it did little to prevent the general lawlessness which became more and more rampant as the institutions of justice became less and less workable. In some parts of the country the breakdown was almost total; in these areas the Garda stations themselves were the only areas held by the law– like little islands in a great sea of crime and disorder.

It was in Co. Clare that the bitter war between Republicans and police reached its highest point of intensity. The Clare area was the one district where even at the best of times the uniformed and unarmed guards had failed to gain anything like the complete acceptance of the people. Even in wild and rebel Kerry the unarmed guard had come to be accepted as part of the way of life in the small towns and villages, but in Clare it was different. Ambushes on Guards were not unknown, guards' families were intimidated and in December 1925 yet another unarmed guard, Thomas Dowling, had been shot dead near Fanore, Ballyvaughan. Dowling had been mistaken for another member of the force who was considered by local poteen makers to be over-zealous in the execution of his duty, and he died in his place while coming back to his station after a night patrol.

Most of the trouble in Co. Clare centered around the area of Kilrush and its immediate environs, where the director of the IRA was T.J. Ryan. Events in the county during 1927 and 1928 had necessitated building up the S branch in the area to a level well above the national average. In late 1928 a local man suspected of passing information on to the police was taken away and never seen again. In 1928 the superintendent at Kilrush, William Geary, was dismissed on suspicion of passing information to the IRA. More than 70 years later, Geary, who emigrated to the USA, was cleared by the government and awarded full pension rights as well as a cash sum.

Partly in response to an ever-increasing level of the IRA activity in the county and partly to guard against repercussions over the sacking of the superintendent, the S Branch in Clare was built up in strength until virtually every leading member of the IRA in West Clare was under almost permanent surveillance. Finally to complicate an already difficult situation, a serious industrial dispute involving bitter clashes and violence developed in Kilrush during the latter months of 1928.

On 11 July 1929 the Clare situation flared up again and claimed its third victim when Detective Tadgh Sullivan was killed at Tullycrine near Kilrush. The detective had been called to a quiet country road where, according to a note received at his station, there was a box containing arms which a farmer had discovered and which for fear of alarming his neighbours, he had not brought into town. When Sullivan opened the box he set off a booby-trap bomb and was killed instantly. Another guard was injured. Once again, the most intensive investigations failed to produce any charges for the killing – showing again, as O'Duffy was constantly pointing out to the government that conventional police methods and conventional police results simply did not apply in this type of situation.

O'Duffy could do no more than authorise increased surveillance and harassment, but in the remote districts of Co. Clare that did little to satisfy the embittered comrades of Tadg Sullivan and Tom Dowling for whom life had become well-nigh impossible with provocation and insults being thrown in their faces by men, women and children.

Later in the year Neligan and O'Connell became aware of the intentions of a number of members of the S Branch in the county to settle the Kilrush business once and for all by bringing T. J. Ryan for a one-way boating trip on the Atlantic. Plans had already been advanced to the stage where a boat had been secured for the purpose but a swift intervention from headquarters put an end to the project. Nevertheless, the fact that such an appalling course of action had been even contemplated was an indication of the level of demoralised lawlessness to which both police and I R A had descended in the area.

In July, a week after the murder of Detective Sullivan, de Valera passed a statement to a member of the Senate, setting out his findings after a trip to Co. Clare. De Valera asserted that there were 'constant assaults, harassment and intimidation by detectives of Mr T. J. Ryan, Cranny, Kilrush Co. Clare' and went on to instance a whole host of atrocities which, he alleged, had been committed by the Guards—both uniformed and plain clothes—in the district. Near Lisdoonvarna, de Valera stated, uniformed and plain clothes guards had taken suspects into a field and beaten them. In South Clare an old man was alleged to have been taken out of his house and kept virtually naked on the roadside for several hours. Ryan himself, it was claimed, had been subjected to incessant victimisation by the police even to the extent of their having cut a hole in the thatch of his roof to keep an eye on him.

The Minister for Justice, James Fitzgerald-Kenney who had succeeded O'Higgins, refuted the allegations, quoting without much relevance but with great emphasis from a statement issued by the Bishop of Killaloe on the murder of Detective Sullivan. Fitzgerald-Kenney told the Senate that Ryan was the leader of an association in Clare which was out to upset ordered and disciplined government by force of arms. He declared:

'I am satisfied that the police in Clare are perfectly disciplined and are doing their work in Clare admirably.' The ghost of Kevin O'Higgins was raised in the debate when Senator Robinson suggested that the previous minister at least tried to keep discipline in the force 'but was done in by his own men'. 'Frankly and without innuendo', he continued, 'I certainly believe it was his own people who did him in. There is no proof that it was anybody else.'

The Clare situation was not to rest there, however, and it was to continue as a frequent topic for debate in the Dáil right into the de Valera administration. On 31 July 1929 the assaults on and harassment of T. J. Ryan were again raised in the house with detailed evidence of injuries which he had received. With incredulous smiles coming even from the sternest Cumann na nGaedheal back-benchers, Fitzgerald-Kenney explained to the house that the most exhaustive police enquiries had shown that Ryan had sustained his injuries when kicked by a cow on his own farm. The absurdity of the claim could not be allowed to pass and it became a standard tale against the Guards and S Branch. The episode further derived a new title to be used derisively for the S Branch over the next three years— 'Fitzgerald-Kenney's Cows'.

The worsening situation in Clare was the first lever in the process which was finally to bring the Free State back to the old condition of permanent emergency legislation with the insertion of Article 2a of the constitution—the situation which O'Higgins had sought to get away from in 1925. In a reflexive reaction to the killing of Detective Sullivan and the continuous attacks on the Guards in Co. Clare, superintendents throughout the country, together with the detective units, began to organise conferences at which co-ordinated pressures against the I R A were arranged. Throughout the latter half of 1929 and during the early months of 1930 prosecutions for I R A membership, illegal drilling and the like increased substantially. The campaign was conducted with special vigour by the police in the South—in Cork, Waterford, Limerick and Tipperary.

At the end of 1929 the Superintendent of the Tipperary district, Séan Curtin, a highly efficient, capable and locally respected officer, began to make preparations to prosecute a particularly flagrant case of illegal drilling in the area. Curtin decided to prosecute under a section of the act which O'Higgins had put on the statute book at the formation of the Special Branch in 1925. The local I R A became aware of his intentions to prosecute and they sought permission from headquarters to eliminate him. Inexplicably, I R A headquarters agreed to authorise his killing and the local battalion was instructed to make the necessary preparations. The headquarters decision to shoot Curtin must remain somewhat of a mystery. He was doing no more and no less than any of a score of other superintendents in various districts throughout the country, and indeed, he had hardly been left with any choice in the decision whether or not to prosecute, so flagrant was I R A activity in the Tipperary district. On 30 March, two hours after he had finished writing his report to Deputy Commissioner Coogan, he was shot dead outside his home at Friarsfield, just outside Tipperary town.

O'Duffy, Neligan and Curtin's colleagues were mystified by the shooting. Curtin had been an efficient officer but he had not been the scourge of the I R A which the Republican press was subsequently to paint him. The I R A and their supporters, on the other hand, saw the assassination of Curtin as the first step towards the overthrow of the Free State system by attacking it at the very level at which it was attempting to enforce its laws.

The killing of Curtin brought home forcefully to every Gárda officer the possibility that he too could become the victim of an I R A assassination squad, and for a time many District Superintendents and Chief Superintendents took the precaution of carrying their .38 revolvers—a personal issue—with them whether on or off duty.

The killers of Superintendent Curtin were not found and on 20 July one of his prospective witnesses in the drilling case, John Ryan of Tipperary, was found shot dead with a placard on his body bearing the inscription 'Spies and Informers Beware'. Again there were no arrests. O'Duffy, Neligan and Coogan organised divisional conferences of superintendents and O'Duffy again made representations to the government, passing on the views of his officers throughout the country. Everywhere the Guards were powerless, without any confidence in the courts and without any guarantee that once proceedings had been opened against criminals, they would have any effect other than to rebound upon themselves as had happened with the unfortunate Curtin. Furthermore, Republicans had discovered that a remedy against Gárda harassment was available to them through the civil courts, and a spate of civil suits for wrongful imprisonment, assault and false arrest effectively robbed the police of their last weapon, unremitting surveillance and intimidation. O'Duffy's demands from the government were clear. He wanted a new emergency powers bill, setting up military tribunals in the place of the jury system. He wanted certain organisations—primarily the I R A—declared illegal, and he wanted wider powers of search, arrest and detention for the police.

The government had been remarkably slow to accept O'Duffy's way of looking at things and had sought alternatives to the introduction of draconian new legislation where it was at all possible. The crime figures as adduced by O'Duffy did not show any significant increase and, in fact, had shown decreases in several vital areas. O'Duffy agreed in conferences with Fitzgerald-Kenney and Cosgrave that the absolute level of crime was dropping but that the incidents of crime were becoming more vicious, more violent and more serious. The biggest obstacle seemed to be the vulnerability of the jury system, and it was towards this sensitive element of the legal process that the I R A had directed most of their attention of late. A mailing campaign had been started by the Cumann na mBan, half appealing to jurors, half warning them of the dangers of co-operating with the Free State courts and police. One juror in a case of attempted murder of a guard had been shot in the stomach by a group of men who called to his

home at Terenure in Dublin and several witnesses in anti-
I R A cases had been killed.

The government considered for a time the possibility of
introducing an act which would enable the Supreme Court,
on the affidavit of the Attorney-General, to decide whether
certain areas of the country should have trial by jury suspended
for a certain period. A similar scheme had been considered in
1925 by O'Higgins but dropped in favour of the Treasonable
Offences Act. The new proposal would not give the government the final say in suspending the normal processes of law,
but it would enable it to initiate a judicial review of the state's
security situation.

Early in 1931 the judiciary was sounded out on the proposed bill, which had the approval of Cosgrave, McGilligan
and Fitzgerald-Kenney. But of the three judges of the Supreme
Court, only one—Hugh Kennedy, a former Attorney-General
—was in favour and the scheme had to be dropped.

The alternative, the Constitution (Amendment No. 17) Bill,
which was to insert Article 2a into the constitution, was introduced in the Dáil on 14 October 1931. The new bill was a
wide-ranging emergency powers measure which gave the
government the right to suspend trial by jury and to replace
it with summary tribunals which would be manned by army
officers. Numerous organisations, including the I R A, Saor
Éire, Cumann na mBan and the Women Prisoners Defence
League, were proscribed. The only significant exception was
Sinn Féin, which Neligan regarded anyway as a collection of
helpless eccentrics, easily penetrable by agents and perhaps,
in a roundabout way, an aid to the police intelligence system.
The measure became law on 17 October 1931, the government
went through the necessary motions of proclaiming a state
of emergency, and Article 2a became operational.

The final round was now to be played out between the
Cosgrave government and the irreconcilable proponents of the
Republic. O'Duffy and Neligan adopted a two-pronged
strategy for the day-to-day implementation of the new act.
At local level there was to be a substantial increase in the

numbers of rank-and-file I R A men taken into custody, inter-
rogated, detained and, if necessary, charged—usually with
illegal drilling or with membership of an illegal organisation.
The basic idea was to make life hell for the rank-and-file
supporter of violent Republicanism. The new act enabled the
police to do this without fear of legal repercussions as had been
the case hitherto. The bulk of this work was to fall on the
uniformed branch, while the detective branch was to concentrate on serious prosecution of local leaders and national
organisers.

T. J. Ryan of Kilrush was one of the first into the net. He
was probably a lot safer in jail than at home in Clare. George
and Charlie Gilmore were convicted of membership of an
illegal organisation and followed him very swiftly. Leitrim
inevitably blew up again when the local organiser, Seán Farrell,
was taken in and there was further bitterness and recrimina-
tion when a Republican named Vaugh who had been kept
in police custody for three weeks died the morning after his
release. As far as the I R A were concerned, Vaugh had been
beaten to death, although medical evidence was subsequently
to show that he died from a combination of illnesses which the
guards had indeed ignored and neglected during his period
in custody.

But the operation of Article 2a was demonstrably successful
in the narrow, operational police sense. Violence diminished,
the I R A was forced underground, and O'Duffy was able to
report satisfactorily to the government. But the cost in terms
of police-community relations had been enormous and the
police thmselves knew it. A *Gárda Review* of the period
featured a cartoon of a uniformed guard with cloven feet, a
goatee beard and horns, and the caption 'Am I really as bad
as they say?' In many areas of the country, the early months
of 1932 marked the lowest point yet reached in relations between the Gárda Síochána and the people of rural Ireland.
There were no-go areas in a number of towns in Cork and
Kerry—districts where the Guards could not enter and
where their very appearance resulted in violence.

The Cosgrave government had reached the very peak of its unpopularity, and in the eyes of the majority of the people it was no longer acceptable. The Guards themselves had grown tired of the Cosgrave government through repeated pay and allowance reductions and threats of such reductions. In January 1932, only weeks before the election which was to bring Eamon de Valera to power, a proposal for a further reduction of Gárda pay by five per cent was greeted with fury in the force. The Representative Body resigned and its area committees began to canvass relatives of guards to vote against Cosgrave in the election (the Guards themselves having no vote).

The wheel had nearly come full circle since the first idealistic venture of the unarmed guard among the people ten years before.

10   A New President and a New Commissioner 1932-33

THE election of February 1932 which ousted the Cumann na nGaedheal government after almost ten years of uninterrupted rule, was fought on negative rather than positive issues. The government pointed to their record in the field of industry and economics and went to very little trouble to assure the voters of anything in the future. The Fianna Fáil party pointed to the 100,000 unemployed and questioned the government's concern for anybody but themselves, and both sides made capital of the security situation. Cumann na nGaedheal constituency organisations ran newspaper advertisements warning of the threat of Bolshevism and Communism from Fianna Fáil and asking whether the country wanted to be taken over by gunmen and desperadoes. Fianna Fáil pointed to the government's campaign of legal repression and declared it the policy of a bankrupt administration. It was perhaps in the area of security that the most immediate changes would be expected if a Fianna Fáil government was elected. The I R A anticipated the release of their members in Free State prisons and the wholesale decimation of the police force, in particular the Special Branch. Neligan would go, O'Duffy would go and true justice would be seen to be done on behalf of the wronged sons of the Republic. To the Cumann na nGaedheal side, such a change would mean the triumph of evil and sinister Communism and the dismantling of the structures by which the state was protected. De Valera was to surprise both sides.

The results of the election had given de Valera a qualified victory over Cosgrave. He had seventy-two seats to Cosgrave's fifty-seven and he was dependent on the support of the seven Labour Party members for his majority.

The first indication of de Valera's skilful and ambivalent attitude towards the security of the state was given as early as 9 March, when he announced among his cabinet line-up the appointment of James Geoghegan as his Minister for Justice. Geoghegan was a mild-mannered, almost self-effacing, man. A barrister by profession, he had undoubted professional talents and he was in some ways the exception in a cabinet composed in the main of recently converted gunmen and guerillas. Geoghegan was not the man to fight with O'Duffy and Neligan. There would be no confrontation between the government minister responsible for security and his executive, but on the other hand there would be no strong man between de Valera and the security organs of the state.

The position of O'Duffy, Coogan, Murphy, Neligan and the other chiefs of the Gárda Síochána had now become quite invidious. The men whom, only six brief years earlier they had tracked down, persecuted, arrested and imprisoned were now their political masters. The condition of officers at divisional and district level throughout the country was only marginally less unhappy. These were the men—just about two hundred in all—who had been the spearhead of Kevin O'Higgins's campaign of law and order since the end of 1922. These were the men who had decided at local level, where it mattered, who was to be prosecuted, who was to go to jail, who was to be subjected to the eternal round of detention, interrogation release and re-arrest. But the plight of the Special Branch men was the worst of all, for they were protected neither by rank, as in the case of O'Duffy and his chiefs, nor by the officer's commission, as in the case of the Superintendents and Chief Superintendents; the S Branch were the arch-monsters whom the victors might reasonably single out for exceptional punishment.

The heart of many a detective and District Superintendent must have sunk with apprehension when on 9 March, immediately after de Valera's election as President of the Executive Council had been approved by the Governor General, Arbour Hill barracks was visited by the Minister for Defence, Frank

Aiken, and the Minister for Justice, James Goeghegan and the men held there by order of the military tribunal were released. On 18 March the operation of Article 2a of the constitution was suspended, but significantly, the act which authorised its use was not repealed. De Valera was keeping one foot on either side of the stream. The message as far as the Guards was concerned, however, was clear. It was 'Hands off the I R A'.

There were of course no official circulars to that effect, no orders, written or verbal, but the moral was drawn very swiftly from one or two instances in which guards were either foolish or principled enough to try to continue their prosecutions against members of the movement. Once the operation of Article 2a was suspended the Guards were in the position of having to rely entirely on common law procedures for their prosecutions. This meant the forwarding of case files to the Attorney-General's office for directives on the manner of prosecution. The Cumann na nGaedheal Attorney-General, John A. Costello, had been replaced by Fianna Fáil's Conor Maguire and the few guards who did forward files for directives found it impossible to get an answer. The moral was clear enough, and the Guards adapted slowly to it and settled down to a period of enforced coexistence with the I R A all over the country. It rankled deep both among the uniformed and detective branches and in country districts the Republicans lost no opportunity to rub the Guards' noses in their loss of power.

In Listowel, Co. Kerry, as soon as the results of the election became known, local I R A supporters trooped down to the Gárda station and ordered the guards to leave as the new Republican police force which de Valera was bound to replace them with would be due within a matter of days. An impromptu baton charge across the floor of the station's public office made it clear to their visitors that the guards were not prepared to anticipate their departure quite to that extent. In a number of towns in Tipperary and Cork members reported to their officers that patrolling guards were being jostled into the gutters and off the footpaths. In villages in Co. Galway delegations of local Republicans approached local sergeants with 'instructions' as to how policing affairs were to be carried out from now on. In Cork City young guards reported that they were spat upon in the public street by Republicans against whom they were now powerless to act.

It became evident at a very early stage that as part of his balancing act to hold the I R A in check while broadening and consolidating his base of support, de Valera was prepared to allow the Guards to suffer for their sins in the past. Shortly after the election he went on a victory tour of the South and visited Skibbereen, Co. Cork, where the district officer, Superintendent Ward, drew up a guard of honour of his men to receive him. The local I R A drew up another guard of honour who lined up on the opposite side of the street. When de Valera arrived he took the salute, inspected the I R A detachment and then passed on into the town, completely ignoring the Gárda group.

The vulnerability of the Guards had become a point of some concern to the leader of the Labour Party, William Norton, upon whose seven-man party de Valera was dependent for his majority. There was a strong mutual respect between Norton and Neligan and a similar relationship between Norton and O'Duffy which had been fostered during the years of the Labour Party's single-handed opposition in the Dáil. Shortly after the new government had come to power, Norton asked to meet both men and offered them assurances that as long as de Valera was dependent upon him for his majority, they would remain in office provided they continued to serve the Fianna Fáil government as well as they had served the Cumann na nGaedheal one. What Norton did not know and what presumably would have made him regard O'Duffy in a less favourable light was that only weeks beforehand O'Duffy had been actively considering the possibilities of a coup to prevent de Valera from coming to power in the first place.

There is little doubt but that the less stable side of O'Duffy's volatile character had become uppermost during the last three years of the Cosgrave administration. His clashes with the government had become more hysterical and more frequent, his self-centred vanity more of an embarrassment and a cause of concern both with his senior colleagues in the Guards and elsewhere. In 1928 he had marched virtually the entire officer corps of the Guards off to Rome where they paid homage to the Pope and exchanged salutes with Il Duce Mussolini. Later he marched another contingent off to Lourdes and Biarritz, where most of their time was spent being photographed with local dignitaries, the pictures being reproduced *ad nauseum* in the Irish newspapers and in the *Gárda Review*.

O'Duffy's doctrinaire Catholicism, his obsession with the evils of drink and his insatiable appetite for self-adulation had by this time reduced the *Gárda Review* to the level of pure and unquestioning hagiography. A not untypical editorial of December 1928 ran :

It is impossible to overlook or to ignore the fact that the Gárda Síochána, from its distinguished chief down, is inspired by something more, by something grander and greater, than a mere conformity with regulation. A paid policeman is one thing. A policeman who feels that in performing his daily or nightly round of duty is fulfilling the law of Christ is another . . . This pilgrimage [to Rome] was led and organised by our police chief, General O'Duffy, whose genius has made the Gárda Síochána the miracle that it is. No competent and impartial observer will deny that the Gárda is the nearest approach to a miracle that cold and scientific analysis can discover.

Asking rhetorically what lay behind the success of this tremendous endeavour, the *Review* replied : 'There can be only one answer—the Faith of our Fathers. The General knew that under the surface lay an indestructible substratum of Christian principle.'

In later years too O'Duffy had begun to clash with the cabinet. In 1926 he had fought with O'Higgins over the disciplining of guards in Waterford. Later there were differences, voiced in the media, over pay and conditions for the force. By the time Cumann na nGaedheal had gone from office he had come round to the Labour Party's way of thinking in the debate nine years earlier and had suggested that the Gárda should be put under local instead of central control.

In fairness, it was not all O'Duffy's fault. Given almost a free hand in the early years of his commissionership, he was to find, once the big crisis of 1922–23 had passed, that the Cumann na nGaedheal cabinet and the officials of their Finance and Justice departments were insistent on keeping a strict, almost stifling, hold over the administration of the Gárda—especially in matters financial. Since O'Duffy had refused the functions of accounting officer for the force, to be tied in with his role as Commissioner, he found himself in the position of having to account for every penny to the Secretary of the Department of Justice, Henry Frighil. On numerous occasions O'Duffy clashed with accounting officers in the Departments of Finance and Justice over accounts and expenses claimed by his officers. If one of his officers certified a claim 'on his honour', that was enough for O'Duffy. He would fight it through to the last halfpenny with the civil servants.

In the wider scope of things too O'Duffy was up against the strong personalities of cabinet members and senior administrative officials who did not share his view of the special role of the unarmed police force in Irish society. To the Cumann na nGaedheal cabinet, with the exception of O'Higgins and possibly one or two others, the police was no different from any other department of the public service. It was an arm of government in precisely the same way as was the Board of Public Works or the Department of Agriculture. O'Duffy clashed with them all: with Blythe, the Minister for Finance; with Frighil, the Secretary of the Department of Justice; with Kennedy, the Attorney-General.

Matters had finally reached the stage by the end of 1931 that several leading members of the government resolved that O'Duffy would have to be relieved of his post as Gárda Commissioner if Cumann na nGaedheal were returned to power.

Blythe proposed that he should be given the alternative of heading a commission to investigate the mineral resources of the country (originally he had been an engineer by profession) or becoming the Irish ambassador to Washington, a post which would have probably have appealed much more strongly to O'Duffy. But in the event it was the Cumann na nGaedheal government which it cannot be denied—he had served well had reached the decision to remove him from office. But he was under no illusion as to his future under a de Valera government. He might have a brief respite while de Valera would get the feel of the ropes, but as soon as it was safe to do so, de Valera would replace him. Almost as soon as the results of the February election became known O'Duffy began to explore the possibility of keeping de Valera out of power.

It would be less than fair to the man to suggest that O'Duffy's sole motive in this endeavour was to preserve his own office. His anguish at the spread of disorder and crime in the Free State in the previous five years was genuine and he drew little if any distinction between Fianna Fáil and the IRA in the allocation of responsibility for the state of the country. It would be tantamount to surrender to the forces of anarchy to allow people as unfit (in O'Duffy's view) as Fianna Fáil to take control of the destinies of Ireland.

According to David Neligan, O'Duffy had canvassed views among some senior army officers about establishing a military government if Fianna Fáil won the election. But it is important to stress that no corroboration of Neligan's account has come to light. According to Neligan's account, some of these officers had a proclamation printed at the Ordnance Survey Office in the Phoenix Park, calling on the citizens of Saorstát Éireann to stand behind a military government under the leadership of Eóin O'Duffy and explaining why the normal democratic processes had to be suspended. O'Duffy also mentioned the matter cautiously to the army Chief of Staff, Michael Brennan, a brother of Paddy of Kildare mutiny fame. Brennan was taken aback and even more worried because he suspected that he was not the first army man to be consulted on the plot. He immediately ordered a few transfers of senior officers whom he suspected might be likely candidates for O'Duffy's approaches and then called back to see O'Duffy, warning him that at the first sign of any improper action the army would arrest him.

If Neligan's account had any substance in reality, it is difficult to imagine what might have deterred O'Duffy from his planned course of action. Neligan claimed credit for changing his commissioner's mind in the course of a discussion among a number of senior officers at the Depot mess some weeks before the election.

According to Neligan, he was about to leave the lounge in the mess when O'Duffy, in a huddle with a group of officers at the other end of the room, rose and called him over. On the table was the proclamation to the citizens of Saorstát Éireann. O'Duffy indicated it with a gesture and said: 'Well Dave, what do you think? Neligan read it and quickly replied: 'You don't expect me to have anything to do with this?' and walked towards the door. O'Duffy followed him as Neligan went down the steps towards the front door of the mess and said: 'You know, Dave, you'll the first one to go under de Valera.'

Neligan drove immediately to the home of Professor James Hogan, head of the History Department of University College, Cork, a mutual friend of O'Duffy and himself. He explained what he had seen and heard at the depot and asked Hogan to talk to O'Duffy. Hogan went immediately to the depot and took up the cudgels with O'Duffy. They argued and fought most of the night. Hogan drawing on the theory of democracy and the sacredness of its institutions, O'Duffy countering with the point that de Valera and his followers had paid little attention to the principles they now demanded for themselves. Finally, towards morning, the contest ended and Hogan emerged, exhausted but victorious. Ten days later Neligan was summoned to see W. T. Cosgrave who told him he had heard reports that O'Duffy was planning to do something foolish. Was it true, he wanted to know, was O'Duffy going to lead a coup? Neligan neither denied nor confirmed the report but simply assured Cosgrave that things were now under control. The President was apparently satisfied to leave matters at that.

But in spite of Fianna Fáil's fears that they would not be allowed to take office without opposition—and the anticipated threat was much broader than the individual one from O'Duffy—the transfer of power went smoothly and the threat of resistance from the army and police, which, after all, were Cumann na nGaedheal institutions, receded quietly. On the surface, at any rate, the Guards accepted the changeover quietly enough. The new Minister for Justice and the new Attorney-General were featured on the cover of the *Gárda Review* and Geoghegan was feted by the headquarters staff when he arrived to make his first official visit to the depot— among his hosts being O'Duffy, Neligan and Coogan. O'Duffy and the force as a whole, it would appear, did their best to function normally under common law, but the very range of their duties was now so confined that they had little enough to do anyway. Membership of the I R A and its associate organisations was no longer an offence, drilling and training could not be penalised except under the Treasonable Offences Act, and before any charges could be brought under that law they would have to be referred to the Attorney-General's department where they were almost inevitably set aside. Above and beyond this, there was already a marked reduction in political crime in most areas and it was generally considered the wisest course of action for local guards to look the other way at any Republican activity which might possibly come within the scope of some obscure act. From February to October 1932 the normal processes of the criminal law were by-passed in the Irish Free State through a tacit understanding between government and police that what had been crime before the change of government was crime no longer and was rather the legitimate by-product of the unfulfilled ambitions of Republicans.

But the Cumann na nGaedheal party in opposition did not accept the transmutation as easily or unreservedly as that. Through the summer and autumn of 1932, Cumann na nGaedheal members lashed furiously at the government for what they alleged was its dual standard on law and order. In August Dr T. F. O'Higgins, in an interview with the *Irish Times* listed twelve incidents during the months of July and August which he said showed that the Fianna Fáil government was not prepared to bring the rule of law to bear on its own supporters and which showed that members and supporters of the previous government were in physical danger. The list included an armed attack on a farmer in Co. Leitrim by self-styled Republican police, the unexplained release of an I R A supporter called Dempsey who had been charged by the Guards with unauthorised possession of arms and convicted by the courts, and the attempted shooting of a Cumann na nGaedheal supporter at Loughrea, Co. Galway. On 4 September the former Minister for Justice, James Fitzgerald-Kenney, speaking at a political meeting in Co. Mayo, charged his successor, James Geoghegan with failing to stand up to the I R A and with interfering with the course of the law. In the course of his speech he declared :

It is his duty to maintain the supremacy of the State in this country; it is his duty to face any man or body of men who wish to upset by armed violence the institutions of the state; it is his moral duty to do so because it is the duty of any government to maintain order and put down sedition. But the Minister for Justice has not done anything of the kind.

We are told that the I R A can publicly and freely train; that they can recruit as many men as they wish and are entitled to get as many arms as they like. This association which has been condemned by the bishops is now to have full and free power to lead astray the young men of the country. [Fitzgerald-Kenney then recounted the Dempsey case.] The Minister for Justice is wanting in the discharge of his duty which rests upon his shoulders of preventing seditious doctrines being preached in this state; he has made a complete surrender.

He might also have added that the Guards, apart from not prosecuting I R A men, were not even offering normal protection in many instances to supporters of the former government where such protection implied positive action against I R A or Fianna Fáil supporters. In the Francis Xavier Hall in Cork on 30 April when Cosgrave and Patrick McGilligan had tried to address a meeting of their supporters, they were shouted down by hecklers proclaiming 'No Free Speech for Traitors'. A force of guards present in the hall was too small to restore order effectively and the meeting had to be abandoned. Some weeks later, when General Mulcahy, the former Cumann na nGaedheal Minister for Defence, was about to address a meeting in Gloucester Street, Dublin, a crowd rushed the platform, toppling the speakers and flailing them with sticks and bottles. Mulcahy retreated to safety using an upturned chair to hold off his assailants. A number of guards drawn from the detective branch and from the various districts around the Metropolitan Area stood by without interfering in what was clearly an intrusion on the rights of free speech. Whether officially or unofficially, the guards had been given to understand that they were not to intervene, and the meeting broke up in disorder.

Some indication of the unspoken—and certainly unwritten—instructions under which the Guards were now operating as a result of government policy was given on 29 August at Navan by the Minister for Defence, Frank Aiken. Patiently and at some length he explained how Fianna Fáil was seeking to kill violence by kindness. He went on :

Ever since the government has assumed office a number of nervous people wanted us to crack a lot of heads, as was the policy of the late government when people who were a danger to them got their skulls opened.

We have refrained from coercion because we believe that it is a bad father who always uses the rod and we have allowed ourselves to be criticised by some of the daily newspapers and by small cliques throughout the country and allowed a lot of anti-national propaganda to be spoken and written up in the press simply because if we took the steps Cumann na nGaedheal took and put all these people into jail and suppressed their newspapers we would be doing more harm than good.

Notwithstanding the opposition of a few individuals, we will win. We want to get willing obedience to the law and we also want willing loyalty to the state.

How long Fianna Fáil might have been prepared to wait for the return of the prodigals must remain problematic, for by October a new organisation of Cumann na nGaedheal supporters, the Army Comrades Association, whose avowed purpose was to defend the right of free speech, had appeared on the scene and was already helping to set the pace of events throughout the country. De Valera was about to find himself in the cleft stick situation which he was seeking to avoid with the I R A wing of his supporters.

It was becoming vitally important for de Valera to broaden his base of support beyond the I R A wing if he was to escape from his dilemma of running with the I R A hare and hunting with the Free State hounds. As 1932 wore on it became apparent that the Guards were not going to acquiesce in their dual role for ever. Two sacrificial offerings of the force which de Valera gave up to the I R A during this period as part of his elaborate juggling act were to rebound badly in his face and brought discontent within the Guards to a dangerous pitch. The first incident concerned the disciplining of two Special Branch detectives in the now infamous Kilrush area and the other concerned the charging of Inspector E. M. O'Connell under the Official Secrets Act.

Kilrush had not been quietened by the change of government, and industrial trouble, in which T. J. Ryan's supporters had undertaken an active role, was added to the other un-savoury elements of the situation there. The premises of Daniel Ryan, a local trader had to be placed under round-the-clock police guard as a result of differences between the owner and the employees over rates of pay and conditions of employment. The Republicans, emboldened by their new-found immunity from police prosecution, had begun to drill and parade openly in the streets of the town, and tense verbal confrontations between the I R A men and the Guards had become common. On the afternoon of 15 August detectives and Republicans clashed in the streets over the hanging of posters on public lamp-posts. The usual abuse was exchanged and there was a good deal of pushing and jostling about.

What happened between then and 11 p.m. was to become the subject of a government enquiry and the most bitter controversey both within the Gárda force and outside it. What was not in dispute was that shortly after 11 p.m. T. J. Ryan and George Gilmore, who was in Kilrush in connection with a Republican meeting and Feis, were brought, suffering from gunshot wounds and other injuries, to the local hospital under guard by the members of the local S Branch unit. The two men were charged with the attempted murder of two detectives, Muldowney and Carroll, who had been guarding Daniel Ryan's premises earlier in the evening.

But two days later it became known that the charges against Ryan and Gilmore had been dropped by the state and that instead the two detectives, Muldowney and Carroll, were being suspended from duty pending an official enquiry. Deputy Commissioner Coogan was immediately despatched from Dublin to investigate the situation. The Minister for Justice, Geoghegan, shortly afterwards announced that a full public enquiry into the episode would be held in Kilrush starting on 7 September.

The enquiry in Kilrush had something in it for everyone. It confirmed the Cumann na nGaedheal supporters and the Guards themselves in their belief that the forces of anarchy had the state by the throat, and it showed more clearly than ever

for the I R A-Fianna Fáil axis that the Guards were truly a
gang of bloodthirsty Free State hacks. Its pages of evidence
can have done little to effect any reconciliation between the
two sides, but the revelations at the enquiry throw an intrigu-
ing light on the kind of relationships which existed between
Republicans and police in at least one country community.

The evidence at the enquiry revealed a relationship of the
most extreme bitterness and hatred between police and Republicans in the Kilrush area. The attitudes of both sides were
characterised by violence, vituperation and intimidation. The
detectives, it would appear, lost no opportunity of harassing
and abusing the I R A men; the I R A men, in turn, lost no
opportunity of ridiculing and belittling the police. The community was split apart: people drank in separate pubs, children fought vicious battles on their way out of school; where
one side or the other had the opportunity to harm their opponents it was taken with gusto. In the course of the enquiry
Superintendent Feeney gave it as his opinion that there was
more perjury committed in the courthouse in Kilrush than
in the rest of Ireland put together!

The incident of 15 August does not appear to have been
untypical except in so far as that it went beyond the usual
dimensions of punching, abuse and the use of cudgels, batons
and gun butts. The two detectives, Carroll and Muldowney,
claimed that in shooting at and injuring Ryan and Gilmore
they were exercising their right of self defence. Ryan and
Gilmore, however, insisted that the attack on them had been
sheer unprovoked aggression. The enquiry found for Ryan and
Gilmore, thereby accepting their allegations that the two
detectives had set upon them and their friends and shot them
without provocation, beyond the exchange of the usual abuse
and insults. The detectives had claimed that Ryan, Gilmore
and their companions had approached the protection post
in military formation, that shots had been fired by a
member of their party at the detectives and that they had
fired in self-defence, first over their heads and later at their
feet.

The enquiry found, however, that no shots had been fired at the detectives and they accepted Ryan's and Gilmore's assertions of subsequent ill-treatment at the hands of the detectives in their station—a hotel which had been taken over in the town.

The finding against Muldowney and Carroll, which on the basis of the evidence seemed reasonable enough, sent a wave of anger through the force and especially through the S Branch. It was a significant reaction, for on the evidence produced at the enquiry, the two men had certainly exceeded the spirit and letter of the law, not to mention their professional duty. The use of what could almost be called terror tactics and their accompaniment by extreme violence had unhappily become almost accepted by the force as a whole. It was evident that something was wrong. But the immediate consequence of the enquiry was not the dismissal of relatively unknown and unimportant detective officers but the sacking of Dave Neligan, their Chief Superintendent and head of the Special Branch.

Neligan had been particularly upset by the Kilrush enquiry. The two detectives, he agreed, had exceeded the disciplinary limits authorised for the force, but in his view they had suffered the most extreme provocation, not necessarily on the night of 15 August but over a period of years in the district. Their colleagues had been killed and maimed; their wives and children reviled in the public street, in the schoolroom and even in the church; their homes had been daubed and damaged; and finally, since the change of government they had been subject to a flood of personal vilification and open insult to their faces. Early in December he organised a collection within the force for the dismissed guards to compensate temporarily for their loss of livelihood.

The government was furious and yet delighted at Neligan's leaving himself open. Together with O'Duffy, he was called before the then Minister for Justice, Geoghegan, who was accompanied by Seán T. O'Kelly. He was peremptorily suspended from duty, but on full pay, pending a final decision as to his future by the Executive Council. He had breached Gárda disciplinary regulations by taking up an unauthorised collection within the force but the government was more concerned, he was told, with his apparent flouting of its decision to discipline the two detectives. For the time being Coogan was to take charge of Neligan's department. The force seethed; there were tentative suggestions to O'Duffy that there should be a mass resignation of officers. O'Duffy demurred, pointing out that the government would be only too happy to have another two hundred well-paid positions for their many followers. Neligan was subsequently placed in a section of the Land Commission where, in his own words, he was never told for thirty years what he was supposed to be doing in an office all to himself.

The second indication of de Valera's tightening grip around the administration of the Gárda Síochána did not come until after he had consolidated his parliamentary majority in the general election of 24 January 1933. He won 77 seats out of a total house of 153, giving him the narrow majority of one, even without the Labour support, which he still enjoyed in any event.

On the morning of 19 February the newspapers announced the dramatic arrest of Neligan's second in command, Inspector E. M. O'Connell, together with Colonel Michael Hogan of army headquarters, under the Official Secrets Act. No official details were released but there was sufficient 'leakage' to give the impression that some devilish plot against the state was being hatched out between army and police.

Dublin was allowed to seethe with rumours for a day or two while Inspector O'Connell and Colonel Hogan were remanded to Mountjoy jail. The pieces began to be filled in by informed newspapers and journalists; O'Connell and Hogan had been engaged in some operation to leak official Gárda information from the depot; dozens of detectives had surrounded the plotters' homes the night the arrests were made; further arrests were always a possibility.

In reality the situation was quite different. O'Connell was

a highly efficient professional police officer who had shared the burden of running the S Branch with Neligan for the ten years since 1923. Perhaps even more signficantly, he was, apart from his personal loyalty to Neligan and O'Duffy, a thoroughly non-political administrator. There was nothing to suggest at the time of his trial or later that he had served Fianna Fáil, like its predecessor, with anything other than efficiency and enthusiasm. He had indeed been hauled out of his bed in the early hours of the morning by a rather bewildered and embarrassed colleague from the detective branch who had warned him to say nothing as he had been sent to arrest him. The pointlessness of a midnight arrest was later mentioned by O'Connell, who added that he might as easily have been taken into custody the following morning when he walked into detective branch headquarters in the Park as he had done every morning for the previous ten years. Hogan too was a respected officer, a brother of the Cork don whom Neligan had called in to deal with the rebellious O'Duffy. He was a personal friend of both Neligan and O'Connell.

For three days rumours of the 'Secrets Case' were rife in Dublin. Then there was a further sudden shock announcement from the government. On 22 February O'Duffy was dismissed. There was never any official indication that the two episodes were even being connected in the minds of the government, but the inference was there for all to see. Something, somewhere in Gárda headquarters, was very wrong.

O'Duffy's successor was Colonel Eamon Broy, then holding the rank of Chief Superintendent. He was promoted over the heads of four Deputy or Assistant Commissioners; Coogan, Murphy, Walsh and Cullen. Broy had hitherto been a shadowy figure within the Civic Guard. A former member of the D M P detective branch, he had, like Neligan, been one of Collins's important contacts during the War of Independence. For a brief period after the Civil War he had headed the Free State air force—whence he owned his title of Colonel—and on the amalgamation of the D M P and Gárda Síochána in 1925 he had been made Chief Superintendent in charge of the newly

G

formed Dublin Metropolitan Division. On Neligan's suspension as head of the S Branch at the end of 1932 he had been put in charge of the political detectives and in that capacity he was O'Connell's direct superior at the time the alleged secrets leakage took place.

This dramatic chain of events, the Kilrush enquiry, the suspension of Neligan, the arrest of O'Connell and Hogan, the removal of O'Duffy and the rapid promotion of Broy had the newspapers and the general public—not to mention the police themselves—in a complete daze. There were rumours that a coup had been discovered, that wholesale dismissals of Gárda officers were due to take place. *An Phoblacht*, the organ of the Republican movement, never slow to capitalise on any difficulties the Guards might be in, broke their endless commentary and analysis on police affairs to maintain an incredulous silence.

But there was a complete official silence until 14 March, when, with the newspapers calling for an explanation of the government's action, Cosgrave moved a motion of censure in the Dáil, criticising the dismissal of O'Duffy.

There was no question of O'Duffy not having been efficient. His intelligence reports to the Executive Council had continued almost unchanged after the coming of Fianna Fáil to power. He had supervised a mammoth police operation on the occasion of the Eucharistic Congress in Dublin in the previous June which celebrated the 1,500th anniversary of St Patrick's mission in Ireland. Even more impressively, he had maintained a rigorous impartiality on the part of the Guards during the general election campaign of January 1933, ensuring freedom of speech for both parties in pursuance of de Valera's declaration that the election campaign would have to be free and unimpeded. That in itself had not been easy; in the early stages of the campaign there had been wild riots and baton charges in Dublin in which the Guards had been overwhelmed. De Valera had called in O'Duffy and told him that he would have the army to back him if necessary, but that eventuality did not arise. On 22 January at Tralee, when a Republican crowd

tried to shout down an election meeting which was being
addressed by Cosgrave, the Guards swept the street in a sudden
baton charge which left fifty people injured but allowed the
meeting to go ahead without further interruption.

Cosgrave's motion of censure over O'Duffy's dismissal was
debated at length in the Dáil and the first indication of the
government's point of view was given. O'Duffy, it was revealed,
had been offered an alternative post in the public service
which was to be equally well paid. He had, however, refused
it. But de Valera could not be drawn on the specific reasons
for O'Duffy's dismissal. Perhaps there were none; perhaps
he had simply taken advantage of the atmosphere of intrigue
and anticipation which had been generated by the O'Connell-
Hogan case to ditch a man who was certainly going to be an
embarrassment to him anyway; perhaps de Valera was saying
all he had to say on the matter when he replied to Cosgrave's
motion :

It is because we realise that the ultimate responsibility for peace
and order depends on us that we are going to see to it that those
who will have the immediate responsibility will be people in
whom we have full confidence. Let us note that—without any
of the bunkum—full confidence. Deputy Cosgrave asked me
was there any characteristic in the quality of the new occupant
of the office that the old occupant did not have. I say, yes,
one, that he was not the chief of police for ten years under the last
administration. . . We want a chief of police of whom no
section of the community can say that that man is deliberately
and politically opposed to us, and is likely to be biased in his
attitude because of past political affiliations.

It was probably less than accurate for one of the Dublin
newspapers to allege that in sacking O'Duffy de Valera
was yielding to the pressures of violent minorities. It was
true that since Fianna Fáil had come to power there had been
an almost constant stream of demands from various Republican groups for his removal. Some of the comments from the
floor at the Fianna Fáil Árd Fheis in November of the same

year can give an indication of the grassroots feeling against O'Duffy in Republican circles.

Referring to the payment of a national pension to the General, a delegate from Donegal stated : 'We find it almost impossible to spark up any enthusiasm in the country for this act. O'Duffy more than any other man was responsible for the Treaty being accepted and for the reduction of this country to civil war.' There was 'loud applause when Mr McDevitt went on to say that some people suggested that General O'Duffy should not only be deposed but transported and never allowed to come back'. Mr Colwell (Kells) described General O'Duffy as the most remarkable scoundrel in the world. Mr Clarke (Kerry) remarked that General O'Duffy had visited Kerry recently and 'left it very quickly'.

Yet de Valera had retained O'Duffy for the greater part of a year, which hardly indicates any great and immediate desire to satisfy the howls of his more bloodthirsty supporters. Certainly, once the sacking of O'Duffy became known it could do de Valera little but good among the backwoodsmen who rejoiced to see the final fall of their *bête noir*. But it was a risky way of gaining a little indulgence from the gunmen, upon whom de Valera was anyway becoming less and less dependent, for there was always the chance that the dismissal of O'Duffy, together with the Kilrush affair and the arrest of O'Connell and Hogan, might prejudice the loyalty of the Guards as a whole. There was something more than the mere sacrificing of a guy to the gunmen in de Valera's dismissal of O'Duffy at this stage.

It was evident, even at this early stage, that there was a rapid parting of the ways between the constitutional Republicans and the I R A. In the autumn of 1932 the I R A had begun a campaign to disrupt the political activities of Cumann na nGaedheal as implied by the slogan 'No Free Speech for Traitors'. By setting his face against this policy in the 1933 election campaign de Valera was cutting the I R A adrift to some extent. He did that even further by announcing at Navan early in January that no section of the community, other than the forces of the state, would be allowed to arm itself: 'All arms shall be completely at the disposal of the majority of the elected representatives of the people.' It had become clear that at some stage in the not too distant future de Valera was going to have to take on the I R A in no uncertain manner. Over and above this, in May 1932 the Army Comrades Association had been transformed into an organised force for the protection of the right of free speech in the Free State. The final explosive element in the mixture was put in when on 1 July de Valera defaulted on the payment of land annuities to Britain as specified under the terms of the Treaty. It was evident that de Valera was going to have his own security problems in the early 1930s, and for these he needed the services of a police and security machine whose loyalty and sympathy would come a good deal higher than those of the Neligans, the O'Connells and the O'Duffys.

It is in this light that the dismissal of O'Duffy makes most sense. The signs of an impending confrontation were there for everyone to see—a confrontation which would make the disturbances of the late 1920s seem calm by comparison—and the government needed its own men directing the police and detective services. With O'Duffy, Neligan and O'Connell gone, the process was almost complete.

The final touches were added during 1934 when selected members of the S Branch, mainly detective sergeants, including Philip MacMahon and Michael Gill, about half a dozen in all, were reverted to uniform, demoted and transferred to obscure rural stations or innocuous desk jobs where their political knowledge was neutralised. Gill and McMahon, both ironically to become heads of the Special Branch under subsequent Fianna Fáil governments, did not accept the government's decision with docility. The reduced detectives subsequently began legal proceedings against the Minister for Justice for wrongful reduction in the ranks. The matter was finally to be settled amicably and the officers concerned were restored to their former ranks.

Meanwhile the hapless O'Connell and his alleged partner

in crime, Colonel Hogan, had been brought to trial under the Official Secrets Act. The facts of the case, as revealed at the trial, bore little or no resemblance to the widely spread rumours of vicious intrigue and threats to the state. It transpired that Hogan's brother, the Cork professor, was working on a booklet examining Communism in Ireland and had been loaned material for his purpose from the files of the S Branch in the Phoenix Park. The material consisted largely of sample pamphlets and handouts which the S Branch had filed and which could have been bought off the side of the streets at any time during the previous ten years. Neligan had allowed the handout of the material for what he considered bona fide academic purposes and the process had merely been continued under Broy. At the trial Inspector O'Connell protested that the whole business had been transacted in the open, so much so that he had openly handed the envelope of material to his clerk with the instructions to have them brought around to Colonel Hogan's office. The material contained in the envelope he described as 'a load of tripe'.

Not unexpectedly the jury returned a verdict of 'not guilty' without even retiring and O'Connell and Hogan left the courtroom as free men. O'Connell, however, was not to be entirely exonerated; he was reduced to the rank of sergeant for reasons which were never explained to him. He was not to get his rank back until the inter-party government of John A. Costello came to power.

Thus by the end of March 1933 the Gárda Síochána had been suitably lopped and trimmed to serve the needs of the de Valera administration. There was a new Commissioner, the old heads of the S Branch had gone and the handful of S Branch officers who might have been regarded as a threat to the new regime had been packed away to a variety of harmless posts. In addition, de Valera had appointed a new Minister for Justice, Paddy Ruttledge, a harder, stronger man than Geoghegan. The Civic Guards, as a whole, found that if they did not bother de Valera, he would not bother them. They could hardly be classed as potential revolutionaries : most of them were now settled in their early or middle thirties with newly acquired wives, families and mortgages, and they were happy enough to try to work the new system. There was even a murmur of enthusiasm from the force's Representative Bodies when the Guards were excluded from a pay cut which de Valera's Minister for Finance, Seán MacEntee, proposed for public servants. The master juggling act had succeeded again.

11 The Broy Harriers 1933

THE trouble which de Valera expected as 1932 drew to a close was not long arriving. In the closing months of the year and early in 1933 the I R A, emboldened by their continuing immunity from prosecution or intervention by the Guards, increased the frequency of their attacks on Cumann na nGaedheal meetings and dances and other functions organised by the newly expanded Army Comrades Association. The A C A had spent the winter consolidating its strength throughout the country and its recruiting meetings had become focal points for serious disturbances. The Guards were in the middle, lacking firm leadership and clear direction. There were nightly reports of disturbances especially from Cork, Tipperary and Limerick. On 10 October there were baton charges in Kilmallock, Co. Limerick, when the Guards sought to prevent an I R A crowd from breaking up an A C A meeting. On 30 October there was serious rioting accompanied by baton charges in the streets of Mallow, Co. Cork, when the Army Comrades and Republican groups came to grips, with the Guards holding the middle ground.

The ambiguous relationship with the I R A which the coming to power of the Fianna Fáil government involved for the Guards was now further complicated by the emergence of the strengthened Army Comrades Association. It had been possible—but only barely—for the Guards to coexist for almost a year with the I R A and that coexistence depended upon the Guards' ability to swallow their pride and allow themselves be metaphorically and sometimes physically kicked about. But the increasing frequency of street confrontations between Republicans and the A C A was now going to eliminate any possibility of the Guards continuing their passive acceptance of I R A violence. Their dilemma was now acute. If they refused to intervene in the nightly violence, they would be abdicating their role as police officers whose primary responsibility was to the law. If they moved against the I R A, who were at this stage still originating most of the violence, they would be as likely to find themselves disowned by the Attorney-General's office or their own headquarters. If they attacked the A C A—in these months at least—they would be merely adding a new and ominous dimension to the I R A's campaign of intimidation.

Most local superintendents therefore adopted the policy of ensuring that the A C A were given freedom of speech whereever possible while using only the bare minimum of force which was necessary to achieve that objective. Nevertheless, in many instances that minimum of force was quite a lot. The Mallow riots of 30 October were the first instances of the Guards using force to secure the right of free speech for the A C A, but the unpleasant realisation that the honeymoon was coming to an end did not dawn on the I R A until 6 November in Cork when W. T. Cosgrave, whose last appearance in the St Francis Xavier Hall had ended in riot, decided to address another public meeting in the city.

Cork had been one of the most unruly districts in the country since the coming of Fianna Fáil to power, and its Republicans now showed a fire and zeal which was markedly absent during the Special Branch raids and swoops of the previous year. Since the change of government the traditionally peaceful city area had witnessed several serious assaults and violent attacks on Cosgrave supporters, and the police, as elsewhere in the country, had contrived to be looking in the other direction at the appropriate times. But the local officers were resolved that no interference with Cosgrave's meeting would be tolerated this time and about two hundred guards under Chief Superintendent Carroll were drafted in. I R A supporters had been marshalling in the Grand Parade since early evening under the direction of Tom Barry, the legendary commander of the 3rd West Cork Brigade, one of the I R A's most feared fighting units during the War of Independence.

Shortly after Cosgrave began to speak just after eight o'clock the first stones began to fly from the Republican crowd, and Carroll's men, in two waves, began to move down the street. The crowd turned to face the police and three or four men fell under a hail of missiles, but by the time the second wave of police hit the crowd with batons flailing the street was already emptying. Forty civilians and a dozen guards were injured but, remarkably, there were only two arrests. This absence of large-scale arrests was to be a feature of Gárda policy against the I R A in these months. It reflected a lack of confidence on the part of the police that their prosecutions would be allowed to go ahead. The distinction between Fianna Fáil and I R A was an academic one in the eyes of most of the Guards at this stage, and taking supporters of the government through the courts in large numbers was an unproductive practice.

The Guards' lack of faith in the courts was, if understandable, probably less than justified. Conor Maguire, the Attorney-General, after an initial period of indecisiveness, had already begun to prosecute very firmly for cases of disruption and violence at political meetings.

De Valera himself had set the tone of government policy at the Fianna Fáil Árd Fheis in November when he appealed to his supporters to accept the principle that their opponents also had the right to organise and hold public meetings. He urged the Fianna Fáil party to 'set its face against action which would prevent our opponents from being heard'. After the Kilmallock riots of 9 October thirty-one persons had appeared in court charged with various offences, and after the scenes in Cork on 6 November, a congratulatory directive had been received by the local detective department from the Attorney-General's department.

On the whole, however, it was a period of indecisiveness and uncertainty during which the Civic Guards were obliged, for the most part, to sit back and watch crime and violence increase on both sides of the political divide. Nor was there any clear directive from de Valera, Ruttledge or Broy as to what the Guards were to do in situations of potential violence. The only occasion on which de Valera had specifically asked O'Duffy to step up police action had been during the general election campaign of 1933. Conor Maguire also called on the Guards to be firm in putting down crime, telling them : 'The nation's honour is at stake. . . It ought to be possible for everybody to come here and state his programme without interference. That is fair play and justice.'

As a general rule, law enforcement policy for these months varied from division to division as each Chief Superintendent or Superintendent took it upon himself to decide how best to keep bloodshed off the streets without antagonising either his former or his new political masters.

A few officers brought things to their logical conclusion in the courts in the full knowledge that they were risking the displeasure of the government but for most of the two hundred middle-grade officers spread throughout the countryside police activities between August 1932 and June 1933 represented no more than a simple holding operation pending the parting of the ways between de Valera and his militant I R A supporters.

From de Valera's accession to power in August 1932 until the summer of the following year the pace of political events in Ireland—particularly on the streets—was set by the I R A. But from the end of July 1933 it was the Army Comrades Association which was to make the running in the struggle for political power and the I R A was to find itself dwarfed by the organisation which had arisen largely in reaction to its own existence. In a period of six to eight months the I R A ceased to be the major security threat to the de Valera government and by the autumn of 1933 the Civic Guards were facing a new and unknown quantity which they did not know whether to regard as friend or enemy.

The A C A had been growing steadily since the end of 1932 and had already developed into a powerful national body by the time O'Duffy ceased to be Commissioner of the

Gárda in March 1933. His views of the organisation were not
flattering and on several occasions he had warned the
government that it was extensively armed and dangerous,
but it is probable that after his dismissal by de Valera he
regarded it as the only instrument by which proper government could be restored to the state.

In spite of O'Duffy's natural policeman's reservations about
the A C A and in spite of the readiness with which members
of the former Cosgrave government would have been prepared to ditch him had they been returned to power in 1932,
the A C A had little difficulty in persuading him to accept the
leadership of the organisation in July 1933. O'Duffy was
no doubt confident of his ability to eliminate whatever blem-
ishes he saw in the organisation, and his dismissal by the de
Valera government left him in no doubt that the new government was not fit to rule. It was his duty, he believed, to rid
the country of the divisive influence of party politics.

The appointment of O'Duffy as head of the A C A was
the greatest boost which the movement had received to date,
although in some respects the decision of the organisation to
invite him to lead them was a gesture of despair. It reflected
a belief on the part of the Cumann na nGaedheal party and
their adherents that the January election had sealed their fate
as a political force for some time. Cumann na nGaedheal had
become rather threadbare of talent since the assassination of
Kevin O'Higgins and there was nobody among its ranks capable of filling the void left by his death. O'Duffy, with his
colourful personality, his immense organising ability and his
noted sporting, military and police career, might be the catalyst
necessary to start a movement which could hurl de Valera
and his assorted supporters into political oblivion.

The leadership of the A C A was a tempting offer to this
vain and egocentric man and it was precisely the kind of
challenge that O'Duffy would relish. Nobody had questioned
his anguish and concern at the rise in violence and crime and
the spread of what he saw as antichristian ideas under de
Valera. Here he was asked to lead a crusade against these

evils; he was being entrusted with the task of rescuing and protecting the glorious heritage of the Catholic Irish people. It was a challenge which he took up with eagerness but which was to prove in the long term too much for his stability and balance. It was a challenge which brought out in O'Duffy the very worst of those symptoms of which his critics had long complained during his years as Commissioner of the Gárda Síochána. But it would be some time before this became apparent; and with the announcement that General O'Duffy was assuming leadership of the Army Comrades Association there was a massive increase in membership and activity throughout the country.

The appointment of O'Duffy as Director-General of the A C A was the final drawing of the lines for the struggle which was to continue until 1935 between the two major forces in modern Irish politics. For years left-wing elements, Communists, Saor Éire and the I R A had strengthened themselves and built up their resources until their influence had spread through Irish life in great disproportion to their relatively small numbers. The outrage and anger of the right wing had heretofore been expended in non-productive, disorganised ways but now, with the creation of a strong, disciplined new movement, the right wing was going to hit back.

On 20 July 1933, the day he was formally announced as Director-General of the A C A, O'Duffy outlined the constitution of the movement, the name of which was now to be changed to the National Guard. It was to have a strong accent on youth and the formation of the character of young Irish men and women. It was pledged to promote the unity of Ireland, to oppose unreservedly all Communistic and alien influences, and to maintain public order. It stressed its basic recognition of the legitimacy of the Free State and promised co-operation with its agencies, army, police and civil service. It guaranteed certain advantages to farmers and undertook to 'awaken throughout the country a spirit of combination, discipline, zeal and patriotic realism which will put the state in a position to serve the people efficiently in the economic and social spheres'. As early as April 1933 the movement had adopted as its symbol the blue shirt or blouse, and already de Valera had made it clear that he regarded this as a uniform and that, as such, its wearing would not be permitted.

But the new organisation had confronted the Guards with something new. Here was a movement which clearly stood by the law—at least at this early stage—and which had even supported the Guards on the streets. Superintendent Holland of Kilmallock had given it as his opinion in the court case which followed the October rioting there that had it not been for the action of Blueshirts—as they had already become known—his tiny force of guards would have been overwhelmed. Moreover, they had not committed any offences so far, beyond being involved in a few riots, and even those had not been of their own making. And, above all, there was the immeasurable bond of sympathy and understanding between the Guards and the Blueshirts. They had both originated from the Treaty side and they were both bitterly opposed to militant Republicanism whether sponsored by the I R A or by Fianna Fáil. The Blueshirts and the Guards were natural allies.

There were to be instances in which Blueshirts in the Midlands and the West were allowed the use of Gárda facilities such as phones and transport, but the alliance between the police and the new organisation could never be a true one and these were isolated occurrences. The rigid discipline of O'Duffy and his unceasing exhortations to the Guards to remember that they served no party but the government it pleased the people to elect had gone too deep for the force to be swayed. At best, there was to be a sympathy within the Gárda with the ideals of the Blueshirts and their supporters but the Fianna Fáil government had no way of knowing that such sympathy would not be translated into action. It was as much to test the Gárda-Blueshirt relationship as anything else that the government in late July ordered a revocation of personal guns held by former Cumann na nGaedheal ministers and certain Blueshirt supporters.

The significance of the revocation order was symbolic more

than real and it served as a useful test run for the Fianna Fáil government to gauge public opinion and feeling within the police force. On the morning of 30 July police directed by Superintendent Charles Dunleavy called on the homes of former Cumann na nGaedheal ministers in Dublin with revocation orders for the arms which most of them had held since the assassination of Kevin O'Higgins. There were, as might have been expected, cries of indignation from men who had been at the best of times obvious targets for the guns of assassins and revenge squads and who, now out of office, were more vulnerable than ever.

The Dublin Guards carried out their work effectively and thoroughly. It was as well, for unknown to the raiding parties of detectives, the weapons were carefully checked when returned to stores to ensure that their serial numbers tallied with those of the guns issued six years previously. Any attempt to withhold weapons, with or without the collusion of the police, or to substitute others would have been immediately spotted.

The real test of the police, however, was to come in the following two days when superintendents all over the country were instructed to take similar measures against Cumann na nGaedheal supporters in many districts. There were raids in Limerick, Ballina, Claremorris, Galway, Oughterard, Dundalk, Tipperary, Listowel and Cork. In Ballina, for some still unexplained reason, the Free State air force circled the town while the raiding operation was in progress and arms which had been issued to local banks for their protection were also called in. The operation went smoothly and without incident. The government could not have been anything other than entirely satisfied.

Among the guns called in had been the official weapon still held by General O'Duffy, as well as several personal automatics and revolvers which he had collected during his years as Commissioner of the Police. He had at first refused to hand over the guns, pointing out rather reasonably that having held the position of chief of police for ten dangerous years he was in constant danger of revenge attacks. Moreover, he stressed, if there were any weapons in need of seizure by the police they were the guns now being flaunted almost openly by the I R A.

There was a great deal of sympathy within the officer corps of the Guards for O'Duffy's point of view. Even if the Blueshirts were armed, they had heretofore used those arms only in self-defence, and even that had occurred less than half a dozen times. In virtually any Gárda district in the country the Guards, if they so wished, could swoop on half a dozen genuine gunmen whose firepower was far in excess of that of the small arms held under licence by the supporters of the former government. But nobody was under any illusions—least of all the Guards—as to the purpose of the revocation orders. Apart altogether from testing the police, their purpose was to show the Blueshirts that Fianna Fáil was in charge and that the government would not tolerate the emergence of a military body in opposition to its forces.

Meanwhile street fighting had become an almost nightly occurrence in Dublin as I R A supporters continued their efforts to silence the National Guard and Cumann na nGaedheal and as the newly militant forces of the right wing began a series of attacks on Communist and allegedly subversive groups. Driven on by events on the continent, anti-Communist hysteria reached a peak in Dublin in the spring and summer of 1933. Indeed, it was commonly believed in the detective division of the Guards that de Valera had been ticked off by the papal nuncio over his treatment of Inspector O'Connell and Colonel Hogan, who had been, after all, in the vanguard of the campaign against atheistic Communism and its attendant evils.

On the night of 29 March—coincidentally the date of the acquittal of Hogan and O'Connell—crowds attacked the Connolly Hall in Great Strand Street in Dublin, the headquarters of the revolutionary workers' group. Over two hundred guards had to be called in to disperse the crowd which had been whipped up by the exhortations of speakers, in-

cluding one or two priests, at the corner of Abbey Street and
O'Connell Street. There was fierce fighting as the demon-
strators hurled rocks, timbers and firebombs at the hall. The
guards replied with repeated baton charges and Connolly Hall
was left standing for at least one night. The following night
the attack was repeated and the guards were obliged to use
their vehicles as battering-rams to break the rush of the
mobs. There were more baton charges and the skirmishings
continued later on in the area of the city centre. But the ring of
police around Connolly Hall held firm and although the
firebombs caused extensive damage to woodwork and the
exterior of the building, it was not damaged structurally. There
were similar sporadic outbursts during the following three
months and a particularly bad outbreak of violence was to
occur in July. A group calling itself St Patrick's Anti-Communist League was prominent in the disturbances, and one
speaker on behalf of the League told his listeners at Abbey
Street Corner that two thousand Communists roamed through
Dublin on Friday nights distributing Soviet anti-God money to
the Communist cells throughout the city.

Thus by July the political climate was tense, uncertain and
foreboding. The Blueshirt organisation had grown in strength
and consolidated itself in opposition to the I R A-Fianna Fáil
alignment. The I R A had emerged into the open, at least
temporarily, under the umbrella of Fianna Fáil, and de Valera
was quietly biding his time, broadening his base of support and
edging towards the point where he would be able to shed the
I R A and drive them back into the political wilderness.

In July 1933 the Gárda Síochána was passing through the
most dangerous period of the transition from Cumann na
nGaedheal government to Fianna Fáil government. The worst
fears of de Valera's critics—and the Guards were among the
most vigorous of these—had been realised. The I R A had
emerged emboldened and restrengthened. Violence on the
streets had increased and the normal processes of law had been
set at nought in de Valera's endeavours to avoid an immediate
breach with the I R A. The former Commissioner of the force,

its very spirit and guiding light, had set himself firmly on a course of political action whose primary aim was to topple the government from power. In short, the country was dividing as it had not been divided since the Civil War. The middle ground was rapidly shrinking and the community was splitting, going either for de Valera or O'Duffy.

The possibility of a mass upheaval of the Guards to support O'Duffy was never very great, but what was remarkable at this juncture was the absolute decision of the members of the force to continue in support of a government with whose policies they disagreed and whose origins they detested. It would be naïve to suggest that the Guards were all motivated by an unshakeable adherence to the strict principles of parliamentary democracy. The nature and structure of the force, with its strength divided into small station parties, most of which consisted of between two and ten men, was such that a widespread revolt within the Civic Guard would have been almost impossible to organise, and the best any rebel group could hope for would be a spontaneous movement of support among their colleagues elsewhere once news of any attempted coup reached them. Even if the Guards had wanted to turn against the de Valera administration, they would have found it extremely difficult to organise any large-scale gesture.

Moreover, most of the Guards were now men in their middle and late thirties, with young families and wives to support— hardly the stuff that revolutions are made of, especially the kind of revolution which could turn out to be confined to one station or division while the remainder of the force looked on.

But on the other hand it would be less than fair to ascribe the Guards' acceptance of de Valera's right to rule as mindless indifference or simple self-interest. The pressures on the force to turn against the Fianna Fáil government were considerable, and O'Duffy had begun to argue plausibly that the privileges and the rights of a democracy could hardly be extended to a party which had long refused to accept the principle of democratic rule. In a number of districts, particularly in Tipperary and North Cork, prominent Blueshirts had made clandestine approaches to Gárda officers with offers of guaranteed promotion once a change of government would be effected, provided in the meantime they co-operated with the movement. And if the likelihood of the Guards resigning *en masse* to support O'Duffy was slight, there was always the much more real possibility that the force's basic sympathies with the Blueshirts would effectively prevent them from operating with full enthusiasm and efficiency on behalf of de Valera. There were, of course, a small number of incidents of this nature, but on the whole the Guards were to serve the new government as efficiently as they had the old. The principles inculcated by O'Higgins and O'Duffy had gone deep into the force and the stability of the Guards in these vital months was to be one of the major factors in the resolution of the Blueshirt crisis.

O'Duffy was to put the Guards to the full test of their loyalty to the principle of a non-political police force very shortly after his acceptance of the leadership of the National Guard. On 25 July he announced that on 13 August the organisation would hold a commemorative ceremony on Leinster Lawn in memory of Griffith, Collins and O'Higgins. The annual commemoration had been a tradition under the Cumann na nGaedheal government but it had not been held in 1932. When O'Duffy mentioned his expectation that 20,000 Blueshirts would be marching, the possibility of a coup and an attempted takeover of government buildings began to be mentioned freely in political circles. Whether de Valera subscribed to the fears that O'Duffy might attempt such a coup is uncertain but it is clear that the government decided that on 13 August there must finally be an open confrontation with the Blueshirts.

Immediately O'Duffy had made his announcement, Commissioner Broy was summoned to meet de Valera and Ruttledge, the Minister for Justice. They wanted to know what the attitude of the army and the Guards would be if O'Duffy managed to gain even temporary control of the centre of power at government buildings. If O'Duffy chose to make Leinster

House another General Post Office, Ruttledge put it, would the supposedly non-political forces of the state refuse to move against him? Broy was sure the Guards would not initiate any moves against the government. He did not know what would happen in the event of O'Duffy declaring a provisional government from the seat of power. The lot of the Guards had become an invidious one in the past twelve months. Their leaders had been sacked, their members disciplined, and all over the country they had been exposed to the abuse and vilification of their enemies of ten years standing. Broy's own mind on the attitude of the Guards was undecided, and his uncertainty did little to reassure de Valera and Ruttledge.

There was a serious weakness in de Valera's hold over the Guards, for he had not yet managed to replace the intelligence link between police and government which he had destroyed by dismissing O'Duffy and Neligan and by relegating O'Connell to the uniformed ranks. Nor was Broy the best man to keep the government informed of the thinking of the force. He had served all his time in a mainly administrative capacity in charge of the Dublin Metropolitan Division and later at the Phoenix Park depot. He was not well known in the force and he knew none of the officers outside of the Dublin area except for brief meetings at conferences in the depot. Moreover, he had something less than the full support of the detective branch after the dismissal of Neligan. After Broy had been promoted to Commissioner to succeed O'Duffy the direction of the detective branch had been divided between Chief Superintendent Garret Brennan and Superintendent Tom Woods, both skilled and tried police officers but neither with the correct political credentials to be taken fully into the confidence of a Fianna Fáil government at this level. If the Guards as a whole were going to revolt in favour of Eóin O'Duffy, the chances of the government knowing about it beforehand were not very great. The Guards were a great unknown as far as Fianna Fáil were concerned. They had little, if any, knowledge of what was going on within the organisation. The only course open to the government was to give the force an emergency injection of suitable new political blood.

The possibility of infiltrating the Gárda with party supporters had been considered as early as December 1932 because some members of the government felt the Guards might be too enthusiastic in the use of the baton on I R A supporters during the election campaign. But O'Duffy was still Commissioner at that time and would never have countenanced such a course. The suggestion was dropped.

But it was raised again—possibly by de Valera himself—at the end of July as the prospect of a serious clash at O'Duffy's commemorative parade became more of a reality. It was agreed that a definite Fianna Fáil presence would have to be established immediately in the Gárda Síochána. The obvious place to put it was in the Special Branch.

The man entrusted with the task was Oscar Traynor, then on the fringes of government and yet not of it. (He was to become Minister for Posts and Telegraphs later in the year.) Traynor, a tough, capable party-man had sufficient political experience to know precisely what was required in the new police and at the same time he had sufficient contacts with and plausibility among the gunmen to know whom to pick. The initial aim was to bring in a body of men who would serve the dual purpose of supervising the old 'Free State' detectives while simultaneously providing a dependable protection corps for the defence of government buildings and Leinster House. The whole process of selection, recruitment, induction and training for the new recruits took less than three days in all.

O'Duffy's parade was due for Sunday, 13 August, and recruitment began on the previous Thursday night, although rumours had been flying about for several days. Since 1 August the ideal of the unarmed policeman had been unofficially declared dead by the Fianna Fáil government, and fifty extra guards, armed with .303 rifles had been allocated to special protection posts in the vicinity of Leinster House. The newspapers reported that the government was planning

to create a new branch of the Gárda; the government however, would go no further than a confirmation that the force
had been allowed to fall below strength and was now being
brought back up to its authorised level. On 6 August Ruttledge announced that the extra guards at Leinster House were
not 'members of a new body but are drawn from the same
bodies as were formerly called on to provide guards at Leinster
House and government buildings. . . The only result of our
strengthening the Guards is that recruiting may be started
to fill the places of those who have been transferred from
normal duties.'

Thus the legal niceties of the situation were settled. This
was not simply an imposition of party followers on the police
organisation. These were duly recruited policemen, bringing
up to full strength an overworked and undermanned
police force. The only difference was, of course, that these
men, because of the urgency of the security situation, would
be appointed directly by the Commissioner without undergoing
the normal physical and educational tests.

The first group of new police were all either Dublin men
or living in Dublin. Without exception they were noted and
active supporters of Fianna Fáil and many had been until
recently members of the I R A as well, engaged in conflict
with the very police of which they were now to become a part.
Almost without exception they had had unpleasant experiences
at the hands of Fitzgerald-Kenney's 'Cows' and a few had
actually served jail sentences under the Free State government
for their activities. In the main they were from working-class
and lower middle-class districts of the city—the typical areas
of urban Fianna Fáil support. Groups were also selected from
places of employment where there was a tradition of active
Republicanism. Large contingents came from the railway
works at Inchicore, the Dublin Port and Docks Offices and
Clery's, the big department store in O'Connell Street. More
than a dozen members were recruited from a North City
swimming club.

Throughout Friday and Saturday Traynor conveyed his

recruits to the Phoenix Park depot, where they were formally sworn in as policemen. Each man was then issued with a .45 Colt revolver and two hundred rounds of ammunition. They were then transported to the Castle where they received their entire police training in the form of a ten-minute lecture from Chief Superintendent Clarke. Then, armed with the ancient powers of the constable and their .45s, they were rushed off to take up positions around Leinster House. Later in the day selected numbers of the new policemen were allocated to take over protection duties with the members of the Fianna Fáil government and the Guards formerly provided by the 'Free State' Special Branch were taken off and transferred to other duties.

The effect of the new enlistments on the Gárda force as a whole was traumatic. At the Special Detective Unit in Dublin Castle veteran detectives gazed in shocked amazement at their new colleagues dismounting from a lorry which had pulled into the Castle Yard. Almost without exception, they could recognise every face as those of the men whom they had sought out and pursued over the previous ten years. These were the men whom, apart from charging them in open court, they had spied upon, hauled into the Bridewell for long nights of questioning, or knocked from their bicycles with the glancing blow of a patrol car. And apart altogether from the sheer unsuitability of these men for police work, the old Guards asked themselves, how could they possibly be expected to work together as colleagues?

The new policemen themselves were not over-happy about the prospect of walking into what they can perhaps be forgiven for thinking of as the lion's den. Some former members of the D M P detective branch had overheard former members of the S Branch remark wishfully that they would be sorely tempted to shoot the unwelcome recruits as they arrived in the Castle and the D M P men had passed on the warning. Thus the new arrivals entered the Castle with more than a little apprehensiveness and with their Webley revolvers gripped tightly in their hands.

By the morning of Sunday, 13 August, Dublin was securely in the hands of the Fianna Fáil administration through its newly recruited police. Two thousand guards were on duty throughout the city, and Leinster House and government buildings were safe under the guns of the Praetorian Guard, as some of the original police had begun disparagingly to entitle the new detectives (though they were shortly to be universally known by their more famous soubriquet of the 'Broy Harriers').

Three quarters of an hour after midnight on Sunday the government invoked the notorious Article 2a of the constitution to ban the parade and awaited the National Guard's reaction. O'Duffy demurred quietly and the parade was cancelled. The immediate crisis was past, but the struggle between Fianna Fáil and the Blueshirts was only beginning its most vicious and violent phase.

12 Guards versus Blueshirts 1933-35

THE political struggle between the Fianna Fáil party and its Republican adherents on the one side and the Blueshirts and their Cumann na nGaedheal supporters on the other which engrossed the Irish Free State from 1932 to 1935, presented the Gárda Síochána with a problem of public order quite unlike anything which had ever before been experienced by any police force in Britain or Ireland. Virtually the entire community, rural and urban, was divided along bitter party lines which left little room for moderation. The extreme Republicans, imbued with all the lethal determination of a a cause which could not be questioned, refused to concede the legitimacy of Cumann na nGaedheal or Blueshirt viewpoints. The Blueshirts, for their part, were coming to the belief that since the law was being administered in a partisan and unjust manner, it no longer bound them. And yet it was not war. The courts were still functioning, the police still patrolled, the administration of the state went on virtually uninterrupted. When the struggle would be resolved these tools of government would be there to be picked up by the victor. In the meantime—and the dilemma was particularly acute for the police—they had to fend for themselves, largely without leadership, and try as best they could to steer an even course between the two major political groupings.

The period from February 1932 to July 1935 can be divided into four very distinct levels of police action. From the date of de Valera's accession to power until the calling of a general election of January 1933 there was an undeniable police tolerance of I R A violence throughout the whole country. Very often this tolerance was at the expense of a hitherto non-violent A C A, but it was not entirely a matter

of the Guards complying with unwritten and unspoken instructions from their new political masters. The emergency
powers granted to the police under Article 2a of the constitution had been suspended and prosecutions against the I R A
under the ordinary criminal law were extremely difficult because of the ever-present threat of intimidation of witnesses
and jurors. Moreover, the instructions from the Attorney-
General's department, which the Guards were obliged to seek
before proceeding with a prosecution, were often ambiguous
and always slow in arriving, thus having the effect of acting
as a definite brake on the police.

The second period, from January 1933 to August 1933,
saw the Guards take a tougher line against the I R A,
beginning with the general election campaign. But prosecutions against the I R A were still relatively rare and
the A C A's right of free speech was more often secured
through the vigorous use of Gárda batons than through the
normal process of arrest and prosecution in the courts.

The third period, from August 1933 until April 1934, saw
the Guards, now re-armed with provisions of Article 2a, moving with increasing force against both Blueshirts and I R A,
though less frequently against the latter since they were still
a legal organisation, unlike the banned Blueshirts. Nevertheless, although the I R A were still technically within the law,
an increasing number were now being brought through the
courts with the approval of the Attorney-General's department
and, therefore, of the government.

The fourth and final period, from April 1934 until July
1935, saw the ultimate confrontation between the police and
the Blueshirts with frequent shootings, several deaths and
very great violence on both sides. Meanwhile the Fianna Fáil
party had finally split with the I R A and the organisation
had embarked on a series of violent operations which were to
culminate in its being proscribed under Article 2a in June
1936.

The new Fianna Fáil policemen were to become a vital
ingredient of the government's security policy once they took

up duty at the beginning of the third period—immediately after the banning of the parade of 13 August. Irish politics has had a successful reputation as a breeding place for epithets and it was almost inevitable that the new police should become the object of some bright Cumann na nGaedheal mind in an effort to suitably denigrate them. The new Guards almost immediately became known as the 'Broy Harriers'—a combination of their Commissioner's name and that of a famous pack of hounds, the Bray Harriers. Patrick MacGilligan, Cosgrave's Minister for Industry and Commerce, is credited with originating the term when he drew an analogy between the new police and the Black and Tans, the police reinforcements which the Castle had placed among the R I C in the War of Independence. The Black and Tans had drawn their title from another hunting pack and the pun was too good to lose. It had to stick.

McGilligan was being a little less than generous to the new Guards. With a few notable exceptions, they were generally no worse and no better than the men who had filled the ranks of the detective branch since its inception in 1925.

They were older than the recruit policeman should ideally be. Many of them were men in their forties and a few were even in their fifties, with perhaps twenty or thirty years' experience of totally unconnected occupations and for whom police work was something quite new and totally baffling. They lacked proficiency in the many skills which make up the trained policeman and a few still found it difficult to accept themselves as members of a body which they had long detested and reviled. In time, however, many of them were to become first-rate policemen, drawing on the experience of the hunted as well as the skill of the hunter in their new profession. But MacGilligan was probably venting the anger and annoyance of many of the original Guards who now found themselves obliged to work alongside men whom they had looked down upon and classed as criminals. Up to a point, perhaps, their fears and prejudices were confirmed by the very early experiences of the Harriers.

Many of them had joined without any intention of taking up a permanent police career. They were all settled into other lines of work, with wives and families to support and jobs to go back to. For many, the temporary membership of Special Branch was just a gesture, a temporary sacrifice on behalf of the party. A few anticipated that their new role might give them a chance to settle old scores with members of the original S Branch, and this made the exercise worthwhile in the short term. In Dublin Castle it was not uncommon for the Harriers at first to refuse to follow orders from their 'Free State' superiors or to do duty with the original members of the S Branch. In Cork City the intervention of more level-headed Harriers just saved the life of a Blueshirt named Murray who was about to be shot by one of the new detectives. The Harrier, through a combination of drink and excitement, could not remember whether he had been sent to shoot or protect Murray and was dismissed the following day. In one or two districts in Galway and Clare, Harriers presented themselves to their officers with lengthy lists of demands for the better ordering of station life and police work.

Nevertheless, the induction of the Broy Harriers into the Gárda Síochána passed off without serious incident. One or two indignant officers at the depot headquarters in the Phoenix Park were astonished to find on consulting the 1924 Gárda Síochána Act that the whole operation had been carried out in strict accordance with the requirements of law and the Gárda Disciplinary Code.

The immediate threat of major violence or an attempted coup had receded very swiftly after the Blueshirt parade had been banned on 13 August. There was no revolutionary outbreak or declaration of war from the Blueshirts. O'Duffy announced instead that plans were going ahead for the holding of a series of parades in provincial centres on Sunday 20 August, and Ruttledge announced that if the parades went ahead the government would be obliged to ban the National Guard under the provisions of Article 2a. The government again consulted Broy on the advisability of banning the Blueshirts and it was agreed that if the organisation were banned the Guards would be required to operate against it on a nation-wide basis. The Harriers would therefore have to be extended through the country. (They had so far been confined to Dublin.) In the meantime, it was decided that Ruttledge would address the force, taking advantage of a medal presentation ceremony at the depot.

'The government only asks the force to serve the government elected by the people and nothing more,' Ruttledge told the depot staff. 'We do not want to establish either the army or the Gárdaí as partisan political forces. We want to see the Gárdaí and the army as servants of the Irish people and not the servants of any particular government that might come today and get out tomorrow.' Ruttledge's speech was vague and contradictory, telling the Guards on the one hand that they were to serve the government and on the other that they were not, but it was followed up with a detailed circular from Broy to all Chief Superintendents and Superintendents instructing them that the government had decided to proscribe the National Guard and that the most vigorous steps would have to be taken to ensure that illegal meetings would not be held. The Blueshirt parades went ahead as planned on 20 August, and two days later, twenty-four hours before the despatch of Broy's circular, the government announced that the National Guard was banned under Article 2a of the constitution.

The following night O'Duffy addressed a large meeting at Cootehill, Co. Cavan, without any intervention from a sizeable force of Guards and S Branch men who were present. But the next night—24 August—the Chief Superintendent in Waterford prevented O'Duffy addressing a meeting scheduled for the town centre at eight o'clock. A large crowd had gathered but it soon dispersed quietly after some initial jeering and shouting. On the night of Friday, 25 August, another large crowd gathered at Fermoy, Co. Cork, to hear O'Duffy and again the local Superintendent prevented the meeting from beginning. A dangerous confrontation between Blueshirt supporters and Guards seemed inevitable, however, when the crowds refused to disperse without hearing O'Duffy speak. Superintendent Brady finally agreed to allow O'Duffy to make a brief address explaining to his followers that the meeting had been banned and calling on them to disperse quietly. O'Duffy obliged and the crowds broke up. The following Sunday O'Duffy led four car-loads of S Branch detectives on a wild-goose chase around West Cork before finally losing them and addressing a meeting in Bandon.

But this was only the honeymoon. The Blueshirts had not yet decided on a definite policy to counter the government's ban on the organisation, and relations with the Guards had remained good as long as the Blueshirts kept within the bounds of strict legality. The Guards had little complaint about the Blueshirts in most areas, and the Blueshirts had gone to pains to point out that they had no quarrel with the police. Indeed, the Guards had good reason in several instances—as at Kilmallock—to be grateful for the protection of the Blueshirts. But the banning of the organisation in August was the vital turning point in relations between the Guards and the Blueshirts, setting them as it did on a course of certain confrontation which was to last for three years and leave behind it a bitter memory for many years more than that.

From 22 August 1933 the National Guard was an illegal organisation and every Blueshirt a lawbreaker in the eyes of the Guards. From that date onwards the Guards were the potential enemies of the Blueshirts. It was only a matter of time before the situation generated fresh violence, and the I R A, for their part, were prepared to do more than their share in bringing it about.

The month of September 1933 was violent. The I R A were carrying out a campaign against the products of the British brewing firm Bass because of some unsavoury remarks about Ireland which an executive of the company had made in public. The Blueshirts had taken it upon themselves to protect the Bass consignments throughout the country and there were frequent and bloody encounters in the streets. The Guards were pushing prosecutions—of both Blueshirts and

I R A men—through the courts as quickly as possible and for a brief four weeks Broy was able to report to the government that the Guards had things under control. But at the end of September Eóin O'Duffy began to adopt new tactics for the Blueshirts which effectively nullified the efforts of the police and which robbed the prohibition order against the Blueshirts of its effectiveness, as well as injecting a new lease of life into the organisation itself.

O'Duffy had renamed the National Guard the 'Young Ireland Association' and in September the Association merged with the National Centre Party of Frank MacDermot and the Cumann na nGaedheal party to form the 'United Ireland Party —Fine Gael'. O'Duffy was to head the new party and Cosgrave was to lead it in the Dáil. It was evident that the Young Ireland Association was an incorporation of the National Guard and that the United Ireland Party incorporated the Young Ireland Association. And for as long as the Young Ireland Association retained its individual identity within the Fine Gael organisation the prohibition order on the Blueshirts was effectively nullified.

Broy now found himself in precisely the same situation with the Blueshirts as had O'Duffy with the I R A prior to the insertion of Article 2a in the constitution. His police were facing a massive threat of organised lawlessness with little more than the ordinary processes of law at their disposal. In vain he pleaded with the government for a directive for his officers but none was forthcoming. Ruttledge was neither prepared to admit that the Blueshirts had found a loophole nor was he willing to instruct the Guards to proceed under the act. Once more the initiative in maintaining peace was thrown upon the shoulders of the police at local level who were now placed in double jeopardy.

On 24 September in Limerick there occurred what were certainly the most serious disturbances to date when O'Duffy, Cosgrave and James Dillon tried to address a meeting in the city. From the early evening I R A and Fianna Fáil supporters had been gathering in the vicinity of the meeting with the obvious intention of preventing them from speaking. Meanwhile hundreds of blueshirted United Ireland supporters began to range themselves around the platform. In all, the police later reckoned, there were up to 1,500 potential combatants in the street. To deal with the situation Superintendent Reynolds had about four hundred guards drafted in from the divisions of Clare, Kerry, Limerick and Tipperary.

It was typical of the explosive situation with which the Guards were to be confronted over the next eighteen months in towns and cities all over the country. Reynolds had no legal power to ban the meeting and no choice but to let it go ahead. On the other hand, there was a whole range of offences with which he could charge either the I R A leaders or the Blueshirts, but for as long as the two groups held their peace he could not move against either side. It was simply a matter of having to stand by until trouble began.

Shortly before eight o'clock the I R A group attacked the platform and the Blueshirts retaliated with ashplants, staves and knuckledusters. The Guards waded in and a three-sided battle, of a pattern which was to become all too familiar, broke out through the city centre. The I R A withdrew at an early stage and the field was left almost exclusively to the Guards and Blueshirts. Three times the Guards swept the streets and three times the Blueshirts rallied. In one charge Sergeant Morgan went down in a flurry of boots and batons and by the time his comrades came to his assistance he had been stabbed badly in the thigh and abdomen. It was a vicious riot with no quarter given on either side. Unfortunate guards who became separated from their comrades were beaten into unconsciousness, and Blueshirt or I R A prisoners, once taken by the Guards, enjoyed no more pleasurable a fate. There was an ironic turn of events when one of a party of guards who were beating up a prisoner at the back of William Street station suddenly recognised him as Myles Muldowney, one of the detectives who had been sacked over the Kilrush affair a year previously. Muldowney had been employed as a bodyguard for O'Duffy and was unfortunate enough to be caught with a loaded revolver in his pocket by a rear contingent of guards as they left one of the baton charges. Thirty-three people were taken to hospital after the rioting, which went on until the early hours of the morning, but almost miraculously there were no fatal casualties.

Three nights later at Kilrush, Co. Clare, there was more rioting with the Guards again caught in the middle. A group of young Blueshirts had been accosted by men in the main street shouting 'Up the Republic!' the *Irish Times* correspondent reported, and a party of Civic Guards under Inspector Gilroy arrived and formed a cordon to protect the Blueshirts. Shortly afterwards a motor car driven by one of the Blueshirt supporters arrived to take them back to Labasheeda, where apparently most of them lived. It was set upon by a section of the crowd. Stones were thrown and the car windows were smashed by bottles. The guards were eventually obliged to escort the Blueshirts to the police station under a hail of stones and bottles and with cries of 'Up de Valera!', and 'Up the Republic!' from the crowd. Four of the guards were injured by flying missiles and shots were later fired at the station. Finally, the military were called in, and troops with fixed bayonets escorted the Blueshirts out of the town.

Hitherto there had been few charges arising out of the rioting, even though the military tribunals provided for under Article 2a had been set up again to take the place of the ordinary courts. The Guards were in the difficult position that if they prosecuted I R A or Fianna Fáil supporters they would not see the prosecutions concluded succesfully in court or at the military tribunal. On the other hand, since most of the day-to-day violence was still being originated by the Republicans, it would be hypocritical to charge the Blueshirts and let the I R A and Fianna Fáil go untouched. The government, of course, was aware of the Guards' dilemma and for these few weeks was prepared to give tacit support to the police in their policy of rough justice, administered at the end of a baton.

It was a serious and potentially bloody riot at Tralee, Co.

H

Kerry, on the night of 6 October 1933 which finally decided
the Fianna Fáil government to allow the police to utilise the
full provisions of the military tribunal's regulations to deal
with the I R A. The small number of cases which had
been sent through the military tribunals had hitherto nearly
all involved Blueshirts, and the Tralee rioting was to see
the first extensive use of the tribunals against Republican
supporters.

Two hundred guards had fought for five hours in Tralee
with huge crowds which had surged forward again and again
at a platform from which O'Duffy was to have spoken.
O'Duffy himself was badly hurt when a youth reached
through the police lines and slashed his skull with a crowbar.
His car was burned and a grenade was thrown into the Blueshirt crowd. Fortunately it did not go off. The violence was
so great that lorry loads of military had to be sent from Cork
to back up the police under Chief Superintendent O'Duffy
and Superintendent Kelleher; and General O'Duffy and his
aide, Commandant Ned Cronin, had to be given a strong
escort to the county border. On the day following the rioting
an unexploded bomb was found at the rear of the hall where
the Blueshirts were to have had their meeting. Had it exploded, it would have undoubtedly caused a considerable number of deaths and injuries among the crowd.

The Tralee riots, again, had not been marked by any fatal
casualties but the carnage would have been enormous had
the grenade and bomb exploded in the crowded streets.
Moreover, the Guards had taken a terrible hammering, with
over a dozen serious casualties. The government finally ended
its restraint with the Republicans, and fourteen I R A and
Fianna Fáil supporters were sent before the military tribunal.

The Guards, very naturally, were delighted, and superintendents all over the country made preparations to dispose of
their local headaches before the tribunal. But the reaction from
the Fianna Fáil party rank and file was different and perhaps
even more outraged than the government might have anticipated. Public bodies, football clubs and any organisation with

a Republican majority passed resolutions of outrage at this harassment of the defenders of the Republic. A delegation of T Ds from Kerry arrived at government buildings to ask on behalf of their constitutents that the charges be dropped. But de Valera refused to be moved and the delegation went away unsatisfied. *An Phoblacht*, the newspaper of the I R A, which had long been disenchanted with de Valera and already viewed him as a renegade to the Republican tradition, took up the cause of the fourteen Tralee defendants, proclaiming their endeavours to prevent a platform being given to traitors. But once the initial uproar died down, de Valera once more began to enjoy the best of both political worlds, for the charges against the Tralee defendants were relatively light and their sentences were in proportion. Two were in fact discharged under the 'first offenders' scheme and it was popularly believed among the police that the most serious charge of assault with intent to cause grievous bodily harm to O'Duffy was deliberately not brought, since an over-severe sentence might create an even stronger wave of sympathy with the defendants.

The Tralee riots were the cause of vicious allegations and counter-allegations in the Dáil on 12 October, when the government was accused of allowing the country to be plunged into chaos. De Valera's opponents claimed that he was not providing sufficient protection for political figures and that he was allowing mob rule to try to intimidate his political opposition.

He made no detailed reply to the allegations in the Dáil, but three days later, at an unusually well publicised Fianna Fáil meeting in Co. Wexford, de Valera made his government's position towards political violence very clear. To turn to methods of force while the method of election was still open was a gesture of despair, he told his listeners: 'It is no less than a crime against the people.' And then, admitting for the first time that the I R A had been enjoying a degree of tolerance, he went on:

I think you will all admit that the government has not been

too severe in dealing with those people who adopt, or contemplate adopting, force to attain their political aims. But we have a very solemn duty to perform. It is our duty to use all the resources at our disposal to prevent disorder and to avert the violent over-throw of representative institutions. If we failed in that duty we would be guilty of an act of treachery towards the people who entrusted us with power. . . I have repeatedly promised, and I renew that promise today, that we will do our duty.

Almost immediately the police translated de Valera's sentiments into positive action and began to take a stronger line against I R A militants. On 5 November at Balla, Co. Mayo, Superintendent Flynn drew a cordon of guards around a school where a United Ireland meeting was besieged by a Republican crowd. When the Republicans refused to move, Flynn's guards cleared the street in a ten-minute baton charge, and the United Ireland meeting proceeded normally. On 10 December Special Branch detectives near Annagry, Co. Donegal, fired shots at I R A men who had earlier shot at W. T. Cosgrave's car as he made a constituency tour. On 22 January 1934 there were fierce skirmishes in the streets of Athlone as guards baton charged a Fianna Fáil crowd which had attempted to break up an O'Duffy meeting in the town.

But if 1933 had been a violent and confusing year for the Gárda, working without direction and virtually leaderless, 1934 was to bring the force probably to the lowest point in its morale since its establishment in 1922. The Fianna Fáil-I R A axis was splitting very rapidly as a result of ever-increasing hostility between de Valera and his more militant followers. He had shocked and embittered his militant adherents by his policy of eroding support from the I R A, by giving pensions to all veterans of the War of Independence, by his creation of a volunteer service for the army and, above all, by his policy of allowing Republicans to be sent for trial before the hated tribunal. The year 1934 was to see the painful and violent separation of de Valera and the I R A (although another two years were to pass before the I R A was legally proscribed); it was to be marked by a significant further erosion of the principle of the unarmed guard with the establishment of a new armed uniformed corps and with the frequent issue of weapons to ordinary guards; and it was also to bring the Guards, backed by the full vigour of the law, into daily conflict with the Blueshirts and their sizeable and influential supporters among the farming community.

The Free State in July 1932 had defaulted on the payment of the land annuities to Great Britain which had been agreed under the terms of the Treaty of 1921. The move, which was part of de Valera's policy of removing the trappings of colonial rule, resulted in the British placing high import tariffs on Irish goods entering the United Kingdom. In turn, de Valera placed high levies on British goods entering the Free State. The 'Economic War', as it was to be known, was to cause widespread distress and economic hardship through the entire community over the next three years. Exports fell by half and the livestock export trade fell from £18 million in 1931 to £7 million in 1933. By 1934 there were 117,000 people unemployed in the Free State and 30,000 unemployed in Dublin alone. Marches and demonstrations against want and unemployment became frequent in the towns and cities. In November 1932 the Offaly Health Board resigned, declaring themselves powerless to help a crowd of three hundred unemployed men who had appeared at their annual monthly meeting.

But while there was relatively little change in the standard of living of the urban and rural working classes, never at any time far above subsistence level, the larger livestock farmers, who had hitherto enjoyed a degree of relative affluence, suddenly found themselves undergoing extraordinarily hard times. They were cut off from the lucrative cattle markets of Great Britain, and living standards in the ranch-houses and bigger farms began to drop. These were, of course, the groups from which United Ireland and the Blueshirts themselves drew most of their support, and their common opposition to Fianna Fáil was now reinforced by their common worsening economic plight. To counter the hardship brought on by the recession in the cattle trade, farmers in many districts began to withhold payment of rates, hoping at the same time thereby to put pressure on the de Valera government which seemed to them to be hell-bent on wrecking the economic structure of the state.

Although there was no definite policy on the part of either United Ireland or the Blueshirts to withhold rates, this policy was championed in most areas by members of both organisations, and the non-payment of rates became an undeclared issue between the United Ireland alignment and the government.

By the end of 1933, with large sums of rates outstanding in many districts, the government began proceedings against farmers who were in arrears. Sheriff's officers who proceeded to enforce collection of goods or livestock from the offending farmers were physically manhandled and abused and the Guards were called in in large numbers to support the bailiff's parties. The entire twelve months of 1934 were marked by repeated and vicious clashes between guards and groups of farmers, usually headed and organised by local Blueshirt leaders.

Once the police were called in to assist the bailiffs, matters became infinitely more serious for the farmer whose goods were about to be seized. In addition to distraining sufficient stock to cover the arrears of rates, the bailiffs would also take possession of animals or property to cover the costs of their own lorries, the policemen's pay and the transport charges for the police cars. Furthermore, with the depression in the cattle trade, the number of beasts which would have to be impounded to cover even a small rates arrears would be very large as they would fetch only a fraction of their normal market value.

The usual pattern for the Gárda-Blueshirt confrontation was as follows: a Gárda task force would be assembled at the district headquarters and, headed by the local superintendent and several armed Special Branch detectives, would set out towards the property which was to be raided. The Blueshirts, who would have several hours foreknowledge of the assembly of such a large body of police, would fell trees and dig ditches across the roads of their route to delay them, meanwhile alerting as many supporters as possible in the area. In some districts a system of pre-arranged warnings would be sent out by the ringing of church bells. Thus by the time the Guards arrived at the scene there would be a large, hostile and often armed crowd to contend with. Some of the raids were extremely violent. At Bishopstown, Co. Cork, in August 1934 guards under Superintendent Bergin fired ten shots while escorting bailiffs who were executing a writ on the land of a Mr Coverney. A crowd of farmers wielding pitchforks had charged at the police, and as the police cars were engulfed and their windows smashed, the guards opened fire. In September a party of thirty guards under Superintendent Reynolds who were providing an escort for a seizure at Effin, Co. Limerick, were met with a hail of bottles, bricks and stones and were finally charged, cavalry-style, by a troop of Blueshirts on horseback wielding staves. The guards fired over the heads of the horsemen and finally brought down the leading horse with two shots. In October Special Branch detectives fired over the heads of a crowd while protecting a bailiff's party at Kanturk, Co. Cork.

The trouble did not end with the seizure, however, for the confiscated livestock or goods had then to be brought to a sheriff's pound and auctioned. The auctions were, if anything, more violent than the collections, necessitating anything up to a hundred and fifty guards in some cases to protect the auctioneer and any buyer who had the temerity to try to lay hands on his neighbour's stock. More often than not the buyer was a government agent, brought in from outside, who did his business under an alias. Merely ensuring that he left town alive was a task of sufficient magnitude to keep the entire district strength of the police tied up in some instances.

Almost as soon as the Blueshirts adopted their unofficial campaign of non-payment of rates they were to find themselves, as the I R A had been and to some extent were again becoming, the subject of unremitting Gárda surveillance and attention. The final ideological sympathies between the Blueshirts and the police were snapped, for however much they might protest the political nature of their actions as a form of opposition to de Valera's Economic War policy, they were, as far as the Guards were concerned, breaking the law. They were 'beyond the Pale'. As the full force of the law and the strength of the Gárda came to bear on the Blueshirts, United Ireland criticism of the force became more and more frequent in the Dáil. On 9 May and again on 18 May, there were allegations by United Ireland speakers that the Attorney-General was interfering with the Guards and former Cumann na nGaedheal ministers alleged that their police escorts who were supposed to be protecting them, were in fact acting as espionage agents for the government. In June O'Duffy launched a bitter attack on the Guards for their alleged failure to protect one of his meetings at Mullingar, and on 8 July General Mulcahy gave the Dáil a lengthy critique of what he saw as the partisan policies of the police.

The *Irish Times* correspondent in the Dáil remarked of the United Ireland allegations :

There is a significance in the fact . . . that whatever attacks might have been made on the administration of justice generally, they have carefully refrained in the past from implicating the Civic Guards as such. In departing from this policy they supported their case with specific instances. . . Mulcahy was particularly concerned with the methods of the Civic Guards in South Leix. At Ballacolla, which is in this district, the house was informed that it is the practice of persons having disorderly designs against the supporters of the Opposition to congregate upon the window-sill of the local police barracks, while at the neighbouring township of Ballyroan, a Civic Guard who was asked to take a statement from a member of the United Ireland Party who had been assaulted declined to do so on the superficially logical, but hardly convincing plea, that he had no pencil.

There is little doubt that there were some grounds for

complaint by the Opposition. Here and there there were signs that the Guards were beginning to crack under the strain of two years' constant struggle to maintain peace between two organised, armed and often violent groupings, each with its own claim to legitimacy and each demanding of the government and the police the uncompromising liquidation of the other. And there was the sheer physical strain of more than two years of raids, street fights, baton charges and political meetings with guards on duty without a break for anything up to fourteen or fifteen hours at a time. There were long cold and wet nights of checkpoint duty, followed, after perhaps a few hours' sleep, by seizure raids or more political meetings. Provisioning was bad and guards could often go a full day or night without any break for refreshments or a hot meal. Canteens were few and far between and rarely capable of making anything more nourishing than tea.

There were frequent allegations of brutality against the Guards, not all of them unfounded. In April guards in Naas, Co. Kildare, broke up a Blueshirt meeting with what could best be described as unwarranted vigour, and the episode led to accusations and counter-accusations in the Dáil and elsewhere. In Drumsna, near Mullingar, Broy authorised a sworn enquiry into claims that the Guards had maltreated prisoners. There were further incidents in Tipperary, Limerick and Cork. In November, when the government instructed the Guards to break up a demonstration by unemployed workers in Dublin, there were scenes of further violence which reflected little credit on the Guards.

To a large extent the increasing violence between the police and the Blueshirts could be explained by the simple fact that the Blueshirts were now, in many respects, outside the law. In February 1934 a bill had been passed prohibiting the wearing of blue shirts, and many members of the movement were prominent in the campaign to withhold payment of rates. But there was also a marked deterioration in relations between the police and the public at large, once the Broy Harriers began to appear in stations outside the Dublin area. The original two hundred Harriers who had been recruited in the forty-eight hours prior to O'Duffy's parade of August 1933 had been swiftly augmented by a further two hundred recruits from around the country as soon as the crisis had passed. There was, of course, the inevitable scramble for jobs as soon as the word got out that recruitment into the Guards had been set aside for the Fianna Fáil faithful. The recruitment of the second batch of Harriers was, happily, a little less rushed than the former—they enjoyed a full three days' training before being despatched in lorries to various centres around the country.

Most of the Harriers in provincial areas were willing to accept the direction and guidance of their 'Free State' officers. For the latter the main problem appears to have been to find useful employment for these untrained and pretentiously entitled 'detectives', many of whom were quite unsuited to police work. In the main they were accommodated by creating new protection posts and escort duties which they were happy to carry out.

Relations between the two groups of policemen were, on the whole, perhaps better than might have been expected. As a rule, once initial mistrust and hostility was overcome, the two sections worked fairly well together. The older men were in many instances convinced that the Harriers had been sent to spy on them and the Harriers were prudently cautious in dealing with the senior Guards. In the meantime, before the two groups integrated, Harriers and 'Free State' Guards often made separate reports, kept separate filing systems and worked separate patrols. In the very initial stages the Harriers even elected their own sergeants and then passed their decisions along the line to headquarters where the necessary formalities were complied with to confirm their choices.

That the Harriers and 'Free State' Guards got on well at all was surprising, for once the anti-rates campaign got under way it became customary in many districts for the government to send orders directly to their own police—the Harriers—thus by-passing the normal chain of command through

District Superintendents. It was assumed in many districts that the Harriers would take the lead in implementing whatever law enforcement or security policy the government would decide upon, and not a few superintendents abdicated virtually all responsibility, handing over to the Harriers. In other districts where local officers asserted their rank and authority, the Harriers usually complied, but there were clashes which were to become increasingly frequent as 1934 drew to a close and the struggle between the Blueshirts and the government reached its crisis point.

There were no basic policy differences between the original Guards and the Harriers in their attitudes towards the Blueshirts. They were both in agreement that where the Blueshirts broke the law they should be prosecuted. But there was a significant difference in emphasis and approach. The Harriers, being untrained men and only recently converted to the doctrine of law and order, were even less willing than the original Guards to observe the limitations which the law placed on their activities. They were in many instances violent and occasionally brutal, carrying out their orders in the only way they could in the absence of normal police training and discipline. What was worse, however, was that their orders all too frequently came not from professional policemen who might at least see the pitfalls in a given situation but from the government through an assistant principal officer in the Department of Justice. It was an order transmitted through this channel which was to lead to the tragic events at Marsh's Cattle Yard in Cork on 13 August 1934.

It was a typical auction scene of 1934, with a substantial quantity of impounded stock up for sale. A strong cordon of guards surrounded the sale yard and a detachment of Harriers was on duty inside the yard, heavily armed with rifles and revolvers. A lorry, which had been plated with armoured sheeting in a forge at Innishannon, fifteen miles west of the city, was driven through the gates of the sale yard with about a dozen men aboard. They carried ashplant sticks but were otherwise unarmed. Behind them came a cluster of young boys, among them fifteen-year-old Michael Lynch. Without any apparent justification, the Harriers opened fire, hitting seven people and fatally wounding Lynch who died later that day in hospital.

The Harriers had arrived earlier in the day from Dublin, accompanying the buyers who were going to bid for the seized stock at Marsh's Yard. Earlier they had been warned by the Cork City force that demonstrations were expected during the sale and they were, perhaps understandably, somewhat on edge. The leader of the Harriers, a detective called Moore, had asked for extra men to deal with any unexpected trouble, but instead of being given more men his squad was issued with four Lee-Enfield rifles and eight hundred rounds of ammunition. The Harriers were taking their orders directly from the Department of Justice, and the Chief Superintendent in Cork, Fitzgerald, was given short shrift once they arrived in the city. Fitzgerald, for his part, wisely decided to proceed with his own policing arrangements as if the Harriers had not arrived. Hopefully, their intervention was not going to be necessary.

But the tragic sequel to the sale was not simply a question of individual guards losing their heads and firing their rifles in blind panic. Witnesses declared that the Harriers had deliberately fired to kill the men who had come through the gate in the lorry. There were further allegations that young Lynch, having been wounded, had sought the shelter of some tar barrels but was repeatedly fired on by the guards until he was fatally wounded in the stomach.

Marsh's Yard became the *cause célèbre* of the Blueshirts and the bad feeling and hatred which it caused recoiled upon the heads not only of the Broy Harriers but of the Gárda Síochána as a whole. For the remainder of 1934 and right through 1935 relations between the Guards and United Ireland supporters in the Cork area were to become increasingly hostile with frequent brutality and bitterness on both sides. The bad feeling was exacerbated by the government's refusal to hold an enquiry into the incident in spite of pressure from the officer corps of the Guards on Broy and in complete disregard of the most persistent appeals from prominent figures in the area. In June 1935 the Roman Catholic Bishop of Cork, Dr Cohalan, broke the Church's silence on the political struggle and called for a full government enquiry. 'There was not a machine gun or rifle or shotgun among the men in the motor lorry,' he said. 'Michael Patrick Lynch was not of the lorry party at all. Yet the agents of the government fired deliberately at these unarmed men when there was no question of danger of an attack on anybody.' And referring to the wave of anti-Gárda violence which had engulfed the South since the killing, Dr Cohalan added : 'The killing of Michael Patrick Lynch exasperated a multitude of young men. Coercion and crime generate crime and the acts of lawlessness now complained of are not unconnected with the killing of Michael Patrick Lynch.'

The matter might have rested there indefinitely were it not for the decision of Lynch's father to sue Chief Superintendent Fitzgerald and three of the Harriers—Moore, Condon and Rodgers. The decision of Mr Justice Hanna, delivered in April 1937, was a shocking indictment of the Harriers but it probably served to clear the air as the next best thing to a government enquiry. Hanna's judgement may only be fully understood through the reading of lengthy extracts, but there is a lot to be gleaned from the following selection from his judgement. It was clear that the Broy Harriers were not a body for whom the learned judge had developed an undying respect.

From the autumn of 1933, Hanna was of the opinion, a body of armed men, called by courtesy 'Guards' and taking the oath as Civic Guards was formed for the specific purpose of putting into force the powers of the government under Article 2a of the constitution and also, when required, to do special protection duty for individuals. He continued, 'They were not given the training or discipline of the ordinary uniformed guards which is long and effective . . . but I am satisfied on the evidence that these men were selected mainly for their skill and experience with the gun. . . They were uncontrolled and left to their own undisciplined judgement in the use of firearms.'

Chief Superintendent Fitzgerald was 'not quite sure of his position', Hanna went on, and it was clear that the S Branch men had repudiated any authority on his part to interfere with them in any way.

On the 'crucial question of the firing', he concluded:

There is no doubt in my mind that Moore started the fusillade. Coming back from the gate he heard the crash, turned, either called on his comrades to get ready or used some other words which they undoubtedly took as a command or suggestion to open fire on the crowd trapped in the lorry or about the gate. Moore fired forthwith, emptying his revolver at a distance of 25 or 20 yards. He then obtained a rifle from the car and discharged several rifle shots. Condon emptied his revolver and then took his rifle from the car and fired with it out of the window of the sales ring. Rodgers fired from his revolver and continued to fire after being warned to stop by Mr O'Neill, T.D., and until finally stopped by Superintendent Bergin. . . It was alleged that twenty shots were fired in the air, but I do not think any of these men would waste a shot. I believe that all of them fired to kill. . . It is immaterial to this action that the other 'S' men, with the exception of O'Dowd, also took part in this fusillade.

Some of the civilians when they were seeking shelter from the fire ran towards some tar barrels at the right of the gate. One of these was young Lynch. . . He had got into the shelter of a barrel when Mrs O'Neill with great courage ran to help him. . . . After the young fellow had got into some shelter, wounded as he was, some of the 'S' men endeavoured to kill him. Attempted murder is the only expression in law to describe such conduct. . . I certainly cannot hold for a moment that there was any justification for sending fusillade after fusillade of revolver and rifle shots into the men huddled in the lorry and at the three or four men running to escape.

Mr Justice Hanna concluded:

There has been disclosed a very striking and lamentable fact from the standpoint of public safety, namely the deliberate repudiation by these armed 'S' men of the authority and control of the Cork officers. This bears upon their irresponsibility. Surely it cannot be that when seven armed men of ordinary rank are sent out without a sergeant or officer in control to do duty in a disturbed area, where there are a Chief Superintendent and several Superintendents and Inspectors, we are to be told that they are entitled to snap their fingers at those officers and be a law unto themselves. This is not a case of one man or two men protecting the individual but of seven. The fact that Moore and Condon were made sergeants shortly after this occurrence cannot deceive anyone. It is too obvious. An ordinary guard takes years of hard service to attain the rank of sergeant but these two men, notwithstanding their lack of training and knowledge of Guards' duties, are given (I do not say attain) that rank in about a year after joining the force. These 'S' men are not real Civic Guards. They are an excrescence upon that reputable body.

Mr Justice Hanna's judgement was not a blow to the morale of the force, for that was already so low that things could scarcely be worsened. Perhaps in some respects it was almost welcomed by the pre-Broy Guards for it redefined their status and integrity and clearly set a stamp of warning on the direction in which the force was being developed. Since the change of government virtually everything the Civic Guards had attained as a police force in the years 1922–32 had been lost and the police were being forced to view themselves as little more than the unthinking instruments of government security policy. The unarmed guard was a thing of the past, community integration was impossible with the country split in two vicious political camps and the role of the guard as the people's policeman was the farthest thing from de Valera's mind. No sooner had he concluded his struggle with the Blueshirts than he was to turn the resources of the state—and they included the Gárda Síochána—for a final and violent confrontation with the I R A.

By the end of 1935, with the settlement of the Economic War in sight, the level of violence in the community began to fall off. Many areas where Blueshirts and Republicans had faced each other in stormy confrontation over the previous three years were quiet and the Guards were thus able to concentrate their strength and energies in the areas where serious trouble still continued—mainly in North Cork and Tipperary. Cork was still in a mood of justifiable anger over the Marsh's Yard shooting and Blueshirt-Gárda clashes were to continue throughout the county right into the summer months of 1936. But the state of affairs in Cork was exceptional, and two days before Christmas 1935 the government was able to announce that thirty-five prisoners were being released from Arbour Hill detention centre in Dublin because of the 'peaceful conditions' prevailing in the country.

Over the next eighteen months the last traces of the phenomenon of Blueshirtism were to disappear almost as swiftly as the movement had itself grown up in the months after de Valera's accession to power in 1932. In August 1935 the United Ireland Party had split on the issue of O'Duffy's tempestuous leadership and in September O'Duffy himself had resigned, leaving the League of Youth in the unpredictable and inept hands of a small group of malcontents led by Commandant Ned Cronin. It was the end of O'Duffy's role in Irish politics and his abortive attempts to channel the strength of his remaining followers into support for the Spanish Nationalists in the Civil War were followed by his death in 1944 at the premature age of fifty-two.

With the decay of the Blueshirt organisation the lot of the Gárda Síochána in rural areas became an infinitely more pleasant one. The odious tasks of supervising enforced collections and public auctions were ended, and massive public demonstrations with their attendant baton charges and street riots were occasional rather than regular events. Within the force itself a good degree of harmony had begun to develop between the older policemen and the new Broy Harriers and in some districts the arrival of Harriers to augment the existing force had a positive effect on relations between police and people. It does appear that in certain towns in Kerry and Limerick relations between Guards and Republicans had become so bad in the early 1930s that police no-go areas had been allowed to come into existence. These were districts—usually small housing schemes—where the appearance of the Guards in itself was sufficient to cause a riot. As a result the police entered these districts only when directed to do so by the utmost necessity, and even then always in large numbers. There were instances in which the Broy Harriers broke this deadlock in police-public relations. In Tralee, where there was a large body of active Republicans, the Harriers arrived to find a substantial section of the working-class population totally alienated from the Guards. Within a month the Harriers had restored a measure of communication—not with the full approval of their Cumann na nGaedheal colleagues—but nevertheless beneficial in the long term for the Gárda as a whole.

But this benefit to the Gárda Síochána was at best an unexpected by-product of the raising of the Broy Harriers. In virtually every other respect the force was damaged by the turmoil of the 1932-36 period. The principle of a police officer's discretion in instituting proceedings against a suspect was totally overruled by political considerations, and the force as a whole was brought more firmly than ever before under the direct political control of government through the offices of the Minister for Justice and the Attorney-General. During 1934 and 1935 it was accepted practice for the government to by-pass the normal police chain of command by passing instructions direct to the Gárda station parties, and very often such instructions came instead through officials of the Department of Justice. The role of the Commissioner thus lost much of its significance and the important functions of the chief of police tended increasingly to be exercised by the Secretary or other senior officers of the Department of Justice. This tendency was brought to its logical conclusion in 1938 when Colonel Broy was replaced as Commissioner by the Assistant Secretary of the Department, M. J. Kinnane.

There were, furthermore, substantial inroads into the ideal of the unarmed police force. By the end of 1934 both uniformed and detective guards were very frequently heavily armed when taking part in distraining raids or when performing protective duties. Very often, too, platoons of uniformed guards armed with rifles were detailed for duty on the occasions of public processions or meetings. In January 1934 the government had ordered Broy to set up a special armed corps among the uniformed branch of the force—as distinct from the already armed detectives. The *Irish Times* made a scoop of some importance when the paper revealed on 5 January that 'A new section of the Civic Guards, armed with rifles, has been established in Dublin by the Commissioner, Colonel Eamon Broy.' The paper went on to detail the formation of the new unit which was composed entirely of 'young men . . . new to the use of rifles and their carriage'. The newspaper's reporter, who had watched the special corps on parade, described them on the depot square : 'They were being drilled by a sergeant who was also carrying a rifle and four other sergeants were among the recruits under instruction. The detachment carrying rifles, which appeared to be of the Lee-Enfield pattern, paraded with the other recruits at 9 o'clock in the morning and for some time took part in the normal marching and counter-marching exercises. Rifles were carried at the slope.'

Ordinary guards on the beat were frequently being issued with weapons as well, especially in urban areas where the I R A were active. In May 1935 a number of young Republicans who were found painting slogans in Grafton Street in

Dublin drew revolvers on a uniformed guard and were taken aback when he produced his own revolver and fired back at them. In the ensuing gun-battle the guard, John Egan, was wounded, as were two of his assailants. During July, when anti-Protestant rioting broke out in Limerick and Galway as a reprisal for Orange intimidation of Catholics in Belfast, weapons were despatched for use by the police if necessary. The situation in Limerick deteriorated to such an extent that the Guards eventually decided to call in the army. In Galway, where Catholic workers left the mills and refused to return until their Protestant co-workers had been sacked, intervention by local clergy averted major violence, although there were some baton charges.

The Blueshirt threat was receding, but as it did so, the prospect of a violent confrontation between Fianna Fáil and the I R A became inevitable. The I R A was being continually weakened as de Valera built up his own base of support, constantly drawing away by one means or another the fringe supporters of extreme Republicanism. A volunteer reserve for the national army was created, giving young and active men a chance to put on a uniform, fire a few shots and earn the occasional few pounds as well, without being driven into the ranks of the I R A. A scheme of pensions for I R A veterans was set up which was to absolve a multitude of de Valera's ideological sins in the eyes of many of his erstwhile critics.

The I R A hard core, for their part, heartened by the defeat of the Blueshirts and antagonised by what they saw as de Valera's treachery, became bolder and more aggressive as time went on. In December 1934 P. J. McEnery, a Junior Counsel who had prosecuted for the state in a number of military tribunal cases, was taken from his home near Killiney in Dublin by I R A members. He was taken to Arbour Hill, tarred, and chained to the railings with a placard round his neck proclaiming the I R A's disapproval of him.

In March 1935 Republican-inspired elements involved in a strike of Dublin buses and tram-cars fired on uniformed guards in Dublin on two separate occasions without any apparent motivation, and later in the month the Guards mounted a major swoop on I R A officers throughout the country. The government was fast losing its patience with the I R A and over forty of those held in the Gárda swoops were sent to the Glasshouse—the military detention centre at the Curragh military camp. This was the first instance of the Fianna Fáil government moving against the I R A on a coercive basis—as distinct from moving against them after the event of a crime, but it was not to be sufficient to deter the organisation from a course of direct confrontation with the government and the police.

Throughout 1935 the I R A and the de Valera government played a dangerous and sometimes violent game of political shadow-boxing. In February an I R A unit had shot and killed Richard More O'Ferrall, whose father was acting as the agent for the disputed Sanderson Estate, near Edgeworthstown, Co. Longford. The town tenants' association had called on the I R A for assistance in the dispute, and the intention of the I R A unit which called to the More O'Ferrall home on 9 February was well short of murder. A struggle had, however, developed when the I R A men tried to force their way past the front door, and Richard More O'Ferrall was shot in the spine. He died in hospital on 21 February, and a month later the local Gárdaí, assisted by a Special Branch squad from the Castle, arrested four local men and charged them with the killing. Two juries failed to find them guilty, and the whole episode occupied the attentions of the police, the Attorney-General and the government for the greater part of a year. The police—and in particular the Special Branch—believed that the Edgeworthstown murder should convince the government of the necessity for banning the I R A, but de Valera held his hand for a little longer; the ultimate break between Fianna Fáil and the I R A was not to come until the following June. For the time being, the government agreed, every device short of an outright proscription of the I R A was to be used to keep the movement in check.

The old Special Branch in the Castle was reorganised and

strengthened under Superintendents McGloin and O'Neill, and as original Civic Guards and Broy Harriers became unified in the face of the common I R A enemy, the skilled and able detectives of the old regime, displaced from the Castle to make room for the Harriers, were gradually brought back to their old units. Michael Gill, who had been reduced to the rank of detective guard and sent to Waterford, was reinstated in the Castle and shortly afterwards promoted to Inspector. Philip McMahon, who had been shunted off to the depot to an administrative job, was brought back to active enquiries and also promoted. The Special Branch was gradually brought up to a peak of efficiency to be ready for the day when the final inevitable crunch would come. In fact, if not in law, the I R A was an illegal organisation from 1934 onwards and was treated as such by both police and legal officers of the state. It was no mere slip of the tongue when a Senior Counsel, prosecuting five I R A men for various offences in April 1935, described them as belonging to 'an illegal organisation'.

The final incident which brought about the outright proscription of the I R A was the murder in March 1936 of seventy-two-year-old Admiral Boyle Somerville followed by the killing in April of a young former I R A member in Waterford, John Egan. Admiral Somerville's crime was to provide references for local boys in the Skibbereen area who wished to join the Royal Navy and young Egan's offence was to disengage from his local I R A unit at Dungarvan. The two killings—and in particular that of Egan, who was shot down in the street without warning and in cold blood—appalled the country. In May the cabinet decided in principle to invoke the terms of Article 2a of the constitution and it was agreed that the ban should be imposed on the organisation in the days preceding the annual Wolfe Tone commemoration ceremonies at Bodenstown. In this way it was hoped to avoid a confrontation at the commemoration by not allowing the I R A too long to re-evaluate their position after the imposition of the ban. On 18 June, three days before the commemoration, the I R A was declared an

illegal organisation under Article 2a of the constitution.
The proscription of the I R A was not immediately followed
by a flood of arrests, and the Guards proceeded against the
I R A at much the same relatively leisurely pace they had
followed since the abatement of the Blueshirt violence. The
policy of the Special Branch, now composed of twin elements
of Cumann na nGaedheal and Fianna Fáil, firmly welded
together, was to keep an information flow of the highest
quality and accuracy pouring into the ears of their Commissioner and of the government. There were of course the inevitable clashes and skirmishes between I R A men and police
which did little to improve mutual regard and respect. The
zeal with which the Broy Harriers had taken up their security
duties on behalf of the Fianna Fáil government had earned for
them in the eyes of the I R A an even deeper hatred and resentment than that held for the members of the original Special
Branch. Moreover, their lack of experience of dangerous
police duties had already resulted in prisoners being injured as
much through ineptitude as through malice. In June 1937
there was yet another such incident when a party of detectives
making an arrest in Clanbrassil Street in Dublin panicked
and shot dead an I R A man, Peter McCarthy, whom they
were attempting to take into custody. In retrospect it appears
that the incident was genuinely an accident but to the I R A
it was nothing short of cold-blooded killing of a defenceless
comrade.

How the ugly war between police and I R A might have
gone were it not for the decision of the illegal army's leadership to carry out an English bombing campaign in 1939
cannot now be determined but it is certain that even without
the opening of a 'British front' by the I R A, de Valera would
have demanded stronger action from the police because of the
deteriorating political situation in Europe as a whole. On 16
January 1939 the first of the I R A's bombs exploded on
electrical lines and at power stations throughout Britain. Nine
months later on 3 September Britain went to war with Germany, and a completely new set of factors now governed the

relationship between de Valera and the I R A and the relationship between de Valera and the main combatant powers, Britain and Germany. From the beginning it was clear that the de Valera government intended to follow a path of strict neutrality and the existence of the I R A as an active force was the biggest single threat to that policy.

Confronted with the crucial necessity of a watertight security system, de Valera replaced his Minister for Justice P. J. Ruttledge, with Gerry Boland, a tough hard-working veteran who had stood by de Valera's side since the dreary days of opposition in the early 1920s and who had plenty of experience dating from those days of the things which made a police security operation effective. It was a double advantage that he had learned about security from the receiving end, for in the days of David Neligan's S Branch men Boland had been a marked man by the Cumann na nGaedheal authorities. Chief Superintendent Seán Gantley was placed in charge of the Special Branch at Dublin Castle and Chief Superintendent Patrick Carroll, a practised and highly competent officer, was appointed to the vital post of Chief Superintendent 'C3' with overall responsibility for political crime and the security of the state.

Gantley, a supremely efficient and capable officer, found that the Special Branch section was weak in many points and that not a few of the detective staff were simply putting in their time with little or no effort. In the short period of a few months he had reformed the unit, transferring several members whom he considered unsuitable and improving the information and command systems. He was to meet an untimely end in 1948 when he was accidentally shot by one of his own detectives while leading a raid on a foundry premises in Dublin's dockland where an armed criminal was reported to be hiding.

In a situation of international warfare the Guards now found that in addition to the endemic problem of the I R A there was also a problem of espionage on behalf of the major powers. A small squad of eight men, comprising some of the Special Branch's most able and painstaking investigators, was set up as a counter-espionage unit, working in close liaison with the intelligence section of the army. Over the next four years this unit carried the burden of protecting the security of the state from the combatant powers, and while it fulfilled its functions with impressive efficiency, its methods of operation throw an interesting sidelight on Irish neutrality.

The problem of counter-intelligence in neutral Ireland during the Second World War was essentially one of catching German, British and American agents. But while German agents, once taken into custody by the police, were interned for the duration of the war, British and American agents, almost without exception, were quietly released and returned to England or allowed to slip across the Border into Northern Ireland where there were U S military bases. Usually the Allied agents were given a thorough grilling by Special Branch or army intelligence officers before they were allowed to go free, and while the information thus elicited with the application of only a very little pressure was limited, it was nevertheless valuable to the Irish authorities in tracking down German agents and their contacts. The Germans, were, of course, of infinitely more concern to the Gárda and army than were Allied agents, for the likelihood of any significant link-up between the I R A and the Allies was small while a similar link-up with the Nazis could utterly destroy Ireland's status of neutrality. The policy of the Special Branch towards foreign agents during the war years was perhaps one of the clearest proofs of the contention that Ireland was 'neutral for the Allies'.

Meanwhile, the Gárda authorities had been given the task by the government of setting up a locally based security force which would fulfil the civil functions of an unarmed home guard and which would operate as an auxiliary to the police where necessary. Responsibility for the project was given to W. R. E. Murphy, now senior Deputy Commissioner of the force, and by the end of 1940 Murphy had constructed an auxiliary police known as the Local Security Force or L S F. Almost 25,000 strong, it was directed throughout the country by the Gárda's District Superintendents and until 1945 it carried out valuable security and patrol functions, thus releasing the Guards for more pressing police work in the disturbed conditions of the time.

The L S F, of course, had its fair share of catastrophe as might be expected in any such volunteer organisation. Red alerts were periodically flashed to Dublin resulting in full army mobilisation as some over-imaginative member would report huge landings of Germans or Allied troops. Cocks of hay which were caught up by a freak whirlwind in the midlands one evening had become German paratroopers in the eyes of the L S F by the time the incident was reported to Dublin. Board of Works officials on survey work along the west coast were taken for agents signalling to submarines and marched off in spite of their protestations to the local police station. But in spite of these periodic hullabaloos, the L S F on the whole was considered a valuable asset by the government and took credit for numerous successes in locating crews of crashed aircraft, in supervising salvage and search operations in coastal areas and in carrying out all the many routine tasks necessitated by a crisis of national security.

The Guards responded almost immediately to the opening of the I R A's bombing campaign in Britain, sweeping up several dozen men in the period January to April 1939. Most of them were processed through the military tribunal into the Curragh where even in the spring and summer of 1939 conditions were at least tolerable. But once the vital issue of neutrality arose after the outbreak of war in September, the Fianna Fáil government resolved that there would be no element of leniency in dealing with the I R A. The prisons and internment camps would not be allowed to become institutions of higher learning where the I R A could re-group and re-educate themselves. By the end of 1939 I R A prisoners in the Curragh and other detention centres throughout the country, mainly Portlaoise prison, had begun to suffer the full pains of punitive incarceration, conducted with only slight concessions to the principles of humanitarianism or mercy. The open, chatty compounds of former years were gone, and the relatively easy security and the reasonable conditions of food and accommodation were at an end. Prisoners were now confined in individual cells, blocked off from the sunlight and the company of their fellows, in a concrete world without time, without noise, without change. For the less important detainees there was still the Curragh, but even there conditions of extraordinarily strict security prevailed.

It was the conditions in the Curragh and at Portlaoise which, more than any other single factor, provoked the most serious and bloody conflict between the I R A and the Gárda Síochána since the foundation of the state. The period 1940–44 saw more than a dozen guards killed or seriously wounded by I R A guns and an almost equal number of I R A men either killed in open gunfights with the police or subsequently executed.

Supported by extensive powers under the new Offences Against the State Act, the Guards moved in on the I R A with a vengeance during the early months of 1940. The new act, while incorporating virtually all the provisions of the Cumann na nGaedheal legislation of previous years, gave additional powers for the detention of suspects and gave the government extensive censorship rights as well as powers to prohibit the holding of certain inquests. The surveillance and enquiries section of the Special Branch was strengthened until Gantley was sure that the I R A was adequately penetrated. At the end of 1939 Boland was able to report to the government that the police had the whole I R A organisation under surveillance, capable on the issuing of the appropriate orders, of rounding up the entire leadership.

The acid test of Boland's claim was to come probably sooner than the police might have wished. On the night of 23 December the I R A cleaned out the army's ammunition store at the Magazine Fort in Phoenix Park, escaping with 1,084,000 rounds which were rapidly distributed around the country almost before the security authorities had grasped the full dimensions of the raid. But once the police machine had become activated, the missing ammunition was recovered with a speed which can have left no doubt as to the effectiveness of the security network which the police had woven about the country. By the end of January the Guards had in fact recovered more ammunition than was actually stolen in the raid, and, as an added bonus, over two dozen I R A men were taken into the net on various charges. Perhaps of greater satisfaction to the police themselves was the capture of an I R A radio transmitter in Dublin, found in the course of searches for the Magazine Fort ammunition.

The bulk of the Magazine Fort ammunition was recovered by the Guards through simple routine detective work based on extensive and unrelenting surveillance of the I R A over the previous year. Even in the smallest towns and villages active I R A men were the subject of almost constant attention from the police and not infrequently from paid police agents among the civilian population as well. Not only did the Guards employ agents out of official funds, but many were paid out of guards' personal salaries on the frequently realised expectation of the policeman that he could make good his loss out the official reward fund which was distributed periodically among zealous and particularly efficient officers.

There were, as might be expected, instances of violence arising directly out of this intensive police vigilance on men who were, more often than not, armed and nervous. On 2 January 1940 Guard Tom Roche was shot dead in Patrick Street in Cork while shadowing Tomás MacCurtain, son of the Lord Mayor martyred during the War of Independence. In August two Special Branch detectives, Richard Hyland and Patrick McKeown, were shot dead in Dublin while raiding an I R A training centre located at 98a Rathgar Road. A third detective, Pat Brady, was seriously wounded. Two other members of the raiding party, Detective Bob Mullally and Detective Dick Wilmot succeeded in arresting three of the I R A men who had been using the house, and two of the captured men, McGrath and Harte, were subsequently executed for the murder of the two detectives.

Each month was now marked by fierce and bloody skir-mishes between the I R A and the security forces, in particular with the Guards. In April the I R A succeeded in placing a bomb in Special Branch headquarters in the Castle which injured five detectives when it exploded without warning near the radio room.

In May there was a wild gun-battle in Merrion Square when an I R A party shot up two detectives who were carrying confidential mails to the British Embassy. Firing from the cover of the lamp-posts, the two detectives, William Mc-Sweeney and William Shanahan, held off the attackers with their revolvers and sustained serious wounds themselves. Both men were subsequently awarded medals in recognition of their defence of state mails. During the autumn there were bank raids in Dublin with further exchanges of gunfire be-tween the police and the raiders. Most of the I R A's casualties were in Portlaoise prison or the Curragh internment camp, where half a dozen men either starved themselves to death or died in violent incidents during the course of the war. But they had their casualties on the streets as well. In August 1940 an I R A prisoner, John Kavanagh, was shot as he escaped with two others from Cork jail. In July 1943 another I R A man, Jackie Griffiths, was shot dead in circumstances which have never been fully explained when he encountered a Special Branch patrol in Holles Street in Dublin.

The uniformed section of the Gárda Síochána was, of course, largely insulated from these violent incidents which were concentrated for the most part in the two cities of Dublin and Cork. For the ordinary guard the war years were a period of dull and unpleasant routine work, necessitating long and irregular hours of duty. Under the Emergency Powers Act a whole host of new regulations had to be enforced by the Guards. They had virtually full responsibility for supervising rationing in certain vital areas and there was a major problem of black-marketeering which also fell on the shoulders of the force. But on the whole the Guards were enjoying a period of relatively good relations with the community, which was perhaps surprising in view of the ferocity and viciousness with which the I R A-Special Branch vendetta was being played out in Dublin. Perhaps the most cold-blooded episode of that vendetta centred on the killing of Detective Sergeant Dennis O'Brien as he left his home at Rathfarnham, Co. Dublin, on the morning of 9 September 1942.

O'Brien had been a Broy Harrier whose intimate and recent knowledge of the Republican movement had been put to full and effective use in tracking down the I R A, once the political go-ahead was given in late 1939. Rightly or wrongly, the I R A believed that he had been personally responsible for the debacle at Rathgar Road in August 1940 in which the two detectives died and which resulted in the executions of McGrath and Harte. Nor was this his only crime in the eyes of I R A. Together with Gantley and Inspector Michael Gill, O'Brien had been one of the most relentless and thorough scourges of the movement, pulling off one coup after the other. As O'Brien walked to his car at 9.45 on the morning of 9 September a volley of shots swept across the garden wounding him in the head and chest. He was dead within minutes.

The killing of Detective Sergeant O'Brien was possibly the only fully premeditated and cold-blooded street killing of this turbulent period. A straight gunfight was one thing, and both I R A and Special Branch had lost men in this fashion, but the shooting of O'Brien was a deliberate planned assassination. The full circle of tragedy was completed, as might have been expected, by an arrest and execution—of Charlie Kerins, Chief of Staff of the I R A—in December 1944.

There was little grieving even in the Special Branch for Dennis O'Brien, for he was over-zealous even in the eyes of his own colleagues. But the killing showed the utter ruthlessness which had become a feature of the I R A-police confrontation during the war years. Yet in killing O'Brien the I R A were ironically testifying to the effectiveness of the police operation in breaking up the organisation over the previous three years. It was a revenge killing, nothing more. O'Brien was shot not because of a particular thing he knew or because of a particular case he was prosecuting but because he had been too good at his job. O'Brien and the rest of the Special Branch had made fully effective the draconian system which de Valera and Boland had built to defend themselves against the I R A. Those who would threaten by force the delicate balance which kept Ireland neutral in the war could only be dealt with by the harsh and often brutal discipline of Portlaoise and the Curragh. And without the Dennis O'Briens, the Michael Gills and the Seán Gantleys that system would not have worked. The moral rights and wrongs of their role can be argued indefinitely, but their influence in the execution of government policy at a time of the greatest national crisis cannot be denied. By the time Europe made its peace they had effectively eliminated the I R A as a force in Irish politics for about twenty years to come.

Sources

PUBLISHED material on the history of the Gárda Siochána is very limited, particularly for the early period, and many official sources which could clear up major mysteries remain closed to the researcher. I have therefore depended to a considerable extent on personal interviews with participants in the various incidents recorded, although many people who could have told me much preferred to remain silent for their own good reasons. I give below a list of the persons who assisted me either by way of personal interview or with advice and guidance, and I also include a limited list of published sources and a small critical bibliography.

A number of former members of the Gárda Siochána and the Dublin Metropolitan Police supplied me with signed statements, documents and photographs relating to specific aspects of the book. In particular these related to the Kildare mutiny, the Royal Irish Constabulary, the setting up of the Special Branch in 1925 and the operation of Oriel House in 1922-23. Many former members of the police forces and a number of political figures supplied me with information from personal journals or official records still in their possession. Discretion forbids that these should be detailed.

INTERVIEWS AND ACKNOWLEDGEMENTS

Upwards of two hundred personal interviews were carried out, of which approximately thirty might be said to have been particurlarly valuable. A number of persons were especially helpful in difficult and sensitive areas of my research, and to these I offer a word of particular gratitude. They include Mr

Seán Hughes and Mr E. M. O'Connell who were helpful with their recollections of the Royal Irish Constabulary and the Dublin Metropolitan Police; Colonel David Neligan, Mr Harry Nangle and Mr Phillip McMahon who told me much of the early days of the Special Branch; Colonel Paddy Brennan and Mr Jim O'halloran who traced for me many of the mysteries arising out of the Kildare mutiny; Mr Thomas Collins and Mr James Moore who assisted me in interpreting several particularly difficult questions.

The following are those upon whom I leaned most heavily for personal recollections and experiences: Mr Robert Baxter, the late Mr Gerald Boland, Col. Austin Brennan, Col. Patrick Brennan, Mr Francis Burke, Mr Patrick Carroll, Mr Thomas Collins, Mr John A. Costello, Mr Ernest Blythe, Mr Alfred Flood, Mr Seán Hughes, Mr Joe Kinsella, Mr Patrick McGilligan, Mr Philip McMahon, Mr James Moore, Major-General W. R. E. Murphy, Mr Harry Nangle, Col. David Neligan, Mr Jim O'Halloran, Mr E. M. O'Connell, Mr Philip O'Donoghue, Mrs Una O'Higgins-O'Malley, Mr Thomas O'Leary, Dr Thomas O'Neill, Mr Niall Osborough, Mr Edward Reynolds, Mr William Roe, Mr Thomas Woods.

I would like to thank Mr Michael Conway and Mr Jack Marrinan of the Representative Body for Guards at Dublin Castle for their constant assistance and advice. For stimulating thought on at least a few of the topics covered in this book I thank Inspector Tom O'Reilly of the Representative Body for Inspectors and Sergeants, and for assistance with research and photographs I would like to thank Superintendent Patrick Carey and his staff at the Gárda Press Office. I also received valuable assistance from Mr Thomas O'Leary and his staff at the Gárda Pensioners Association. I cannot overstate my gratitude to a small group of friends at University College, Dublin, who were never to busy to help out with some of the historical and political questions raised in the book. In particular I would mention Mr Brian Farrell, Mr Tom Garvin and Mr Maurice Manning, all of the Department of Ethics and Politics. I must also thank Mr Tony Lennon and his staff of the *Irish Times* Library whose already busy lives I made even more complicated, and a word of thanks, too, to the Chief librarian of Independent Newspapers, Mr Des Spillane.

Finally, to Brian and Aine McCarthy of the Innishannon Hotel who gave me peace and quiet at thier home, and to my wife and mother to whom I denied those facilities while writing this book, I say thanks for their tolerance.

BIBLIOGRAPHY

The earliest years of organised policing in Ireland have never been comprehensively chronicled and placed in any social perspective. The nearest attempt is Galen Broeker, Rural *Disorder and Police Reform in Ireland* 1812-36, London 1970. It can be profitably read in conjunction with R. B. McDowell, *The Irish Adminstration*, London 1964. The contemporary development of the British police system is well covered, however, and probably the best work to read in conjunction with this book is Charles Reith, *A New Study of Police History*, London 1956.

There are several self-styled histories of the Royal Irish Constabulary, none of which are of any historical value and whose strongest quality insome cases is their unintended humour. George Garrow Green, *In the Royal Irish Constabulary*, London 1905, is about the best of these. The more serious student might be advised to read the *Report of the Committee of Inquiry (Royal Irish Constabulary and Dublin Metropolitan Police)*, H M S O 1914. *The Standing Rules and Regulations of the Royal Irish Constabulary* is available in the major libraries and tells more about the working of the force than any other single volume.

All of the histories of modern Ireland and the years of the Troubles are scanty in their treatment of the question of policing. Donal O'Sullivan, *The Irish Free State and its Senate*, London 1940, contains more than any of the others but its coverage is still very slight. The only honourable exception is James Gleeson, *Bloody Sunday*, London 1963. This little book has never received a greal deal of critical acclaim yet it covers aspects of the war between the I R A and the Crown forces which have been consistently ignored by more celebrated writers.

Of the setting up and development of the Gárda Siochána little, if anything, has been written beyond the occasional article in the *Gárda Review*, dealing with a paticular area or particular incident in the development of the force. Denis J. O'Kelly, *Salute to the Gárdai*, Dublin 1959, is a slender commemorative volume comprising a selection of essays on various aspects of the life of the force. Its historical value is small, but it contains an interesting account by Piaras Béaslai of the progress of the unarmed Civic Guards in the early 1920s.

Three books published in the past five years are indispensable for a full understanding of the events with which the present work deals. They are J. Bowyer Bell, *The Secret Army*, London 1970, Tim Pat Coogan, *The I R A* published almost simultaneously with Mr Bowyer Bell's work, and Maurice Manning, *The Blueshirts*, Dublin 1971. They are complementary to his story, and to understand it they too must be read.

For those who wish to go further into the background of the events outlined in this book I can do no better than recommend an examination of the files of the *Gárda Review* and in particular the issues of the years 1929-30 in which Eóin O'Duffy details the founding and setting up of the Gárda Siochána. For an account of the Kildare mutiny I recommend an excellent series of articles published in *An Siothadóir*, the journal of the Gárda Pensioners' Association, by the late Superintendent Seán Liddy in 1970.

The papers of the late General Richard Mulcahy, at present being catalogued, amplify many aspects of matters referred to in this book. The serious student of the early years of the Irish Free State will have to refer to this collection. The present author has been able to make use of some information contained therein.

A limited but stimulating selection of documents pertaining to the Republican Police is available at the State Paper Office in Dublin Castle.

Publishers Note

The above sources and bibilography are republished as they appeared in the 1974 edition. The State Paper Office has since become The National Archives of Ireland.
The author's introduction to this edition includes a list of more recently published relevant materials.

Index